The Deeds of God in Ṛddhipur

The Deeds of God in Ṛddhipur

Translated from the Marāṭhī and annotated by
Anne Feldhaus

with introductory essays by
Anne Feldhaus and Eleanor Zelliot

New York Oxford
OXFORD UNIVERSITY PRESS
1984

Library of Congress Cataloging in Publication Data

Main entry under title:

The deeds of god in Ṛddhipur.
Includes index.
1. Mahanubhava. I. Feldhaus, Anne.
BL1277.842.D43 1984 294.5'92 83-21949
ISBN 0-19-503438-4

The preparation of this volume was made possible (in part) by a grant from the Translations Program of the National Endowment for the Humanities and the American Institute of Indian Studies.

[redacted]

Printing (last digit): 9 8 7 6 5 4 3 2 1

Printed in the United States of America

For
Huberta LeSaint Feldhaus,
Louis Feldhaus, and
William LeSaint

Acknowledgments

Three scholars of Marāṭhī literature helped me in preparing this volume, and I wish to express my gratitude to them. Dr. S. G. Tulpule went through the whole text with me, correcting the first draft of my translation. Dr. V. B. Kolte answered numerous questions about the most difficult passages. And Dr. I. M. P. Raeside read the completed version and made several helpful suggestions. The final decisions were my own, as is the final responsibility.

Extracts from the translation, and an earlier version of part of the introduction, were first published in the *Bulletin of the School of Oriental and African Studies, University of London,* 45 (1982). I am grateful to the editors of the *Bulletin* for permission to reprint these materials.

I am also grateful for the criticism, advice, and encouragement of Raoul Birnbaum, Delwin Brown, Dilip Chitre, Paul Courtright, David Dell, James Fitzgerald, Sam Gill, Mahant Gopirāj Manānubhāv, Jack Hawley, Mahant Nāgarājbābā Mahānubhāv, Cynthia Read, Ludo Rocher, Daniel Snell, Günther Sontheimer, Frank Southworth, Guy Welbon, Eleanor Zelliot, and other friends and colleagues in India and America. Eleanor Zelliot's encouragement took the most concrete form; I am particularly grateful for the historical essay she contributed to the introduction.

This book is dedicated to my mother, my father, and my Uncle Bill—with thanks for their humor.

Tempe, Arizona A.F.
March, 1984

Contents

The Deeds of God in Ṛddhipur

Introduction

I. THE MAD GOD OF ṚDDHIPUR

> The Gosāvī used to go up to a small well. He would stand at the edge and look at his holy face in the well. He would talk to himself. He would say things to himself. He would comb his beard with his fingernails. He would laugh. He would put his holy hand into the well. Sometimes he would sit at the edge of the well, dangling his holy feet.
>
> He would play this way, and then he would leave.
>
> (*The Deeds of God in Ṛddhipur,* 288)

> The Gosāvī went out by the eastern gate. When he was near the Paraśurāma temple, to the northeast of it, he farted.
>
> And the Gosāvī said, "Die, buttocks! Die! Why are you shouting?" and he slapped his buttocks and laughed.
>
> Then he left.
>
> (*The Deeds of God in Ṛddhipur,* 101)

These are two of the 323 chapters which comprise the unusual biography translated here. It is a religious biography, written by and for members of a religious group; and its subject, Guṇḍam Rāüḷ, called "the Rāüḷ" and "Śrīprabhu" as well as "the Gosāvī," is someone the group believes to be God incarnate. And yet, as these passages illustrate, it is a book with a sense of humor.

Its sense of humor distinguishes this book from much traditional religious biography, which is often intended primarily to present a religious ideal or to illustrate a particular virtue.[1] Although its subject is God, and the remembrance of his life a work of piety,[2] *The Deeds of God in Ṛddhipur* does not seek to idealize him or to present him as a model for the faithful. Rather, it shows him as rude, greedy, petulant, childish, crazy—and funny—as well as, occasionally and arbitrarily, helpful and kind. Far from providing a model or ideal of human conduct,

Guṇḍam Rāüḷ's behavior violates human standards of conduct: he is not polite, serious, sane, or even consistent.

It is because Guṇḍam Rāüḷ is God that he need not conform to human standards. His aberrant behavior is as much a sign of his divinity as are his miracles and the devotion he elicits in his followers. The humor of the book derives not only from the "funniness" of Guṇḍam Rāüḷ in a conventional perspective, but from the basic theological perspective implicit throughout: Guṇḍam Rāüḷ is a "funny" man because he is not really a man. He is God.

It is the Mahānubhāva sect for whom Guṇḍam Rāüḷ is God, and to whose Old Marāṭhī literature[3] *The Deeds of God in Ṛddhipur* belongs. This sect, which is native to the Marāṭhī-speaking region of Western India (Mahārāṣṭra), was founded in the late thirteenth century. Its founder was named Cakradhar. Guṇḍam Rāüḷ was Cakradhar's guru, and the person to whom Cakradhar entrusted his disciples after his death. Both Cakradhar and Guṇḍam Rāüḷ are understood by Mahānubhāvas to have been incarnations of the one God, Parameśvara ("supreme Lord").

The Mahānubhāvas are one of several sects resulting from the devotional (*bhakti*) movements of medieval India. These movements proclaimed a God not bound to the stone of temples and their images, nor restricted by the rules of ritual purity. Such a God can be addressed in the language of the people, not just in the Sanskrit of the erudite and the religious professionals, and can be approached by members of all castes and both sexes. Some in medieval India went further. For Kabir,[4] for instance, God transcends the distinctions between religions: he can be worshipped by both Muslims and Hindus. For some devotees of Kṛṣṇa,[5] God's behavior transcends the rules of morality.

The Deeds of God in Ṛddhipur pursues the proclamation another step. In narrating the life of Guṇḍam Rāüḷ, the text shows that God transcends not just the rules of ritual and morality and the hierarchies of caste, sex, and learning but the conventions of politeness and sanity as well. For the text shows that Guṇḍam Rāüḷ was God, and it shows that he was mad.

Madness

By calling Guṇḍam Rāüḷ mad, I mean that his behavior, as reported in this text, goes beyond the sort of unorthodoxy typical of other figures (including the Mahānubhāvas' founder) important in the *bhakti* movements.

Guṇḍam Rāüḷ does, like these others, break pollution rules, disrupt rituals, and treat deities with a lightness bordering on disrespect.

For example, he puts a menstruating woman's sitting mat into a water jar (chapter 16); he washes his hands in a Brāhman's water jar after playing with meat at the butchers' shops (49); and he regularly takes his daily bath and does the auspicious Saṃdhyā ritual at a well used for bathing after funerals (36). In one story, he kicks over the arrangements for the Navarātra festival (102), and in several he plays with temple deities—for instance, with Narasiṃha:

> 112. He plays with Narasiṃha.
>
> One day the Gosāvī went up to Narasiṃha and touched him with his holy hand. Then he kept putting his fingers into Narasiṃha's mouth and saying, "Oh, he'll bite, I tell you. . . . He doesn't bite, I tell you! Oh, he'll laugh. . . . He doesn't laugh, I tell you! Oh, he'll talk, I tell you. . . . He doesn't talk, I tell you!"
>
> The Gosāvī played this way for a while. Then he left.

In one episode (47), the headmen of his village, Ṛddhipur, have the untouchable Mahārs' and Māṅgs' houses moved, in an (unsuccessful) attempt to prevent the Gosāvī from wandering from these houses directly to those of Brāhmans; and in another, a band of five hundred *saṃnyāsīs* refuses to enter Ṛddhipur because, they say, the Gosāvī pollutes everything there (279).

But the Gosāvī's behavior is not just unorthodox; it is rude. He is rude even to his disciples and to people he does not know. He curses. He calls people names. He is greedy, demanding, and petulant. He is especially obnoxious about food, which he even steals on occasion; and he does not hesitate to criticize his devotees' cooking. The following story catches well the frustration of serving as the Gosāvī's cook:

> 147. He makes fun of hard bread by calling it a piece of wood.
>
> One day the wheat flour would not knead right. The *poḷī*-bread came out hard and tough. Then a plate was prepared for the Gosāvī. The Gosāvī sat in his place. Then he took the *poḷīs* in his holy hand. The Gosāvī examined them closely and said, "Oh, drop dead! It's a lump of dirt! A lump of dirt! Oh, it's a piece of wood! A piece of wood, I tell you!"
>
> After this, the Gosāvī sat silently in his place. Ābāïseṃ said, "Another time I'll make them right, Lord! Beat your servant girl, thrash me, Lord, but please don't throw them out, Gosāvī. Please eat them now!"
>
> The Gosāvī agreed to her request. Then he ate them. He rinsed his mouth and chewed pan.

Sometimes the Gosāvī threatens—or even does—physical harm to people; at other times he is kind and helpful, as when he helps housewives and mothers with their tasks. There is a whole set of such stories (7, 9, 28, 39, 40, 72, and 129), typified by the following:

39. He pours cold water into hot.

One day a woman who was all alone was bathing her baby. She was hoping to herself, "If the Gosāvī comes along, he'll pour some cold water in with the hot."

At that point, the Gosāvī came along. He took a copper water pot in his holy hand. He poured cool water from the water jar into the hot water.

After some time, she said, "That's enough. That's enough, Rāüḷ." Then she bathed her baby. She laid it in its cradle and put it to sleep.

Then the Gosāvī left.

But there is a larger number of stories in which the Gosāvī is neither helping nor hurting anyone, stories in which he is simply playing, talking to himself, or doing some strange little thing. He plays with children (5, 10, 12, 13, 21, 27, 99, 110, 142, and 159); he sorts the weights in the goldsmiths' shops (306) and the coins in the money changers' (305), and he mixes up the spices at the grocers' (53); he sits on a rock called his "thinking rock" and decides where to go next (34, 201, 263, and 264); he sits on other rocks and pretends they are horses (18, 60, 154, and so forth); he plays with his reflection in water or in a mirror (76, 158, 288, and 295; cf. 260); he chides a squeaky gate (98); he gets up from his place just as his meal has been served, runs a considerable distance, breaks a thorn off a particular tree, and returns (100); and he upbraids his buttocks when he farts (101).

In response to such behavior, the townspeople in a story[6] will occasionally say: "*rāüḷ veḍā, rāüḷ pīsā*" ("The Rāüḷ is mad, the Rāüḷ is possessed") (7, 9, 70, 91; cf. 15). Sometimes someone hit on the head by the Gosāvī will claim to have learned something from the experience. But most often there is no comment, and certainly no attempt to explain the behavior away. In fact, the large number of such stories makes the Gosāvī's madness one of the major points of the text.

Divinity

Another major point is the Gosāvī's divinity. This is indicated by stories of miracles and wonders he performed, by stories of the devotion of his followers, and by special language used to refer to him.

The miracle stories are numerous. They include stories of his extraordinary personal characteristics, such as the radiance which at times streams from his body (e.g., in 4, 15, 31, and 32), or his quickness as a student: he learns in a day what others cannot learn in a month, and in a month what others cannot learn in a year (2). He puts a cat into a trance (*stīti*) just by looking at it (43), and does the same for an untouchable Māṅg just by stepping on his back as he prostrates himself in the road (73).

In addition, the Gosāvī has extraordinary powers of perception. These include the ability to foresee deaths, fires, and other future events, and the ability to discern secret thoughts of his disciples, as well as an uncanny knowledge of where to find such things as underground water sources (48, 164), buried silver (312) or gold (95), camphor kept in a particular box in a particular house in a distant town (293), or, most frequently, a kind of food for which he has a whim—usually out of season (149, 150, 151, 219, 220, 221, 222). In 208, for instance, the Gosāvī helps a man find his stolen bull:

208. He tells about a stolen bull.

One day a man's bull was lost. He looked everywhere, but he couldn't find it. So he said, "Now I'll go to the Rāūḷ. If the Rāūḷ tells me where the bull is, then he must be Parameśvara."

So he came and prostrated himself. Then he said, "Rāūḷ, my bull is lost. It can't be seen, Lord."

The Gosāvī replied, "Oh, drop dead! Go on! It's sitting behind the Mahārs' quarter, I tell you."

So he went, and found it sitting there. Then he said, "He really is Īśvara."

The Gosāvī's power over disease is illustrated in several stories of cures: of a cripple (284), of a dumb boy (285), of a disciple bitten by a snake (131), and so on. In one story (8), he makes a hundred-year-old (*satānīka*) woman lactate; in another (91), he gives a long-lived son to a woman all of whose previous babies have died. Most striking, though, are the stories (8, 57, 96, 245, and 300) in which he raises the dead. Although most of these stories are about humans, in one of the most amusing of them it is a dead donkey that gets revived:

96. He tells a donkey to bray.

A donkey had dropped dead outside the monastery, at its southwest corner, to the south of the Kamaleśvara temple in the courtyard. The Gosāvī went there. The Gosāvī touched it with his holy hand. Then the Gosāvī said, "Hey! Get up! Get up! Bray! Bray! Bray, I tell you!"

And it got up. It went off braying. And the Gosāvī laughed.

The Gosāvī's power over nature extends beyond the ability to cure the sick and raise the dead. In several stories, he stops the rain (209, 210), or keeps himself (211) and someone else (71) dry while others get soaked. In one instance (266), he causes the sun to rise more quickly and burn more warmly than usual. And there is a set of what might be called horticultural miracles, in which the Gosāvī's glance turns bitter gourds to sweet (231) or in which he replants, successfully, dried-out vines that he had uprooted three days before (24, 58, 301).

Finally, the text reports a set of apparently miraculous events of an economic sort. There is a large set of stories in which foods or other wares sampled by the Gosāvī sell more quickly (25) or more profitably (26, 52, 53, 143, 173, 216, and 307) than usual. One of the more elaborate of these stories is the following:

> 173. He scatters a cartload of jaggery.
>
> Someone from a neighboring village had brought a cartload of jaggery to sell. The Gosāvī went up to it. He put his holy hand into the jaggery. And the man grabbed his holy hand without knowing [whose it was].
>
> And the Gosāvī acted angry. He took hold of the cart and heaved it over, then smashed the jaggery with his holy feet. He ground the jaggery into the dirt.
>
> The man stood to the side. Afterwards he went to make a complaint to the village headmen. When he had made his complaint, the headmen said, "Complaints against others are taken to the Rāüḷ, but to whom can we take a complaint against the Rāüḷ? The village belongs to the Rāüḷ; the Rāüḷ can take care of it. If you had let him take some, you would have doubled your profits. But, even now, go and offer some to the Rāüḷ."
>
> So he went. He offered some to the Gosāvī. He collected all the jaggery, sifted it with a winnowing fan, and sold it. His profits doubled.

Neither here nor in any of the other such accounts does the text specify the mechanism by which such a rise in price occurs. One might expect that the food sampled by the Gosāvī is considered more valuable because it is thereby his *prasād,*[7] but the text itself, which mentions the *prasād* of the Gosāvī in numerous contexts, does not bring in the idea here. Thus it appears that there is supposed to be some sort of miracle involved.

The point of all of these miracle stories seems to be to show the Gosāvī's power; and in some of the accounts, as in the story of the stolen bull (208) cited above, there is an explicit statement that the miracles show him to be God (Parameśvara, Īśvara, and so forth).

The other sort of story of which the point is the Gosāvī's divinity is the sort which tells of people's devotion to him. Numerous disciples, townspeople, and officials give the Gosāvī countless offerings, generous hospitality, and endless personal services, from carrying his palanquin (passim), fetching his water (130), and cooking his food (passim), to combing and delousing his hair (80), soothing his stomach-aches (87), and massaging and bathing him daily. His worship (*pūjāvasvara*) seems to have been performed regularly, as part of a daily routine, by the disciples who lived with him; his devotees hoped for his *darśan* and took as *prasād* food which he had tasted. Individuals are mentioned who had their own devotional routines: some, for instance (163, 262; cf. 91), would not eat a meal without first eating the *prasād* of the Gosāvī; and one, Govindbhaṭ, offered the Gosāvī two garlands every day. Govindbhaṭ's story is the shortest in the book:

223. He accepts Govindbhaṭ's worship.

Every day Govindbhaṭ would make two garlands, and he would offer them to the Gosāvī. This was his regular observance.

There are stories which record not just the actions but the declarations of those impressed by the Gosāvī, and there are two conversion accounts (Kothaḷobā, 193; Lakṣmīndrabhaṭ, 213).

Throughout the text, the theme of Guṇḍam Rāüḷ's divinity is reinforced by the use of a special terminology to refer to the parts of his body and to his emotions and bodily functions. Instead of having a hand (Marāṭhī *hāta,* from Sanskrit *hasta*) like everyone else, the Gosāvī has a "holy" hand (Sanskrit and Marāṭhī *śrīkara*). He also has "holy" feet (*śrīcaraṇa*), a "holy" mouth and face (*śrīmukha*), a "holy" head of hair (*śrīmuguṭa*), and, altogether, a "holy" body (*śrīmūrti*). Instead of going to sleep (*nījaṇeṃ*), the Gosāvī "accepts repose" (*pahuḍa svīkaraṇeṃ*), and instead of eating a meal (*jevaṇeṃ*), he "has a repast" (*ārogaṇā karaṇeṃ*). Whereas everyone else comes and goes (*yeṇeṃ* and *jāṇeṃ*), the Gosāvī "proceeds" (*bījeṃ karaṇeṃ*), and whereas everyone else sits (*baisaṇeṃ*), the Gosāvī "has a seat" ([*-si*] *āsana hoṇeṃ*/*asaṇeṃ; āsanīṃ baisaṇeṃ*). Similarly, he "takes on" laughter (*hāsya svīkaraṇeṃ*) and "acts" angry (*kopu naṭaṇeṃ,* e.g., in 38, 64, and 88) or afraid (*bhaya naṭaṇeṃ,* e.g., in 237). Finally, at the end of his life (322), he "accepts" old age and the disease of which he dies (*vṛddhatva svīkaraṇeṃ, bāhīritīcā upadro svīkaraṇeṃ, grāṇī svīkaraṇeṃ*).

Factual Information

This is clearly a biography which is more concerned with portraying its subject's character than with narrating the events of his life. We learn from the episodes only a few of the basic facts. In the first chapter, we learn the names of the Gosāvī's parents, what kind of Brāhmans they were, that they had lost several children before the one they named Guṇḍam was born, and that they themselves died about a year after his birth. In the same chapter, we learn that Guṇḍam was raised by a maternal aunt and uncle, and that after his thread ceremony, he was placed under the tutelage of an Upādhyāya at Ṛddhipur. Elsewhere we learn of various journeys the Gosāvī took outside of Ṛddhipur and of difficulties he caused for the headmen of Ṛddhipur, and we learn about some of his devotees. Finally, we are told that he died of diarrhea and was buried, and that his disciples secretly moved his body, while the village headmen built a temple over the original grave.

The order of the episodes is only loosely chronological. The Gosāvī's birth is reported in the first chapter, and his death in the second-to-last; he is clearly a child in some of the earliest stories and clearly an old man in some of the latest. And some sets of stories form distinct sequences. The two longest of these sequences are the one from chapter 225 to chapter 247, which relates a journey the Gosāvī took with his disciples, and the one from chapter 102 to chapter 120. In the latter sequence, the Gosāvī destroys the arrangements for a festival in Ṛddhipur (102), his disciples get him invited to Deūḷvāḍā (102), he stays in Deūḷvāḍā (104–119) while the disciples negotiate the purchase of a temple in Ṛddhipur which will serve them as a monastery (115), and then the Gosāvī returns to Ṛddhipur (119), only to refuse at first to stay in the monastery (120). Other sequences occur when, as with a set of stories about Kothaḷobā (193–198), the story of the Gosāvī's receiving a new disciple is followed by stories about the disciple and his relations with the Gosāvī and other disciples.

But other stories follow one another not because they narrate a sequence of events but because they share a common theme or a common set of characters; and many stories are placed together for no reason that I have yet discerned. Moreover, in some cases, the order of the stories violates chronological order. For instance, Ābāïseṃ, who is first sent to serve the Gosāvī in 212, has been in Ṛddhipur serving him in dozens of previous chapters. And Keśav Nāyak is alive in 268, more than a hundred chapters after his death in 165.[8]

Among the factual omissions of the text, a noteworthy one is the fact that Guṇḍam Rāüḷ was initiated as a renouncer (*saṃnyāsī*) in the tradition of Śaṅkara.[9] But even more surprising is the text's failure to narrate the meetings between Guṇḍam Rāüḷ and the Mahānubhāvas' founder, Cakradhar. We are told of several disciples being sent to Guṇḍam Rāüḷ by Cakradhar ("*our* Gosāvī," the text calls him). But only indirectly, and very late in the text (322), do we learn that at the end of his life, Cakradhar entrusted his disciples to Guṇḍam Rāüḷ.

Guṇḍam Rāüḷ in Other Mahānubhāva Texts

Other early Mahānubhāva texts provide facts omitted in *The Deeds of God in Ṛddhipur.* They also elaborate on the divinity and the madness of Guṇḍam Rāüḷ.

Mahānubhāva theology stresses the uniqueness and absoluteness of Parameśvara, the one God, by contrast to the multiplicity and relativity of the many gods.[10] Parameśvara is the sole source of liberation (*mokṣa*), which he provides by descending to earth and giving people his presence (*Sūtrapāṭha,* "Pūrvī"). The one God has made a number of such descents (*avatāra*s), and Guṇḍam Rāüḷ was one of them. Thus, for Mahānubhāvas, Guṇḍam Rāüḷ is divine because he is an incarnation of Parameśvara.

According to the *Sūtrapāṭha,* the collection of the sayings of Cakradhar, there are and have been an infinite number of incarnations of Parameśvara (XI.18–19; cf. X.212). But Guṇḍam Rāüḷ is one of only five human incarnations who are named. The others are Cakradhar, Cāṅgdev Rāüḷ, and the Hindu deities Dattātreya and Kṛṣṇa.

The *Sūtrapāṭha* names three ways in which Parameśvara incarnates himself: "Parameśvara takes on a Māyā-body [the body of an incarnation] in three ways: he takes it on in a womb, or he raises a corpse, or he pushes out a *jīva* [from a living body]" (X.104–05). The first chapter of *The Deeds of God in Ṛddhipur* states that Guṇḍam Rāüḷ was a womb incarnation, an incarnation of the first type (*garbhīcā*). But Kolte[11] and Muralīdhar Śāstrī Ārādhya[12] both explain that Guṇḍam Rāüḷ's incarnation was of the third type (*davaḍaṇyācā*) as well as the first; they claim that he replaced a soul (*jīva*) already in his mother's womb.[13]

After taking on a body, an incarnation next, according to the *Sūtrapāṭha,* receives *śakti,* power. Cakradhar's biography, the *Līḷācaritra,* gives a detailed account of Cakradhar's receiving "*jñāna śakti*" and "*parāvara śakti*" from Guṇḍam Rāüḷ. Their encounter, the first and decisive meeting between the two, took place in the prepared-food bazaar at Ṛddhipur:

> There were two rows [of stalls], to the east and the west. There were tall houses(?) to the north and the south. Our Gosāvī [Cakradhar] was in the western row, facing east. Śrīprabhu [Guṇḍam Rāül] was in the eastern row, facing west. His garment was half wound around him from the waist, half draped over his shoulders. The folds of his garment were not tucked between his legs. His beard reached to his navel. His hair hung loose. His left eye was half-closed. A finger of his left holy hand was bent.
>
> When our Gosāvī saw Śrīprabhu, he bowed down. And he embraced himself.[14]
>
> And seeing our Gosāvī, Śrīprabhu said, "This is the way I like it, I tell you. Now it's right, I tell you."
>
> In one of his holy hands, Śrīprabhu had a *seṃguḷeṃ;* he had a *buḍaḍeṃ*[15] in his other holy hand. He was taking bites and spitting them out. He was laughing. He was looking at the sky. Our Gosāvī looked at Śrīprabhu's play (*līḷā*). Śrīprabhu looked at our Gosāvī, and the Gosāvī lowered his holy head.
>
> There had been a *seṃguḷeṃ* and a *buḍaḍeṃ* in Śrīprabhu's holy hands. He had finished eating the *seṃguḷeṃ;* the *buḍaḍeṃ* was still to be eaten. Then Śrīprabhu said, "Hey, there! Take it! Take it, I tell you! Take it, I tell you! Hey! Take it! Take it!" and he made *prasād* of it and gave it to him.
>
> Our Gosāvī, taking it as great *prasād,* prostrated himself, held it with both hands, and bowed. And Śrīprabhu placed his holy hand on our Gosāvī's holy mouth. With that, our Gosāvī received knowledge-power (*jñāna śakti*) and high-and-low powers (*parāvara śakti*).[16]

The Deeds of God in Ṛddhipur contains no similar account of Guṇḍam Rāüḷ's receiving *śakti,* but the *Līḷācaritra* does. According to this account, Guṇḍam Rāüḷ received *para* and *avara* (*śakti*s) from

Cāṅgdev Rāüḷ, another of the Parameśvara incarnations, when Cāṅgdev placed a winnowing fan on Guṇḍam's head and hit him with
a broom:

> Śrīprabhu Gosāvī sat down on the bank of the Gomatī. . . . Śrī
> Cāṅgdev Rāüḷ Gosāvī came along there, sweeping the lanes and the
> empty lots. He had a winnowing fan on his holy head, and a broom
> in his holy hand. He threw the dirt into the Gomatī. He placed the
> winnowing fan on Śrīprabhu's holy head, then he struck him with the
> broom. With that, Śrīprabhu received *para* and *avara* (powers).[17]

The reception of both *para* (high) and *avara* (low) powers classifies
Guṇḍam Rāüḷ, according to another typology, as the most complete
kind of incarnation. *Sūtrapāṭha* XI.20 states that incarnations of
Parameśvara can be *paradṛśya, avaradṛśya,* or *parāvaradṛśya* (i.e., they
can "see" the high, the low, or the high and the low).[18] But, after
classifying Guṇḍam Rāüḷ as an incarnation of the high-and-low
(*parāvara*) type, the *Līḷācaritra* passage goes on to state that his lower
(power) was hidden (*achādileṃ*), while only the higher was manifested
(*prakaṭiyeṃ keleṃ*). We will return to this statement, which the text does
not elaborate, in discussing Mahānubhāva explanations of Guṇḍam
Rāüḷ's madness.

By and large, other Mahānubhāva texts reinforce the image of
Guṇḍam Rāüḷ's madness found in *The Deeds of God in Ṛddhipur*. Several
of Cakradhar's comments about Guṇḍam Rāüḷ are recorded in the
Sūtrapāṭha,[19] and descriptions of Guṇḍam Rāüḷ and his behavior are
found in other texts as well. *Sūtrapāṭha* X.80, for example, contrasts
Guṇḍam Rāüḷ (Śrīprabhu) with Cakradhar and Kṛṣṇa, two other
Parameśvara incarnations: "Śrīprabhu is uncouth; I [Cakradhar] am
uncouth and civilized; Śrīkṛṣṇacakravartī is civilized." Commenting on
this *sūtra,* an unpublished commentary quoted by Kolte explains the
statement about Guṇḍam Rāüḷ by giving an extended description of
his appearance and actions:[20]

> "Uncouth" indicates lack of refinement, dissimilarity to humans.
> How was he unrefined? When he stood up, he did so abruptly. When
> he sat down he squatted, or sat crosslegged. When he walked he
> looked at the sky, or ran pitter-pattering. His speech was faltering: he
> would say things like "Go die!" or "Drop dead!" or he would repeat
> the same word over and over again. When he took things, he would
> grab them—as he took the *lāk bhākrī* bread,[21] the *āvaḷā*-fruit,[22] and the
> jujubes[23] by force. When he gave things, he would throw them—like
> the *semguḷeṃ* and *buḍaḍeṃ.*[24]
>
> To dress himself, he would pleat a sixteen-arm-length garment
> and put one end over his head. To cover his shoulders he would
> leave the right side down and take the end over his left shoulder. He
> covered his shoulders with the same garment he wrapped around his
> waist.[25] This was how his clothes were unrefined.

He would put dirty red *kuṃkuṃ*-powder [on his forehead]; he would put civet-cat musk in the part of his hair[26] and in his rolled-up braids. He would put rings in his ears, anklets at his feet,[27] and a chain around his neck.[28] There was oil on his head; his hair was braided; and his beard reached down to his navel.

He used to swing his holy hand in a circle.[29] He would twist the joint. His movements and behavior were all unrefined. This was the guise he had assumed.

And how was his body unrefined? He had no physical beauty, and his coloring was nondescript. And his left eye twitched. The little finger of his left hand was bent. This was the lack of refinement of his body.

Some details of this description are reminiscent of the description of Guṇḍam Rāüḷ found in the *Līḷācaritra*'s account of his first meeting with Cakradhar. Among other descriptions of Guṇḍam Rāüḷ in the *Līḷācaritra,*[30] the most striking, perhaps, are those which report his other meetings with Cakradhar. Like the account of their first meeting, several of the other accounts show Guṇḍam Rāüḷ treating Cakradhar very much the way he treats anyone else. Cakradhar treats Guṇḍam Rāüḷ with respect and deference, eating his leftovers as *prasād,* for instance, when the two are together;[31] but Cakradhar finds it as hard as any other disciple to please the Gosāvī. In "Pūrvārdha" 165, Guṇḍam Rāüḷ acts enraged when Cakradhar greets him with an embrace. In "Pūrvārdha" 167, he repeatedly refuses (but finally accepts) a garment Cakradhar offers him. And in "Pūrvārdha" 166, Guṇḍam Rāüḷ spanks Cakradhar with a stick, apparently angered that Cakradhar has revealed Guṇḍam Rāüḷ's divinity by refusing to accept food offerings without his tasting them first. On another occasion, by contrast, Guṇḍam Rāüḷ is very explicit in pointing out Cakradhar's divinity. The narrative ("Pūrvārdha" 168) makes pointed use of Guṇḍam Rāüḷ's habit of playing with images of deities:[32]

Śrīprabhu [Guṇḍam Rāüḷ] came playing from the open well to the Bhairava temple [where Cakradhar was staying]. From the Bhairava temple he went to the Keśava temple. Then he began to play with the images in Keśava's temple. He put his fingers on their ears, on their nose, on their eyes, and on their forehead, and he said, "This is your ear; this is your ear; this is your nose; these are your eyes; this is your mouth; this is your forehead." Then he said, "Are you God? Drop dead, I tell you! You're not God, I tell you!"

Playing this way with all the images, he proceeded to the Bhairava temple. Bāïseṃ was standing near the Gosāvī [Cakradhar]. The Omniscient one [Cakradhar] said, "My woman, Śrīprabhu is coming. Stand back a little." She stood back. And Śrīprabhu came and played the same game with the images in the Bhairava temple. He put his finger on their nose, he put his finger on their ears, on their eyes, and on their forehead. And he said, "This is your ear, this is your nose, this is your eye, this is your forehead." And then he said, "Are you God? Drop dead, I tell you! You're not God, I tell you!" He went along, playing this way with the images in the Bhairava temple.

Our Gosāvī [Cakradhar] kept sitting motionless. Then [Guṇḍam Rāüḷ] came up to the Gosāvī, put his finger on the parts of [Cakradhar's] body, and said, "This is your ear, this is your nose, this is your eye, this is your forehead, this is your mouth." Having said this, Śrīprabhu put his finger on the Gosāvī's forehead, then said, "Hey, you're God, I say. . . . No, you're not, I say. . . . Yes, this is God, I tell you," and placed his hand on the Gosāvī's holy head. "This is not God, I tell you," he said, pointing at Bhairava. "*This* is God."

In this way, God revealed God.

Then Śrīprabhu returned to the town.

Thus other Mahānubhāva texts as well as *The Deeds of God in Ṛddhipur* make it clear that Guṇḍam Rāüḷ was childish, difficult, and crazy—what I (and they) have called mad (*veḍā*). They also make it clear that their authors believed Guṇḍam Rāüḷ to be a divine incarnation. What is less explicitly clear is how the early Mahānubhāva authors related Guṇḍam Rāüḷ's madness to his divinity, what theological explanations they would have given of Guṇḍam Rāüḷ's behavior.[33]

It is possible that one such explanation is implied in the *Līḷācaritra*'s statement about Guṇḍam Rāüḷ's *para* and *avara* powers. As we have seen, "Pūrvārdha" 15 reports that although Guṇḍam Rāüḷ received both the *para* (high) and the *avara* (low) powers of a Parameśvara incarnation, only the *para* was manifested in him, while the *avara* was "hidden." The implied explanation would be that Guṇḍam Rāüḷ really was a full incarnation, even though he did not appear to be one. He was not essentially different from Cakradhar, for instance; but his behavior differed from Cakradhar's. This was because in Cakradhar, neither of the powers was "hidden,"[34] whereas in Guṇḍam Rāüḷ, one of them was. Cakradhar's version of this explanation is recorded in *Sūtrapāṭha* X.215: "My children, there is nothing he does not know. Even though he knows everything, he [acts as if he] is ignorant."

Another explanation of Guṇḍam Rāüḷ's behavior is implied in Kolte's and Muralīdhar Śāstrī Ārādhya's claim that Guṇḍam Rāüḷ was incarnated by replacing a soul (*jīva*) already in his mother's womb.[35] Muralīdhar Śāstrī, and several other present-day Mahānubhāvas, made this claim in answer to the question why Parameśvara would incarnate himself as a madman. The consequence of the claim is that Guṇḍam Rāüḷ's madness is not originally his own, but is inherited from the *jīva* he replaced in his mother's womb. But despite the frequency with which present-day Mahānubhāvas make this claim, I have not yet found a source for it in the early Mahānubhāva literature.

Nowhere in Mahānubhāva literature, as far as I know, is it denied that Parameśvara can incarnate himself in a madman, nor is it denied that he did so in the case of Guṇḍam Rāüḷ. The following passage from the *Sūtrapāṭha* (X.106), which echoes the refrain of the residents of Ṛddhipur ("The Rāüḷ is mad [*veḍā*]; the Rāüḷ is possessed [*pīsā*]"), places Guṇḍam Rāüḷ in the context of the many incarnations of Parameśvara:

> God becomes a tortoise, he becomes a fish; he descends among the gods, he descends among men, he descends among animals. When he has descended among men, God becomes a madman (*veḍā*), he becomes a possessed man (*pīsā*), he becomes a mute; but a walking, talking God is rare.

But if it were merely an unfortunate accident that in Guṇḍam Rāüḷ, Parameśvara incarnated himself in a madman, Guṇḍam Rāüḷ's biography would not give the emphasis it does to his madness. The fact that the text does not try to excuse his strange behavior, but instead seems to revel in describing it, indicates the assumption that such behavior is, after all, appropriate for an incarnation of Parameśvara.

This seems to be the explicit point in a passage of the *Līḷācaritra* which records a conversation between Cakradhar and Nāgdev ("Pūrvārdha" 589). Nāgdev, who would later become the leader of Cakradhar's disciples, had just come from Ṛddhipur, when Cakradhar asked to see him. Cakradhar asked Nāgdev to describe Guṇḍam Rāüḷ's behavior. Nāgdev answered:

> The Gosāvī gets up early. He walks back and forth, then he goes to Āp Well. On the way he plays with a certain rock.[36] He plays with the Five Pipals. He plays at Ap Well. Then the Gosāvī goes into the town. He goes from house to house. With his holy hands he lifts the pots down from their stack.[37] He tastes the vegetables and other cooked food. He replaces [the pots] in a stack. He says, "Drop dead! Not that way!" and takes them down again. He stacks them again, looks at them carefully, and then says, "Now it's the way I like it, I tell you." As he walks along the road, he looks at the sky, claps his hands, and bubbles with laughter.

After Nāgdev had told several stories of this sort, Cakradhar asked him what he thought of Guṇḍam Rāüḷ (Śrīprabhu), Cakradhar himself, and Nāgdev's original guru, Dādos ("the Mahātmā"). Nāgdev replied, "They're all alike, Lord." After an interruption from a disciple who was outraged at Nāgdev's answer, the conversation continued:

> The Omniscient one [Cakradhar] said, "You have seen the play (*krīḍā*) of Śrīprabhu, and you have seen the antics (*ceṣṭā*) of the Mahātmā. When you think about the two of them, do you see no difference at all?"
>
> Then Bhaṭ [Nāgdev] began to think. And he saw the unfathomable play (*līḷā*) of the Gosāvī, and he saw the tricks (*kucīta ceṣṭā*) of Dādos. Then the Omniscient one said, "Śrīprabhu is one who de-

lights in the self (*ātmārāmu*). Śrīprabhu is the unqualified Brahman (*nīrguṇa brahma*). Śrīprabhu is the eternally liberated Absolute (*nītyamukta vastu*). And the Mahātmā is a *jīva*[38] like other *jīvas*. . . . *Jīvas* must be bound and they must be released. Only when Śrīprabhu releases such *jīvas* are they released. . . . [39] No *jīva* can imitate for a moment the play (*līḷā*) Śrīprabhu plays (*krīḍati*)."

Thus Cakradhar understood Guṇḍam Rāüḷ's strange behavior to be not only consistent with his divinity but an essential expression of it. Cakradhar taught his understanding to Nāgdev and to his other early disciples. These disciples became the devotees portrayed in *The Deeds of God in Ṛddhipur;* and these disciples composed and first read *The Deeds of God in Ṛddhipur.* For these people—the devotees in the text and the devotees who created the text—Guṇḍam Rāüḷ is God, and his madness is a sign of his divinity.

NOTES

1. Frank E. Reynolds and Donald Capps, eds., *The Biographical Process: Studies in the History and Psychology of Religion* (The Hague: Mouton, 1976), p. 3–5.
2. *Smaraṇa,* remembrance, is a practice to which Guṇḍam Rāüḷ's devotees are enjoined by the founder of the sect to which they belong. See Anne Feldhaus, *The Religious System of the Mahānubhāva Sect: The Mahānubhāva Sūtrapāṭha* (New Delhi: Manohar, 1983), p. 64–65.
3. See I. M. P. Raeside, "A Bibliographical Index of Mahānubhāva Works in Marāṭhī," *Bulletin of the School of Oriental and African Studies, University of London,* 23 (1960): 464–507.
4. See Charlotte Vaudeville, *Kabīr,* vol. I (Oxford: Clarendon Press, 1974).
5. See Edward C. Dimock, Jr., *The Place of the Hidden Moon: Erotic Mysticism in the Vaiṣṇava-Sahajiyā Cult of Bengal* (Chicago: The University of Chicago Press, 1966).
6. Never the devotees; and not, directly, the text itself.
7. See the glossary for English equivalents of this and other Indian terms used in the introduction and the translation.
8. This relative inattention to chronology contrasts with a meticulous attention to geography. Precise details are given indicating exactly where a given episode occurred: in exactly which village or, in Ṛddhipur, under exactly which tree or at exactly which corner of a building or courtyard. The Mahānubhāvas' geographical interest is revealed even more clearly in the large number of texts devoted to describing places where the incarnations of Parameśvara visited or lived. See Raeside's "Bibliographical Index."
9. This fact is reported in "Pūrvārdha" 15 of the *Līḷācaritra,* the biography of Cakradhar, ed. V. B. Kolte (Bombay: Mahārāṣṭra Rājya Sāhitya Saṃskṛti Maṃḍaḷa, 1978). In recapitulating *The Deeds of God in Ṛddhipur*'s account of Guṇḍam Rāüḷ's early years, the *Līḷācaritra* adds that Guṇḍam Rāüḷ was initiated by a certain Kamaḷāraṇya, and that his name as a *saṃnyāsī* was Vibudhāraṇya. The ending *-āraṇya* marks him as a member of one of the

daśanāmī ("ten-named") orders of *saṃnyāsīs* in the tradition of Śaṅkara. See R. C. Ḍhere, *Cakrapāṇi* (Puṇe: Viśvakarmā Sāhityālaya, 1977), p. 227–30.

10. See Anne Feldhaus, "The *devatācakra* of the Mahānubhāvas," *Bulletin of the School of Oriental and African Studies, University of London,* 43 (1980): 101–09. For Mahānubhāva incarnation theory, see V. B. Kolte, *Mahānubhāva Tattvajñāna,* 4th ed. (Malkapur: Aruṇa Prakāśana, 1975), chapter 7; and Feldhaus, *The Religious System of the Mahānubhāva Sect,* part I, chapter 3.
11. Kolte, *Mahānubhāva Tattvajñāna,* p. 199; introduction to *Śrī Govindaprabhu Caritra,* ed. V. B. Kolte, 5th ed. (Malkapur: Aruṇa Prakāśana, 1972), p. 24.
12. In an interview on July 21, 1979, at the Śrī Kṛṣṇa Maṇḍir, Gaṇesh Peṭh, Pune.
13. The significance of this claim will be seen in the discussion of Mahānubhāva explanations of Guṇḍam Rāüḷ's madness.
14. That is, Cakradhar embraced Guṇḍam Rāüḷ, both of them being incarnations of Parameśvara.
15. *Seṃguḷeṃ* and *buḍaḍeṃ* are two kinds of deep-fried snack food.
16. *Līḷācaritra,* "Pūrvārdha" 20.
17. Ibid., "Pūrvārdha" 15.
18. The distinction is not further explained in the *Sūtrapāṭha.* See Feldhaus, *The Religious System of the Mahānubhāva Sect,* p. 36.
19. See ibid., p. 34–35.
20. V. B. Kolte, *Śrīcakradhara Caritra,* 2nd ed. (Malkapur: Aruṇa Prakāśana, 1977), p. 37–38.
21. See *The Deeds of God in Ṛddhipur,* 29.
22. See ibid., 157.
23. See ibid., 216.
24. To Cakradhar, in *Līḷācaritra,* "Pūrvārdha" 20, quoted earlier in this section.
25. Kolte (*Śrīcakradhara Caritra,* p. 38; cf. Ḍhere, *Cakrapāṇi,* p. 232–33) suggests that the garment described is a sari, and that this, along with the *kuṃkuṃ,* the parted hair, the braid, and so on, indicates that Guṇḍam Rāüḷ dressed like a woman, and perhaps that he practiced a form of devotion in which a male devotee plays the role of a female lover of god (*madhurābhakti*). But this seems puzzling in the light of the episodes in *The Deeds of God in Ṛddhipur* in which Guṇḍam Rāüḷ criticizes transvestites (140 and 145); as well as in view of Guṇḍam Rāüḷ's apparent lack of devotion to anyone.
26. See *The Deeds of God in Ṛddhipur,* 291; contrast 292.
27. See ibid., 258.
28. Contrast ibid., 259.
29. See ibid., 14.
30. Other *Līḷācaritra* descriptions of Guṇḍam Rāüḷ are found in Cakradhar's instructions to disciples he sends to Ṛddhipur and in disciples' reports to Cakradhar of their experiences there. Several of these accounts duplicate or resemble closely material found in *The Deeds of God in Ṛddhipur* (e.g., "Pūrvārdha" 589; "Uttarārdha" 326), although others provide new details.
31. For example, "Pūrvārdha" 38, 39, 166, and 167.
32. Cf. *The Deeds of God in Ṛddhipur,* 65, 104, 112, 113, 228, 238, 247, 298, and 314.
33. *The Deeds of God in Ṛddhipur* itself, as I have pointed out, makes virtually no attempt at theological rationalization, and the two commentaries re-

portedly making such attempts are very late and/or not readily available (see the end of section IV). I have not had access to either of these commentaries.

34. See *Līḷācaritra,* "Pūrvārdha" 20.
35. That is, he was a *davaḍaṇyācā* as well as a *garbhīcā* incarnation.
36. Cf. *The Deeds of God in Ṛddhipur,* 74.
37. Cf. *The Deeds of God in Ṛddhipur,* 46.
38. A "soul," which can animate a human or animal body.
39. "*Jīva*s must be bound. . ." is *Sūtrapāṭha* XI.38.

II. DIVINE MADNESS: COMPARISON AND ANALYSIS

That God should be perceived in someone as crazy as Guṇḍam Rāüḷ runs counter to the commonly held "relatively modest dogma that God is not mad."[1] To those accustomed to a conception of God as the source of (or subject to[2]) justice, rationality, and order, it will seem strange that Guṇḍam Rāüḷ's behavior should be considered appropriate for an incarnation of God, let alone that it should reveal his divinity. But in the Hindu context to which it belongs, this position, though striking, is not anomalous; and it is not without parallels in other religious traditions.[3] An investigation of some of the parallels, both Hindu and non-Hindu, will help to clarify the religious meaning of Guṇḍam Rāüḷ's madness.

There have been in India many kinds of people whose behavior has paralleled Guṇḍam Rāüḷ's. However, the reasons for their behavior have typically been different from the reason—more precisely, the need for no reason—for his. Gurus, who are to be treated like gods by their disciples,[4] often treat them, in turn, in a rude and arbitrary fashion; this serves to teach the disciples utter subjugation, if not other lessons as well. For instance, in his study of North Indian musicians, Daniel Neuman notes that a music teacher will often try to discourage a disciple of whose sincerity he is not yet sure:

> One test of such sincerity is a trial period in which he has to perform the duties of a disciple without having much—if any—of the reward of being one. In other words, the disciple will serve his ustad [master], wait on him hand and foot, but receive no talim [training] from the ustad.
>
> The trial period is partly a test of devotion to the guru, and it eliminates those who are not truly sincere. It has another very important function, however, the learning of obedience—total obedience—to the guru.[5]

There is an element of a guru's behavior in some of Guṇḍam Rāüḷ's treatment of his disciples. Dāmurt, for instance, specifies the lesson he has been taught when the Gosāvī hits him over the head with a coconut (109); and when the Gosāvī similarly hits Umāïseṃ with a piece of pottery, she is told that he is teaching her—though it is not made clear what the lesson is (133).

Other parallels are to be found in the behavior of renouncers (saṃnyāsīs), who, from ancient times, have withdrawn from the society of householders and their conventions[6] to pursue final release (mokṣa). Perhaps the most extreme example of unconventional (though ritualized) behavior on the part of renouncers is the practices of the Pāśupatas. These are members of a Śaiva sect who are enjoined, at one stage of their training, to engage in a number of practices intended to evoke censure:

> *krāthana* (snoring or acting as if asleep when one is not), *spandana* (shaking one's limbs as if afflicted by "wind-disease"), *mandana* (walking as if crippled), *śṛṅgāraṇa* (making amorous gestures in the presence of women), *avitatkaraṇa* (acting as if devoid of judgement), and *avitadbhāṣaṇa* (uttering senseless or contradictory words).[7]

By evoking censure in these ways, the Pāśupatas claim to achieve a transfer of karma, their demerit being transferred to their critics and the critics' merit being transferred to them.[8]

Guṇḍam Rāüḷ was not a Pāśupata, but he was a renouncer;[9] although there is no evidence that he deliberately aimed to evoke censure, his behavior certainly did set him apart from conventional society. But the renouncers' ultimate goal, *mokṣa,* was not one the Gosāvī had to strive for, since he had it already. From the beginning, he was the "eternally liberated Absolute" (*nityamukta vastu*).[10]

Devotion is the explanation of the behavior of a number of mad saints in medieval and modern India. Of these, one prime exemplar is the medieval Bengali saint Caitanya, a devotee of the god Kṛṣṇa. Edward Dimock writes of Caitanya,

> He was certainly mad, whether this be interpreted as the divine madness of the holy fool, the random madness of the child, or, as one modern historian claims, as epilepsy. He was literally pulled apart by his passion for Kṛṣṇa. . . .[11]

Majumdar describes, for instance, Caitanya's fury at opponents of his fellow devotees (*vaiṣṇava*s): he would

> jump on a tree, then as suddenly jump down and fall on the ground with closed eyes. He grinded his teeth with a horrible noise, somersaulted, and rolled on the ground. He rushed at *vaiṣṇava*-baiters, and they ran away from him as if from a mad man. That indeed was the common opinion. [His mother] was advised to tie him up securely and then apply suitable medicines.[12]

But Caitanya's apparent madness was a result and an expression of his love for Kṛṣṇa and was diagnosed as such by a prominent *vaiṣṇava* of his day, as well as by devoted followers ever since.[13]

Another mad saint, the ninth-century Tamil devotee Māṇikkavācakar, clearly understands his own madness to arise from his love for the god Śiva:

> While unperishing love melted my bones,
> I cried.
> I shouted again and again,
> louder than the waves of the billowing sea,
> I became confused,
> I fell,
> I rolled,
> I wailed.

Bewildered like a madman,
intoxicated like a crazy drunk,
so that people were puzzled
and those who heard wondered.
Wild as a rutting elephant which cannot be mounted,
I could not contain myself.[14]

By contrast with the behavior of such saints, Guṇḍam Rāüḷ's madness is not understood to arise from devotion. Guṇḍam Rāüḷ is not devoted to anyone; others are devoted to him. Rather than the frenzy of devotion, his madness is for his followers a sign of divinity. It is to the Hindu gods, then, that we must look for more direct parallels to Guṇḍam Rāüḷ.

Indian theism has a long tradition of playful, capricious, and destructive deities. Perhaps the oldest of these is Rudra-Śiva. Śiva's madness, implicit in Vedic references to him,[15] becomes explicit in later Sanskrit texts, where "Śiva is often said to be a madman."[16] Śiva's father-in-law Dakṣa, for instance, regrets having allowed his daughter to marry the mad god:

> I gave my daughter to Śiva against my will, for he wanders in the horrible burning-grounds like a madman, naked, his hair disarranged, laughing, weeping, garlanded with bones. I gave her to that madman because Brahmā urged me to do it, but I did not like it.[17]

In the medieval period, Tulsīdās refers to Śiva as "this monstrous lunatic" and "Master Simpleton."[18] And a Bengali poet expresses a side of Śiva's madness reminiscent of a side of Guṇḍam Rāüḷ's. The poet gives words to Śiva's wife:

> You forget me, mother, and all that I endured with my mad husband. Bhōlā is ever laughing and weeping and knows no one save me. He is always eating hemp, and I must stay near him. I cannot keep from worrying and wondering if he is safe or if any harm has come to him.
>
> I have to lift his food up to his mouth, or he would forget to eat. There is nothing left of me, I am spent with worrying about this madman.[19]

Hindu goddesses also might often be called mad in their destructive ecstasy. The "Devīmāhātmya" of the *Mārkaṇḍeya Purāṇa* describes the demon-killing Kālī, for instance, as having

> protruding fangs, carrying a sword and a noose, with a mottled, skull-topped staff, adorned with a necklace of human skulls, covered with a tiger-skin, gruesome with shriveled flesh. Her mouth gaping wide, her lolling tongue terrifying, her eyes red and sunken, she filled the whole of space with her howling. Attacking and killing the mighty demons, she devoured the armed force of the enemies of the gods. Seizing with one hand the elephants with their back-riders,

drivers, warriors and bells, she hurled them into her maw. In the same way she chewed up warriors with their horses, chariots and charioteers, grinding them up most horribly with her teeth. One she grabbed by the hair of the head, another by the nape of the neck, another she trod underfoot while another she crushed against her chest. The mighty striking and throwing weapons loosed by those demons she caught in her mouth and pulverised in fury. She ravaged the entire army of powerful evil-souled Asuras [demons]; some she devoured while others she trampled; some were slain by the sword, others bashed by her skull-topped club, while other demons went to perdition crushed by the sharp points of her teeth. . . .

Then howling horribly, Kālī laughed aloud malevolently, her maw gaping wide, her fangs glittering, awful to behold.[20]

Iconographic representations of such goddesses are often particularly horrible: perhaps the bloodiest is the goddess Chinnamastā ("Beheaded"), who is pictured drinking the blood which spurts from her own decapitated neck.[21]

By contrast with Śiva and these goddesses, Viṣṇu is generally rather sedate. His Narasiṃha (man-lion) incarnation, however, can be fierce to a point approaching madness. The *Bhāgavata Purāṇa* describes Narasiṃha's main demon-(Asura-)killing exploit as follows:

[Narasiṃha] roared forth a terrific and shrill peal of laughter, and with great rapidity, seized the Asura. . . . Just as a serpent would seize a mouse, [he] caught hold of the Asura. . . . At the door of the assembly-hall, he laid him on his thighs, and . . . sportingly tore him with his claws as Garuḍa does to the most poisonous serpents. His indignant and terrific eyes were too difficult to gaze at. He was licking the corners of his wide open mouth with his tongue. His face and mane were reddish due [to] the drops of blood. He resembled a lion wearing the garland of the entrails of an elephant after killing it.[22]

The prime Hindu example of a playful and capricious, though not destructive, deity is the Kṛṣṇa of the Vṛndāvana cycle. From a naughty, lovable baby, Kṛṣṇa grows into a mischievous child and a boisterous, flirtatious adolescent. The following passage from the *Bhāgavata Purāṇa* describes some of Kṛṣṇa's exploits in the words of the women of his village, Vṛndāvana. The similarity to Guṇḍam Rāüḷ is striking, despite the difference in age:

When the wives of the cowherds saw the charming boyish pranks of Kṛṣṇa, they would go in a group to tell his mother, saying, "Kṛṣṇa unties the calves when it is not the proper time, and he laughs at everyone's angry shouts. He devises ways to steal and eat curds and milk and thinks food sweet only if he steals it. He distributes the food among the monkeys; if he doesn't eat the food, he breaks the pot. If he cannot find anything, he becomes angry at the house and makes the children cry before he runs away. If something is beyond his reach, he fashions some expedient by piling up pillows, mortars, and so on; or if he knows that the milk and curds have been placed in pots suspended in netting, he makes holes in the pots. When the wives of the cow-herds are busy with household duties, he will steal things in a dark room, making his own body with its masses of jewels serve as a lamp. This is the sort of impudent act which he commits; and he pees and so forth in clean houses. These are the thieving tricks that he contrives, but he behaves in the opposite way and is good when you are near."[23]

Although several of these deities are sometimes the objects of a more-or-less exclusive devotion, they are found in classical Hinduism in a polytheism which includes serious, benevolent, and predictable deities alongside the playful, destructive, and capricious ones. In classical Hinduism, none of the gods alone—neither the mad ones nor the others—are to be understood as absolute. For the Mahānubhāvas, by contrast, all such deities are essentially different from the Parameśvara who is incarnated in Guṇḍam Rāūḷ. They form a hierarchy which differentiates them, in their multiplicity and relativity, from the unique and absolute Parameśvara.[24] Although Mahānubhāvas admit the existence of the many Hindu gods, they deny their importance and are thus, like some other medieval Indian devotional sects, monotheists.

In their monotheism, they are also like Muslims, Christians, and Jews. Thus, the Western monotheistic traditions provide important parallels to Guṇḍam Rāūḷ's madness, parallels which should help us to understand its meaning.

Judaism, Christianity, and Islam might at first be thought some of the most unlikely sources of such parallels. The God of these traditions is most often seen in them as just and reasonable. Sometimes stern and sometimes merciful, he is invariably, it might be argued, sane and serious. But the saints and prophets of these traditions are often aberrant or foolish, even to the point of being called mad; since their aberrance clearly derives from, and is justified by, their relation to God, this implies the aberrance, foolishness, or madness of God. The prophet Hosea, for instance, who states, "The prophet is a fool, the man of the spirit is mad" (Hosea 9.7) takes a harlot as his wife; this "crazy" deed reflects the Lord's relationship to his people. The Lord loves his people despite their betrayal of him; he is a cuckold, a figure of ridicule.

A holy fool among the early Hasidic rabbis was Rabbi Meshullam Zusya of Hanipol. In the story of Rabbi Zusya's night prayers, it is his attempt to express his love for God that brings out his foolishness:

> Zusya was once a guest in the house of the rabbi of Neskhizh. Shortly after midnight, the host heard sounds coming from his guest's room, so he went to the door and listened. Zusya was running back and forth in the room, saying: "Lord of the world, I love you! But what is

> there for me to do? I can't do anything." And then he started running back and forth again, repeating the same thing, until suddenly he bethought himself and cried: "Why, I know how to whistle, so I shall whistle something for you." But when he began to whistle, the rabbi of Neskhizh grew frightened.[25]

In the Islamic tradition, there are several people whose love for God expressed itself in unconventional, erratic, or mad behavior. The "lunatic"[26] Buhlūl al-Madjnūn al-Kūfī is a good example, as are the Malāmatiyya. These latter were Sufis whose love for God led them, like the Pāśupatas, to court dishonor. They "deliberately tried to draw the contempt of the world upon themselves by committing unseemly, even unlawful, actions, but . . . preserved perfect purity of heart and loved God without second thought."[27]

In the Christian tradition, the paradox of faith (and the absurdity of God) is proclaimed long before the nineteenth-century existentialist Søren Kierkegaard and his successors. Already in the New Testament, Paul, who calls himself and other apostles "fools for Christ's sake" (I Corinthians 4.10), speaks also of the folly of a God who would save mankind by dying:

> For the word of the cross is folly to those who are perishing, but to us who are being saved it is the power of God. For it is written,
>
> "I will destroy the wisdom of the wise,
> and the cleverness of the clever I will thwart."
>
> Where is the wise man? Where is the scribe? Where is the debater of this age? Has not God made foolish the wisdom of the world? For since, in the wisdom of God, the world did not know God through wisdom, it pleased God through the folly of what we preach to save those who believe. For Jews demand signs and Greeks seek wisdom, but we preach Christ crucified, a stumbling block to Jews and folly to Gentiles, but to those who are called, both Jews and Greeks, Christ the power of God and the wisdom of God. For the foolishness of God is wiser than men, and the weakness of God is stronger than men. (I Corinthians 1.18–25)

A recent study by John Saward traces the theme of "holy folly" in Christianity.[28] Beginning with Paul, Saward finds "fools for Christ's sake" in early Egyptian and Syrian monasticism, in the Russian Church, in early Irish Christianity, among the Cistercians and Franciscans, among seventeenth-century French Jesuits, and elsewhere. One of the earliest of Saward's examples, Saint Simeon Salos ("Simeon the Fool," sixth century), began his fool's career as follows:

> On a dung-heap outside the city he found a dead dog. He took off the cord belt that he wore and tied it to the dog's foot. Dragging it behind him, he ran through the city gates, close to a boys' school. When they saw this spectacle, the children began to shout, "the monk's mad!" and ran after him, boxing his ears. The next day,

> which was a Sunday, Simeon took some nuts and entered the church. At the beginning of the Liturgy, he threw them and extinguished the candles. When they rushed to throw him out, he went up into the ambo and attacked the women with nuts.[29]

The parallel to Guṇḍam Rāüḷ's behavior is remarkable, but there is a difference which would be important to Mahānubhāvas as well as to Christians. Christians consider Simeon Salos and the other "holy fools" saints, whereas Mahānubhāvas consider Guṇḍam Rāüḷ to be God. The more direct parallel is to be found on another level, in an idea which underlies the behavior of the Christian holy fools and provides a repeated theme in Saward's study. This is the idea that the folly of the saints is an imitation of the folly of God.[30] This idea, first expressed by Paul, is found as well in the writings of other Christian saints. The seventeenth-century French Jesuit Louis Lallemant states it as follows:

> To say that Our Lord could have redeemed us without suffering at all, could have won everything He has won for us without dying a death as sordid as that of the cross, and yet chose the death of the cross for our salvation—to say that is madness by the standards of human reason. But "what seems folly in God is wiser than the wisdom of all men." How different are the judgements of God from those of men! Divine wisdom is folly in the judgement of men, and human wisdom is folly in the judgement of God. It is up to us to see to which of these two judgements we are going to conform our own.[31]

Guṇḍam Rāüḷ's biography does not call for his disciples to imitate him. Neither does it state as explicitly as Paul and Lallemant the *relativity* of the divine folly, the idea that in the divine perspective, "the foolishness of God is wiser than men."[32] But Guṇḍam Rāüḷ's biography can lead his followers to a realization similar to that expressed by Paul and Lallemant. This realization, of the difference between human and divine perspectives, is the realization of the transcendence of God.

In more general terms, it is the realization of the "otherness" of the holy. Rudolf Otto, who identified the holy (*das Heilige*) as the fundamental religious category, calls it "wholly other" (*ganz andere*).[33] And Mircea Eliade, who defines "the sacred"[34] as "the opposite of the profane,"[35] states that awareness of the sacred arises because it "manifests itself, shows itself, as something wholly different from the profane."[36] In its most basic meaning, then, Guṇḍam Rāüḷ's madness is holy because it is abnormal. Guṇḍam Rāüḷ's extraordinary behavior manifests to Mahānubhāvas the otherness of Parameśvara, his transcendence of human ways.

The Gosāvī moves as freely as he does among men and women of all castes, classes, and age groups because he belongs to none of the categories into which people divide themselves. He himself states this

explicitly in chapter 281, denying in turn that he is a member of each
of the classical Hindu *varṇa*s ("castes") and *āśrama*s (stages of life):

> I am not a man, nor a god or Yakṣa,
> Nor a Brāhman, a Kṣatriya, a Vaiśya or a Śūdra.
> I am not a celibate; I am not a householder or a forest hermit,
> Neither am I a mendicant, I who am innate knowledge.[37]

Moreover, the Gosāvī is not bound by the rules which govern
people's behavior. He is not, for instance, bound by religious rules: by
the need to pay respect to gods of stone, by the need to attend to the
details of ritual, or—most noticeably—by the need to avoid pollution
and maintain Brāhmanical purity. In this, Guṇḍam Rāüḷ is similar to
other leaders of medieval Indian *bhakti* movements. These leaders
taught the primacy of an interior, personal relation with God, a relation to which temples, images, rituals, learning, caste, sex, and ritual
purity were at best irrelevant, and from which they were at worst
distracting.[38]

But to Mahānubhāvas, Guṇḍam Rāüḷ is himself God, and in this
he differs from most other leaders of *bhakti* movements, as well as from
the Christian and other saints discussed above. It is as God that
Guṇḍam Rāüḷ is exempt not only from the ritualized human tech-
niques of contact with the divine, but also from other conventional
human behavior. It is because he is Parameśvara that he need not be
nice, polite, serious, or even sane. If he is God, why should he not be
mad?

Thus, Guṇḍam Rāüḷ manifests to Mahānubhāvas the transcendent
otherness of Parameśvara. In incarnating himself, Parameśvara is free
to do anything, even to become a madman. But, finally, just as
Parameśvara is free to become a madman, so he is not required to do
so in each of his incarnations. Particularly striking in this connection is
the Mahānubhāvas' Kṛṣṇa. For some other sects devoted to Kṛṣṇa, it is
he, with his sexual vagaries and his childish playfulness—his *līlā*—who
illustrates the freedom and transcendence of God. But the Mahānubhāva texts, for whom Kṛṣṇa, like Guṇḍam Rāüḷ and Cakradhar, is an
incarnation of Parameśvara, do not emphasize these elements of
Kṛṣṇa's mythology; they concentrate instead on Kṛṣṇa's more staid
roles as the preacher of the *Bhagavadgītā* and the lawfully married
husband of Rukmiṇī.[39] For the Mahānubhāvas, it seems, Guṇḍam
Rāüḷ's madness has replaced Kṛṣṇa's *līlā* as the expression of the transcendent lawlessness of God.

The biography of Guṇḍam Rāüḷ, for—indeed, through—all its
delightful frivolity, thus makes an important contribution to the theology of medieval Indian devotion. It also provides a strikingly detailed
picture of the world of Guṇḍam Rāüḷ's times. In the historical essay
which follows, Eleanor Zelliot sketches the outlines of that world.

NOTES

1. Salvador de Madariaga, quoted in Clifford Geertz, "Religion as a Cultural System," in *Anthropological Approaches to the Study of Religion,* ed. Michael Banton (New York: Praeger, 1966), p. 13.
2. Socrates' classical formulation of this alternative is found in the *Euthyphro:* "The point which I should first wish to understand is whether the pious or holy is beloved by the gods because it is holy, or holy because it is beloved of the gods." *The Works of Plato,* trans. Benjamin Jowett, ed. Irwin Edman (New York: Modern Library, 1928), p. 46.
3. In this brief essay, only a few of the parallels will be discussed. Among the interesting parallels which will be omitted are the "trickster" figures found in Native American and other traditions. See Paul Radin, *The Trickster: A Study in American Indian Mythology* (New York: Philosophical Library, 1956); Mac Linscott Ricketts, "The North American Indian Trickster," *History of Religions,* 5 (1965): 327–50; and Robert D. Pelton, *The Trickster in West Africa: A Study of Mythic Irony and Sacred Delight* (Berkeley: University of California Press, 1980). See also Enid Welsford, *The Fool: His Social and Literary History* (1935; repr. ed., Garden City, N.Y.: Anchor Books, 1961).
4. P. V. Kane, *History of Dharmaśāstra,* vol. II, p. 322. *Śvetāśvatara Upaniṣad* VI.23; *Āpastamba Dharma Sūtra* I.2.6.13.
5. Daniel Neuman, *The Life of Music in North India: The Organization of an Artistic Tradition* (Detroit: Wayne State University Press, 1980), p. 55.
6. This withdrawal is to a life of conventions and rituals of their own. See Patrick Olivelle, ed. and trans., *Vāsudevāśrama Yatidharmaprakāśa: A Treatise on World Renunciation, Critically Edited with Introduction, Annotated Translation and Appendices.* Publications of the De Nobili Research Library, vols. III and IV (Vienna: Indologisches Institut der Universität Wien, 1976, 1977).
7. David N. Lorenzen, *The Kāpālikas and Kālāmukhas: Two Lost Śaivite Sects* (Berkeley: University of California Press, 1972), p. 185.
8. Ibid., p. 187, quoting *Pāśupata-sūtra* III.7, 8, and 9.
9. *Līḷācaritra,* "Pūrvārdha" 15. See note 9 to section I of this introduction.
10. *Līḷācaritra,* "Pūrvārdha" 589; quoted at the end of section I of this introduction.
11. Edward Dimock, "Religious Biography in India: The 'Nectar of the Acts' of Caitanya," in *The Biographical Process: Studies in the History and Psychology of Religion,* ed. Frank E. Reynolds and Donald Capps (The Hague: Mouton, 1976), p. 111.
12. A. K. Majumdar, *Caitanya, His Life and Doctrine: A Study in Vaiṣṇavism* (Bombay: Bharatiya Vidya Bhavan, 1969), p. 138–39.
13. Ibid., p. 139. Some of Caitanya's followers have understood him to be Kṛṣṇa, or an incarnation of Kṛṣṇa, or an incarnation of Kṛṣṇa and Rādhā, and thus divine in more or less the same way that Guṇḍam Rāüḷ is for Mahānubhāvas. See Edward C. Dimock, *The Place of the Hidden Moon: Erotic Mysticism in the Vaiṣṇava-Sahajiyā Cult of Bengal* (Chicago: The University of Chicago Press, 1966), p. 32. But Caitanya is *also* portrayed as a devotee, while Guṇḍam Rāüḷ is never portrayed as a devotee.
14. Glenn E. Yocum, *Hymns to the Dancing Śiva: A Study of Māṇikkavācakar's Tiruvācakam* (New Delhi: Heritage Publishers, 1982), p. 180–81.

15. For example, *Taittirīya Saṃhitā* IV.5.1.3; IV.5.5; *Ṛg Veda* X.136.
16. Wendy Doniger O'Flaherty, *The Origins of Evil in Hindu Mythology* (Delhi: Motilal Banarsidass, 1976), p. 65. Cf. O'Flaherty, *Asceticism and Eroticism in the Mythology of Śiva* (London: Oxford University Press, 1973), p. 215.
17. O'Flaherty, *Asceticism and Eroticism,* p. 214. *Skanda Purāṇa* 7.2.9.24; *Bhāgavata Purāṇa* 4.2.11–16.
18. *Kavitāvalī* VII.158 and 159. Tulsī Dās, *Kavitāvalī,* trans. F. R. Allchin (London: Allen and Unwin, 1964), p. 192–93.
19. Edward J. Thompson and Arthur M. Spencer, *Bengali Religious Lyrics, Śākta* (Calcutta: Association Press, 1923), no. 98, p. 98, quoted in David R. Kinsley, *The Divine Player: A Study of Kṛṣṇa Līlā* (Delhi: Motilal Banarsidass, 1979), p. 28–29. For further discussion and illustration of "divine madness" in the Hindu tradition, see this and others of Kinsley's works: in particular, *The Sword and the Flute: Kālī and Kṛṣṇa, Dark Visions of the Terrible and the Sublime in Hindu Mythology* (Berkeley: University of California Press, 1975), and " 'Through the Looking Glass': Divine Madness in the Hindu Religious Tradition," *History of Religions,* 13 (1974): 270–305.
20. From *Mārkaṇḍeya Devīmāhātmya* 84, in Cornelia Dimmitt and J. A. B. van Buitenen, eds. and trans., *Classical Hindu Mythology: A Reader in the Sanskrit Purāṇas* (Philadelphia: Temple University Press, 1978), p. 238–39.
21. Alain Daniélou, *Hindu Polytheism* (New York: Pantheon, 1964), p. 280–81; Kinsley, *The Divine Player,* p. 30.
22. *Bhāgavata Purāṇa* VII.8.28–30, trans. Ganesh Vasudeo Tagare (Delhi: Motilal Banarsidass, 1976), part III (Ancient Indian Tradition and Mythology, vol. ix), p. 936.
23. From *Bhāgavata Purāṇa* X.8, in Wendy Doniger O'Flaherty, trans., *Hindu Myths: A Sourcebook Translated from the Sanskrit* (Baltimore: Penguin, 1975), p. 219–20. For studies of baby Kṛṣṇa's most beloved pranks, see John Stratton Hawley, "Thief of Butter, Thief of Love," *History of Religions,* 18 (1979): 203–20, and John Stratton Hawley, *Krishna, The Butter Thief* (Princeton, N.J.: Princeton University Press, 1983).
24. See Anne Feldhaus, "The *devatācakra* of the Mahānubhāvas," *Bulletin of the School of Oriental and African Studies, University of London,* 43 (1980): 101–09.
25. Martin Buber, *Tales of the Hasidim: The Early Masters,* trans. Olga Marx (New York: Schocken, 1947), p. 246. For fool figures in modern Jewish literature, see Ruth R. Wisse, *The Schlemiel as Modern Hero* (Chicago: The University of Chicago Press, 1971).
26. *The Encyclopedia of Islam* (new ed.), ed. H. A. R. Gibb et al. (Leiden: Brill, 1960).
27. Annemarie Schimmel, *Mystical Dimensions of Islam* (Chapel Hill: The University of North Carolina Press, 1975), p. 86. E. W. Lane claims, "From my own observation I should say that lunatics or idiots, or impostors, constitute the majority of the persons reputed to be saints among the Muslims of the present day." *Arabian Society in the Middle Ages: Studies from The Thousand and One Nights,* ed. Stanley Lane-Poole (London: Chatto and Windus, 1883), p. 60. But this statement bears the marks of "Orientalist" exaggeration.
28. *Perfect Fools* (Oxford: Oxford University Press, 1980). See also Alexander

Y. Syrkin, "On the Behavior of the 'Fool for Christ's Sake,'" *History of Religions,* 22 (1982): 150–71.

29. *Vita S. Symeonis Sali Confessoris* vi., ed. L. Rydén (Stockholm, Goteborg and Uppsala, 1963), p. 145f., quoted in Saward, *Perfect Fools,* p. 19.
30. Eliade sees a similar meaning in aberrant religious behavior throughout the world: "Religious man sought to imitate, and believed that he was imitating, his gods even when he allowed himself to be led into acts that verged on madness, depravity, and crime." Mircea Eliade, *The Sacred and the Profane: The Nature of Religion,* trans. Willard R. Trask (New York: Harper & Row, 1959), p. 104.
31. *La Vie et la doctrine spirituelle du Père Louis Lallemant,* ed. F. Courel (Paris, 1959), trans. as *The Spiritual Teaching of Father Louis Lallemant,* ed. and trans. A. G. McDougall (London, 1928), p. 197; quoted in Saward, *Perfect Fools,* p. 116. (Saward's italics removed.)
32. The most explicit statement of this idea in the early Mahānubhāva literature is found in *Sūtrapāṭha* X.215: "My children, there is nothing he does not know. Even though he knows everything, he [acts as if he] is ignorant."
33. *The Idea of the Holy,* trans. John W. Harvey, 2nd. ed. (New York: Oxford University Press, 1950), p. 25f.
34. Also "*das Heilige*" in the German translation in which *The Sacred and the Profane* was originally published.
35. Eliade, *The Sacred and the Profane,* p. 10; cf. Mircea Eliade, *Patterns in Comparative Religion,* trans. Rosemary Sheed (1958; repr. ed., New York: World Publishing Company, 1963), p. 1, 459.
36. Eliade, *The Sacred and the Profane,* p. 11.
37. This verse, which is *sūtra* XI.a61 of the *Sūtrapāṭha,* occurs also in "Uttarārdha" 516 of Kolte's edition of the *Līḷācaritra.* It is the only *Sūtrapāṭha sūtra* found in *The Deeds of God in Ṛddhipur.*
38. For a brief but excellent introduction to the medieval *bhakti* movements, see A. K. Ramanujan, *Speaking of Śiva* (Baltimore: Penguin, 1973), p. 19–37. A detailed bibliography is found in Eleanor Zelliot, "The Medieval Bhakti Movement in History: An Essay on the Literature in English," in *Hinduism: New Essays in the History of Religions,* ed. Bardwell L. Smith (Leiden: Brill, 1976), p. 143–68.
39. Note, for instance, the large number of texts entitled "*Rukmiṇī-svayaṃvara*" listed in I. M. P. Raeside, "A Bibliographical Index of Mahānubhāva Works in Marāṭhī," *Bulletin of the School of Oriental and African Studies, University of London,* 23 (1960): 464–507.

III. THE WORLD OF GUṆḌAM RĀÜḶ

ELEANOR ZELLIOT*

Ṛddhipur, Guṇḍam Rāüḷ's lively and busy village home in the thirteenth century, is now "a crumbling dusty village in the rolling country north of Amraoti."[1] In his day it was bigger and more prosperous, but never a government center or a major town. On the northern fringe of the Marāṭhī-speaking area which is now the state of Maharashtra, it had strong ties to the awakening centers of Marāṭhī culture clustered around the Godāvarī River to the southwest and marked by the Vardhā, Vaingaṅgā, and Paingaṅgā rivers to the east.[2] But it was essentially a backwater, trafficked chiefly by pilgrims from the "Gaṅgā Valley" (the Godāvarī) to Rāmṭek, the important pilgrimage center near present-day Nagpur in the east. Only the accident that its most important inhabitant was an incarnation of God led to the recording, in loving detail, of the common life of the time. What the Rāüḷ ate, whom he met, what he said, lets us see something of ordinary village life in the heyday of a rich and creative medieval Hindu empire.

The regional identity of Guṇḍam Rāüḷ's people was with the area of Varhāḍ, or Berar, and so important was this that "the bards" protest the leaving of the "Varhāḍ deity" when the Rāüḷ is being taken away to even such a familiar place as the Gaṅgā (Godāvarī) Valley, perhaps two hundred miles distant (chapter 235). The Varhāḍ region was part of the Yādava kingdom, and had been for a hundred years, but the hand of that dynasty seems to have rested lightly on the village of Ṛddhipur. By Indian standards, the Yādava kingdom was a modest one, but the Yādavas themselves thought of their rule as a mighty force from the Arabian sea to the central regions of India, and they sent their armies to battle in Gujarat and Malwa to the north and to fight the Hoysala empire to the south. But there seems to have been stability and peace within the kingdom, and the moving out of the Yādava armies, captained by ambitious soldiers from any of the upper castes, evidently enriched the empire rather than draining it. Political power was balanced between the center at Devgiri, near modern Aurangabad, and the feudatory chiefs of the districts, without involving lesser units. The independence of individual villages is what seems to be reflected in the account of the life of Ṛddhipur.[3]

None of the Yādava kings of the Rāüḷ's time—Kṛṣṇa, Mahādeva, Rāmacandra—are mentioned by name in the text. A nameless king is mentioned twice, and in rather fearful contexts. In chapter 69, he plucks out the eyes of a prisoner taken when he raids Aḷajpur (Elichpur), a large town twenty miles from Ṛddhipur that has been the traditional capital of Varhāḍ. In chapter 227, he plucks out the eyes of

*Carleton College, Northfield, Minnesota

Demon-in-Battle Kāïṃdaraṇā, who has been proven more generous than he. In spite of the eye-gouging habits of the king, the general tenor of the stories bears out the idea of a stable and comfortable rule. The official and his troops who march into Ṛddhipur in chapter 75 are benevolent souls who immediately pay homage to Guṇḍam Rāüḷ. A mention of the Yādava capital is made only in chapter 293, when the Gosāvī's disciples go confidently to Devgiri Cantonment to get a certain sort of camphor for him. The power in Ṛddhipur lay in the headmen of the village, and they had given it over to the God who lived there.

True, Ṛddhipur was in the curiously unmarked center of the empire, between the Desh area to the west and the eastern part of Vidarbha. The great monuments of the age are not found there. The inscription-mad Yādavas left only one inscription in the entire district of Amraoti, although several more appear in the Vidarbha area to the east. The temples supposedly built by the Yādava minister Hemādri which, according to legend, mushroomed up everywhere, overnight, stone upon stone without mortar, are represented by only one example, and that on the western edge, in the Amraoti region. So the account of the deeds of God in Ṛddhipur does not give us an idea of life in the heartland of an empire, but rather a reflection of the culture of the time in an out-of-the-way village.

If one looks at the text as if it were an unconscious portrayal of society at the time, one is struck with four things: the variety of food (listed here more than in other religious texts because of its importance to the gluttonous God); the amount of contact of the village with other parts of the empire, with India to the north and south, and with varied travelers; the importance and variety of religious practices; and the freedom of the Rāüḷ with women, many of whom are in trade or business, and with members of all castes, high and low.

The food that the Gosāvī craves—and gets—suggests a prosperous area. The starchy-sweet list in chapter 246, for instance: "pulse cakes with holes, crêpes, nectar balls, rice milk, stuffed wheat cakes, *puri*-bread, pulse cakes without holes, molasses balls, sugared crêpes, and rice milk," together with the goods of the Māḷī (gardener caste) women the Gosāvī so enjoys playing with: carrots and radishes, eggplant, sweet marjoram and southernwood, and the grocers' dried dates and coconuts, peppercorns and cloves, cardamoms and betel nut, to say nothing of the plantains and sugarcane, and the grapes and oranges brought "from the capital at Aḷajpur"—all this indicates a land of plenty. And so it was still when the British recorded its life in the nineteenth century.[4] The *Gazetteer* notes that the land was good for jowar (a kind of sorghum grain) and for oil seeds, and famous for its garden produce. Wheat by that time was a food used only for special occasions, and rice was for the wealthy, but other foods there were in abundance. So rich was Berar (Varhāḍ) and so predictable was its rainfall that the British thought for a long time that the area was immune to the famine that plagued the rest of the Deccan. But then, in British times too, came a drought of the sort so graphically pictured in chapter 214. Here, when "the rains went away," the Rāüḷ tells a small cloud, "Drop dead! Come here! Come here, I tell you!" and the rain falls. And the children and babies are saved.

There are also suggestions in the food lists and in other matters that trade firmly tied Varhāḍ to other areas and brought the Gosāvī and his people in contact with the larger world. The camphor craved by the mad God, for instance, is not grown in India but must be imported from the Far East or Southeast Asia.[5] There is not much indication that Ṛddhipur was part of the production of the long cotton staple produced in Berar which made the finest of Indian fabrics, although the Gosāvī does lay a child "on a heap of cotton" to sleep, and he has jolly fun with the Vanījārs, a group long known as carriers of goods. He also plays with the horse traders and their horses, and the ancient practice was to bring horses from the Kathiawad area in Gujarat in trade for cotton since horses did not breed well in the Deccan area.

Religion as well as trade is part of the great variety and vitality of the Ṛddhipur world. Many of the practices recorded in the account of the Rāüḷ's life—including those he makes such devastating fun of—are still part of Maharashtrian life: the Śrāddha ceremony for the dead; the playful Śimagā (Holi) festival; the designs with colored powder—*rāṅgoḷī*—which are still an important household art; the Poḷā festival in which bullocks are decorated (even today, one can buy colorful cloths made to accommodate the bull's hump). The number of temples, monasteries, and hermitages in what was essentially a small town is staggering: Vājeśvara, Sāmānyeśvara, Keśava, Haṭakeśvara, Kaḷaṅkeśvara, Nagareśvara, Bhairava, Kamaleśvara, Rāmnāth, Paraśurāma, Narasiṃha, Vāghikā, Lambodara, Sīdhanāth, Gaṇapati, Nāgnāth, Gopāḷa, Koḍeśvara, Vaḍajaṃbā, Bandeśvara, and more. Some can be identified as local versions of Viṣṇu or Śiva or their associates, or with the Nāth cult—a careful tracing of the names and a comparison with the gods now worshipped would certainly tell us something about the patterns of Hinduism.

Added to these local practices was an extensive participation in pilgrimage. Ṛddhipur people come and go easily to the "Gaṅgā Valley," which seems to be the Godāvarī River, and to the holy city of Vārāṇasī on the true Gaṅgā in the north as well. A Brāhman comes from the south in chapter 281 because he has read of the incarnation of God in Varhāḍ. The goddess (Mahālakṣmī) at Kolhāpur, many miles to the south and west, is mentioned as having come to visit the Gosāvī and then gone on to Mātāpur (which is probably Māhūr, home of the goddess Reṇukā). An astonishing number of pilgrims come by on their way to Rāmṭek, some of them ending their pilgrimage in Ṛddhipur because the God there offers them more than the cluster of temples on the holy hill farther to the east.

Male and female Mahātmās, yogīs, ascetics, a Bharāḍī, and "five hundred renouncers" whom the Gosāvī castigates as "rolling stones" and "cleaners of harrow blades"[6] appear in the village, and although the writer's point is to show the Gosāvī's relationship with all these as God, the effect upon the reader is something like wonder at the richness of the religious life.

Not only do women as Mahātmās and women who own hermitages stroll through the story, but also washerwomen, water women, and gardener caste women who ply their trade in the Gosāvī's company. Only the Brāhmans seem somewhat restricted, confined to a courtyard when all others, from prostitutes to townswomen, wave lights (105) to welcome the Rāüḷ. The Gosāvī is extraordinarily free with these women, and they with him—surely scrubbing women's backs (129) and toying with a woman's breasts (180) were prohibited behavior to all but incarnations of God! And there is some indication (180, 181) that some of his teasing was to encourage more modesty among the women. The importance of women in trade and in the religious life, however, seems indisputable.

The Gosāvī's almost total disregard for caste matters is striking. He eats at the home of a Kuṇbī, a low-caste peasant, while he is a student studying the Vedas; he often arranges his companions in one line for dining, regardless of caste. Even more striking is his special tenderness for the Māṅg, the lowest of Maharashtra's three chief untouchable castes, and a much-neglected group often ignored in favor of the more numerous and somewhat more respected Mahārs.[7] The Gosāvī drinks from a Māṅg's water stand (23), a most unusual disregard of pollution; he plays in the Mahār quarter (a separate section of the village) and eats sweets in a Māṅg's home (46); he goes to the new quarters of the Mahārs and Māṅgs outside the village when their old homes are razed because he brought pollution from them into Brāhman homes (47); he helps the Māṅgs get water, an ever-present problem for the Untouchables, who may not use the village well (48); he blesses a Māṅg with his foot (73), leaving him a newly created God Rāma; he accepts three cloths from a Māṅg (283). The Rāüḷ's acceptance of Māṅgs as full human beings as well as vessels for the divine goes further than that of any other of the extremely tolerant Maharashtrian holy men—as if to prove he was God indeed.

It is possible to read the Gosāvī's even-handed, if somewhat capricious, irresponsible, and at times insane, behavior with all human beings as proof of his divinity. It is also possible to speculate on the very appearance of such a being in little backwater Ṛddhipur as a reflection of the great developments in the larger Marāṭhī-speaking world. The beginnings of a self-conscious sense of a people (or a nation) seem to be tied to the production of literary works in that people's common language which express an interest in the common life of all (perhaps the best-known example of this being Chaucer's *Canterbury Tales* in fourteenth-century England). The late thirteenth century in Maharashtra witnessed the same development. The beginnings of Marāṭhī literature were established during Guṇḍam Rāüḷ's lifetime, and of the three strains of that literature, two fully reflected the common life of the time.

True, the men patronized by the Yādava court, chief among them Hemādri, wrote in Sanskrit. But in the two cultural centers of the Marāṭhī-speaking area, in the Desh to the west and in Vidarbha to the east, Marāṭhī literature began to bloom. Mukundarāja, who lived at the court of some now forgotten feudatory prince in the Vidarbha region,[8] wrote the *Vivekasindhu,* an exposition in Marāṭhī of the philosophy of Śaṅkarācārya. A Brāhmanical exercise it was, but at least an exercise not only for Brāhmans. Also in that area, the same Mhāiṃbhaṭ who compiled the Guṇḍam Rāüḷ story wrote the life of Cakradhar, the founder of the Mahānubhāvas, in an anecdotal form in Marāṭhī. And around 1290, in a totally different vein from either of these, Jñāneśvar finished his great commentary on the *Bhagavadgītā,* popularly and lovingly known today as the *Jñāneśvarī.* Jñāneśvar's work, completed while he was staying in Nevāse, a town in the Desh not far from the Yādava capital of Devgiri, became the cornerstone text for the Maharashtrian *bhakti* movement, the devotion-centered faith that dominated religious writing for five hundred years and continues to be a major strain in Maharashtrian Hinduism.[9] Jñāneśvar was a Brāhman, but the poets who followed him in writing devotional songs that are sung today were from the very castes that the Gosāvī plays with in his village—Nāmdev the tailor, Cokhāmeḷā the Mahār, Sāvtā the Māḷī (gardener).

The sense of the beauty and the importance of common village life is strong in these works. Guṇḍam, the mad Rāüḷ, did not write, but we know of his life because of the new reverence for the vernacular and for the ordinary people that was part of his age. Is it possible that the very vitality of the Gosāvī's world, its acceptance of the mad, foolish, wise saint as a holy man, its tolerance of his capricious egalitarianism, its pride in his fame, is somehow a reflection of this burgeoning popular culture?

Within fifty years of Guṇḍam Rāüḷ's death, the Marāṭhī-based creativity of his period was gone. Ala-ud-Din Khilji, nephew of the sultan in Delhi, brought his army through the passes near Elichpur (Aḷajpur), not twenty miles from Ṛddhipur, and was able to make a surprise attack in 1294 on Devgiri. He used the legendary riches of that city to mount a successful campaign for the Delhi throne. The Yādava kings were humiliated and then deposed. By the middle of the fourteenth century, the Bahmani kingdom with its capital outside the Marāṭhī-speaking area was in full sway. The Marāṭhā creativity begun in the thirteenth century during the days of the mad God of Ṛddhipur seemed to be halted for a full two centuries.

It was not that the Muslim kings were harsh or cruel rulers; it was that the cultural fabric of the area, so recently woven, seemed to lose its character. There was no royal minister like Hemādri who built temples here, there, and everywhere, and managed to create a rapid script for Marāṭhī and to write an encyclopedia of religious rites and observances. The *vārkarī* movement of the *bhakti* faith based on the *Jñāneśvarī* and the songs of the *sants* continued, but no great new poets appeared.[10] No second Mukundarāja was inspired by a court to write philosophical treatises in Marāṭhī. And the Mahānubhāvas themselves went underground, writing their precious texts in a secret script, not for fear of Muslim persecution but because Brāhmanical orthodoxy became more rigid and firmer in its opposition to their heterodox faith. Not until the middle of the sixteenth century did great Marāṭhī literature with a passionate interest in common folk appear again. The *bhakti sant* Eknāth of that era also lived in a Muslim kingdom, but one which had a base in the Marāṭhī-speaking area and which was more dependent upon local officials and local customs.

My reading of *The Deeds of God in Ṛddhipur* assigns it a place in that thirteenth-century development of the cultural ethos which became the base for the Marāṭhī-speaking state of Maharashtra. Such a mad god could have lived anywhere, but what he did, and the very fact that it was recorded in the tongue of the people, reflects not only a theological idea but a historic culture. The Mahānubhāvas have only recently begun to be studied as an essential part of the history of Maharashtra. As their early literature is translated into English,[11] a wider audience can be drawn into their world, and into the world of the common man in a rich, creative period of medieval India.

NOTES

1. I. M. P. Raeside, "The Mahānubhāvas," *Bulletin of the School of Oriental and African Studies, University of London,* 39 (1976): 585.
2. The idea of two nuclear regions of Marāṭhī culture is expounded in Shankar Gopal Tulpule, *Classical Marāṭhī Literature* (*A History of Indian Literature,* volume IX, fasc. 4) (Wiesbaden: Harrassowitz, 1979), p. 326. Tulpule credits M. S. Mate, "Marāṭhī Rājā koṇāsa mhaṇāve," *Bhārata Itihāsa Saṃśodhaka Maṇḍaḷa Quarterly,* 54 (1973): 79.
3. My interpretation of Yādava affairs comes chiefly from Onkar Prasad Verma, *The Yādavas and Their Times* (Nagpur: Vidarbha Saṃśodhana Maṇḍaḷa, 1970).
4. *Central Provinces and Berar Gazetteer: Amraoti,* compiled by S. V. Fitzgerald and A. D. Nelson (Bombay: 1911), p. 275.
5. Edward Balfour, *The Cyclopaedia of India,* 3 vol. (1858; repr. ed., Graz: Austria Akademische Drunk-U Verlag Sonstalt, 1967).

6. Chapter 279. Is it possible that these "five hundred renouncers" are a version of the "five hundred svāmīs" of Aihole in Bijapur, whose eleventh-century inscription notes that they are a merchant guild much given to traveling as they trade? See Verma, *The Yādavas and Their Times,* p. 278–80.
7. For a medieval *bhakti sant*'s compassion for the Mahārs, see Eleanor Zelliot, "Chọkhamela and Eknath: Two *Bhakti* Modes of Legitimacy for Modern Change," *Journal of Asian and African Studies,* 15 (1980): 136–56.
8. Tulpule, *Classical Marāṭhī Literature,* p. 325–26, places the controversial time and place of Mukundarāja in the late thirteenth century in Ambhore, in what is now Bhaṇḍārā district, just east of Nagpur.
9. The most comprehensive source on this important movement is G. A. Deleury, *The Cult of Viṭhobā* (Poona: Deccan College Postgraduate and Research Institute, 1961).
10. *Vārkarīs* are pilgrims who journey to Pandharpur yearly, singing the songs of the *bhakti sant*s (saints) and following the tenets of that movement. The *bhakti* movement did not become a separate sect, as did the followers of Cakradhar, but remained an integral part of Hinduism as a whole.
11. The *Līḷācaritra,* the life of Cakradhar, which is as full of notes on common life as is the Rāüḷ's biography, is being translated by Günther Sontheimer and S. G. Tulpule. Other Mahānubhāva works which have been translated into English include the *Sūtrapāṭha* (the central Mahānubhāva doctrinal text), by Anne Feldhaus (New Delhi: Manohar, 1983); and the *Gadyarāja,* a text dealing mainly with stories about the God Kṛṣṇa, by I. M. P. Raeside (forthcoming).

OTHER REFERENCES

Fairs and Festivals in Maharashtra. Census of India 1961. Volume X. Maharashtra. Part VII. B. Bombay: Maharashtra Census Office, 1969.

Kane, Pandurang Vaman. *History of Dharmaśāstra.* Vol. I, part II. (Rev.) Poona: Bhandarkar Oriental Research Institute, 1975.

Naik, A. V. "Structural Architecture of the Deccan." *New Indian Antiquary,* 9 (1947):187–329.

Pense, Murlidhar Gajanan. *Yādavakālīn Mahārāṣṭra.* Bombay: Muṃbaī Marāṭhī Grantha Saṃgrahālāya Prakāśana, 1963.

Sherwani, H. K., with P. M. Joshi, ed. *History of Medieval Deccan (1295–1724).* 2 vols. Hyderabad: Government Text-Book Press, 1973.

IV. THE TEXT

The Edition

The version of Guṇḍam Rāüḷ's biography translated here is the edition prepared by V. B. Kolte, entitled *Śrī Govindaprabhu Caritra.*[1] The edition is based on a manuscript dated Śaka 1495 (= 1573 A.D.), and notes a few variants from two other manuscripts. Kolte states that one of the latter two manuscripts is undated, but appears from the age of the paper to be about as old as the base manuscript; he does not describe the other manuscript. In addition, Kolte appears to have consulted several other manuscripts of the text.[2] All of the manuscripts are written in the Mahānubhāva cipher called *sakaḷa lipī.*[3]

Kolte reports that the number of chapters in the manuscripts varies, one manuscript combining as one chapter what others give as two. There is also some variation in contents; some manuscripts give a more extended and others a less extended version of an episode. Such variants are not noted in Kolte's edition, but he states that the manuscript he used as the base manuscript is complete.[4]

Title

Kolte entitles his edition *Śrī Govindaprabhu Caritra* (*The Biography of Govindaprabhu*). This is despite the fact that the colophon of the base manuscript of the edition calls the text *Ṛddhipuralīḷā,* and it is despite the fact that as Kolte himself reports, the text is referred to within the Mahānubhāva sect as either *Ṛddhipuralīḷā* or *Ṛddhipuracaritra.*[5] Ṛddhipur is the town in which Guṇḍam Rāüḷ spent most of his life; "Govindaprabhu" appears to be a Sanskritization of his Marāṭhī name, Guṇḍam or Guṇḍam Rāüḷ;[6] this Sanskritized version of his name does not appear in the text.

Kolte explains that he finds it more appropriate to name a biographical text for the person whose life it recounts than to name it for the place where the person lived.[7] In translating the title as "*The Deeds of God in Ṛddhipur,*" I have rendered the traditional title recorded in the colophon of the manuscript rather than the title which Kolte gives to his edition.[8]

In other respects, I have remained faithful in my translation to Kolte's edition. I have chosen freely between the readings of Kolte's base manuscript and the variant readings he gives from the other two manuscripts; in the notes to the translation, I have pointed out particularly significant differences between the readings.

History of the Text

In 1932, Y. K. Deshpande published an Old Marāṭhī account of the composition of the principal Mahānubhāva hagiographies.[9] Called

"Itihāsa," this account is found at the beginning of a composite manuscript of the texts. The manuscript is undated, but Deshpande estimates that it was inscribed early in the nineteenth century.[10] I can find no suggestion as to when "Itihāsa" was originally composed.

The following passage from "Itihāsa" records the composition of the biography of Guṇḍam Rāüḷ, who is here called Śrīprabhu:

> After our Sarvajña ["Omniscient one," i.e., Cakradhar, the founder of the Mahānubhāva sect] had gone, Bhaṭ [i.e., Nāgdev, the leader of Cakradhar's disciples] spent fourteen years in the presence [*sannidhāna*] of Śrīprabhu. Then, after Śrīprabhu had gone, Mhāïṃbhaṭ, questioning Bhaṭ, wrote down the deeds [*līḷās*] of Śrīprabhu. He questioned the devotees about those that they had experienced. He questioned [other] people about those that they had experienced. He wrote their titles. They [?] were in Ṛddhipur for six months after Śrīprabhu['s death]. Then Bhaṭ made arrangements in Ṛddhipur and set off for Mātāpur.[11]

Thus, according to this account, Mhāïṃbhaṭ researched and wrote the biography using the testimony of Nāgdev and others who had known Guṇḍam Rāüḷ.

Kolte believes that this account of Mhāïṃbhaṭ's authorship of Guṇḍam Rāüḷ's biography is supported by the statement in Soṅgobās's "Anvayasthaḷa"[12] that Mhāïṃbhaṭ wrote "*tinhī rupeṃ caritreṃ,*" three biographical texts or three parts of a biographical text. Kolte argues that the first two are the two halves ("Pūrvārdha" and "Uttarārdha") of the *Līḷācaritra,* the biography of Cakradhar, and the third is *Ṛddhipuracaritra,* the biography of Guṇḍam Rāüḷ.[13] But the *Līḷācaritra* is sometimes considered to have three parts rather than two,[14] and so the reference of Soṅgobās's "Anvayasthaḷa" may not include *Ṛddhipuracaritra.* In any case, Raeside's judgment is that this "Anvayasthaḷa" is "unreliable for the earliest period" of Mahānubhāva literature,[15] the period to which the biographical texts certainly belong. Thus, Soṅgobās's statement gives at most weak support to the "Itihāsa" account of Mhāïṃbhaṭ's authorship of *The Deeds of God in Ṛddhipur.*

On the other hand, another text cited by Kolte challenges the "Itihāsa" account. The text, a "Vṛddhācāra Anvaya" of a certain Dāmodara Muni,[16] states that the *Ṛddhipuracaritra* was written by Keśarājabās (Kesobās),[17] who compiled the sayings of Cakradhar in the *Sūtrapāṭha.*[18] But Kolte discredits Dāmodara Muni's statement by showing him to be clearly wrong about several other related matters.[19]

And so there remains neither a serious challenge to the "Itihāsa" report that Mhāïṃbhaṭ wrote the biography of Guṇḍam Rāüḷ nor any strong external evidence corroborating the report. But the biography itself gives some internal evidence of Mhāïṃbhaṭ's authorship. Some of this is found in the frequent mention of Mhāïṃbhaṭ (in 57 of the 323 episodes), and in the fact that several times his inner thoughts are revealed. For instance, in 197 he is jealous of his wife, and in 271 and 272 he has presumptuous thoughts.

However, neither the frequent mention of Mhāïṃbhaṭ nor the revelation of his inner thoughts constitutes very strong evidence of his authorship of the text. Other disciples, notably Ābāïseṃ and Nāgdev, are also mentioned frequently. And others' inner thoughts are also revealed—for example, Sādheṃ's, in 177; Īśvar Nāyak's, in 251; and those of unnamed housewives, in 39 and 72.

Somewhat stronger internal evidence of Mhāïṃbhaṭ's authorship is found in the account of his researching one of the stories in the text, 252. Here, as always, he is referred to in the third person. But he is referred to in the third person in the *Līḷācaritra* also, and there is ample external evidence that he wrote that.

Thus, what evidence there is seems mostly to support the "Itihāsa" account of Mhāïṃbhaṭ's authorship of the biography of Guṇḍam Rāüḷ.

"Itihāsa" states further that the biography was composed within six months of Guṇḍam Rāüḷ's death. The biography itself records the date of his death, in chapter 322 of Kolte's edition. Here the date is given as the fourth day of the "dark" (waning moon) fortnight of the month of Bhādrapad, in the Vyaya year. Kolte, using calendrical information and other Mahānubhāva manuscripts besides the base manuscript of his edition, determined that Guṇḍam Rāüḷ died late in Śaka 1208 (= 1286–1287 A.D.).[20] If we accept this as the date of Guṇḍam Rāüḷ's death and accept the "Itihāsa" statement that Mhāïṃbhaṭ composed Guṇḍam Rāüḷ's biography six months later, this gives us 1287 A.D. as the date of the composition of the text.

But the text composed in 1287, it seems, is not the prototype of the manuscripts we now have. For the "Itihāsa" account goes on to relate the loss of many of the original Mahānubhāva manuscripts, including the manuscript containing the biographical texts. Robbers stole the manuscripts from a party of Mahānubhāvas who were crossing the mountains on the way to the coastal plain of Mahārāṣṭra, the Koṅkaṇ.[21] Several Mahānubhāva texts report this loss,[22] which Nene dates to 1308, the year in which the Yādava king Rāmadevarāja was taken prisoner and sent to Delhi by Malik Kāphūr, an officer in the army of Ala-ud-Din.[23]

The texts that were lost had to be reconstructed by disciples who had memorized them. "Itihāsa" describes the reconstruction of a number of different versions of the biographical texts[24] but does not specifically mention the reconstruction of the *Ṛddhipuracaritra*. The account in the "Anvayasthaḷa" published by Nene in 1936, however, does mention the *Ṛddhipuracaritra* by name among the texts reconstructed.[25]

According to this account, the *Ṛddhipuracaritra* and other texts were reconstructed by Dattobās of Taḷegaon, a disciple of Haribās. This Haribās is named earlier in the "Anvayasthaḷa" as a disciple of Bānāïseṃ, who in turn is said to have been a disciple of Āṇobās.[26] Āṇobās,[27] according to Kolte,[28] was a disciple of Bāïdevbās, who was a disciple of Nāgdev, the successor to the Mahānubhāvas' founder Cakradhar. Thus Dattobās's line of succession is as follows:

Cakradhar
|
Nāgdev
|
Bāïdevbās
|
Āṇobās
|
Bānāïseṃ
|
Haribās
↓
Dattobās

Allowing twenty years for each generation (except Bāïdevbās's[29]) after Nāgdev, and accepting Deshpande's calculation of Śaka 1234 (= 1312 A.D.) as the latest possible date of Nāgdev's death, Kolte calculates that Dattobās reconstructed the texts by Śaka 1314 (= 1392 A.D.).[30]

In making his reconstructions, states the "Anvayasthaḷa," Dattobās relied primarily on the Hirāṃbā version (*pāṭha*), but accepted variants from Paraśarāmabās and Rāmeśvarabās and other authorities in the sect. The Hīrāṃbā version[31] is identified by "Itihāsa" as one prepared by Harībās (= Haribās), who had learned the text orally from Hīrāïseṃ (or Hīrāṃbīkā), who in turn had learned it from Āṇobās. Haribās used for his reconstructions not only his own recollections but also those of others who had memorized the text.[32]

Thus, by this account, the text we now have dates from the late fourteenth century, was prepared by Dattobās of Taḷegā̃v, and is a composite of several people's recollections of the original work of Mhāïṃbhaṭ. Echoes of the text's history are heard in the passages introduced by such words as "*ekī vāsanā*," which I have usually translated, "According to some. . . ." Such passages record variant oral versions of the text.

Commentaries

Kolte reports having examined manuscripts of two commentaries on the *Ṛddhipuracaritra.*[33] Both of the manuscripts date from the end of the sixteenth century Śaka (= late seventeenth century A.D.). One of the commentaries, the *Hetusthaḷa* of Nyāyabās, is listed by Raeside and dated by him to c. 1353.[34] But according to Raeside, this text, which is "not extant," is concerned with "describing the circumstances in which various sayings of Cakradhar were spoken"—that is, it is a commentary on the *Sūtrapāṭha* rather than on the *Ṛddhipuracaritra.* The other commentary, the *Vastucandrikāsthaḷa* of Gopībhāskara, is not even mentioned by Raeside, although Raeside does list other works of Gopībhāskara and dates him to the mid-seventeenth century.[35] Kolte quotes two sample passages from the *Vastucandrikāsthaḷa;* both passages emphasize the Gosāvī's mercy in mixing with the townspeople of Ṛddhipur.

Unfortunately, I have not yet found copies of either of these commentaries, and so I cannot really judge their usefulness for interpreting *The Deeds of God in Ṛddhipur.* The *Vastucandrikāsthaḷa,* at least, should prove to be of interest in its own right as reflecting attempts, on the part of a later generation of Mahānubhāvas, to understand the behavior of Guṇḍam Rāüḷ.

NOTES

1. 5th ed. (Malkapur: Aruṇa Prakāśana, 1972.) (According to Raeside, "A Bibliographical Index of Mahānubhāva Works in Mārāṭhi," *Bulletin of the School of Oriental and African Studies, University of London,* 23 [1960]: 500, the first edition is dated 1944.) I have corrected my copy of the fifth edition from a copy of the second edition, which contains fewer printing errors.
2. V. B. Kolte, introduction to *Śrī Govindaprabhu Caritra,* p. 1–2.
3. For a description of this cipher, see I. M. P. Raeside, "The Mahānubhāva *sakaḷa lipī,*" *Bulletin of the School of Oriental and African Studies, University of London,* 33 (1970): 328–34. Cf. Feldhaus, *The Religious System of the Mahānubhāva Sect: The Mahānubhāva Sūtrapāṭha* (New Delhi: Manohar, 1983), p. 79–81.
4. Kolte, introduction to *Śrī Govindaprabhu Caritra,* p. 2–3: *govindaprabhūsaṃbaṃdhīcā sarva majakūra śake 1495cyā pratīta aṃtarbhūta jhālelāca āhe.*
5. Ibid., p. 1.
6. "Prabhu" and "Rāüḷ" are both honorifics, the former Sanskrit and the latter Marāṭhī.
7. Kolte, introduction to *Śrī Govindaprabhu Caritra,* p. 1.
8. As Kolte himself notes, the text is one of a series of Mahānubhāva biographies named not for their subjects but for their locations. There seems to be a theological significance to the set of names: since each biography records the life and deeds of a different incarnation of the Mahānubhāvas' one God, the subject of all of them is in a sense the same person, and the texts can be distinguished by the different *loci* of the one God's various activities. It is this significance which leads me to translate the word "*līḷā*" or "*caritra*" in the title *Ṛddhipuralīḷā* or *Ṛddhipuracaritra* as "the deeds *of God.*"
9. In Y. K. Deshpande, "Mahānubhāvāṃce Caritragrantha," *Bhārata Itihāsa Saṃśodhaka Maṇḍaḷa Quarterly,* 13 (September 1932): 45–57. It is not clear whether what Deshpande published is all, or only a part, of the account. See Raeside, "A Bibliographical Index," p. 481.
10. Deshpande, "Mahānubhāvāṃce Caritragrantha," p. 46.
11. Ibid., p. 49–50. *āmaceyā sarvajñāṃ bījeṃ keleṃyā naṃtareṃ bhaṭāte śrīprabhuceṃ caudā varṣeṃ sannidhāna. maga śriprabhu bījeṃ keleṃyā naṃtareṃ*

mahībhaṭī bhaṭātem̐ pūsauni śrīprabhucīyā līḷā līhīlīyā. bhaktācīye anūbhavīcīyā bhaktā pūsīlīyā. janācīyā anūbhavīcīyā janāsi pūsīlīyā. tayācīyā ādi kelīyā. śrīprabhu māgem̐ sā māsa ṛddhipūrī hote. maga bhaṭa ṛddhipūrī vyavasthā karūṇi mātāpūrā nīgāle.

12. Ed. V. B. Kolte, "Anvayasthaḷa," *Mahārāṣṭra Sāhitya Patrikā,* 25 (1953): 25–31.
13. Kolte, introduction to *Śrī Govindaprabhu Caritra,* p. 11.
14. Kolte argues against this view in his introduction to the *Līḷācaritra,* p. 62–63.
15. Raeside, "A Bibliographical Index," p. 470.
16. The text is not listed in Raeside's "Bibliographical Index," and Kolte gives no further bibliographical information about it, except to identify Dāmodara Muni as a disciple of Nāyaṃbās. This Nāyaṃbās could possibly be the same as Nyāyabās, the author of the commentary *Hetusthaḷa,* discussed later.
17. Kolte, introduction to *Śrī Govindaprabhu Caritra,* p. 10.
18. Feldhaus, *The Religious System of the Mahānubhāva Sect,* p. 9f.
19. Kolte, introduction to *Śrī Govindaprabhu Caritra,* p. 11. More recently, Mhāiṃbhaṭ's authorship of the text has been challenged by V. D. Kulkarni, in the introduction to his edition *Śrī Goviṃdaprabhu-Caritra* (Pune: Venus Prakāśana, 1980. The edition is taken directly from Kolte's), p. xi–xviii, and defended by Kolte in "Śrī Goviṃdaprabhucaritra: Kartṛtva āṇi Kāla" (*Navabhārata* 35 [February 1982]: 37–48 and 35 [March 1982]: 1–16).
20. Kolte, introduction to *Śrī Govindaprabhu Caritra,* p. 12–14. That is, in *gata* Śaka 1208 (= *cālū* Śaka 1209). Cf. notes to chapter 322 in this translation.
21. Deshpande, p. 51. *aisem̐ asatā dīlīceni sulatānem̐ cāli kelī. teṇem̐ rājīka bheṇem̐ kavīśvara kokaṇā gele. kamaḷāïsem̐ vālhā rāhīlī. ano bāsa jhāḍī maṃḍaḷātu sīrapūrāsi gele. daṃtte gopāḷa bāsa te kokaṇā na vacatīci. te ghāṭamāthāci rāhīle. kavīśvara kokaṇā jātā mārgī cora uṭhīle. tehī kokaṇīṃcā ghāṭa ūtaratā samasta gurukūḷa nāgavīlem̐. pothīyācī jhoḷī parasarāma bāsāpāsī hotī. tyāṃtūni parasarāma bāsī eka pustaka kāḍhīlem̐. te bhoïvari tanāta gāḷīlem̐. era javaṃ gāḷāvī taṃva eṇem̐ corem̐ parasarāma bāsāciye hātācī jhoḷī āsaḍūni nelī. tyāṃta ādī sahīta pāca rūpem̐ carītrem̐ prakaraṇācī pothī sthānācī pothī itūkem̐ gele.*
22. See Kṛṣṇamuni's "Anvayamāḷikā" (H. N. Nene, "Kṛṣṇamunīcem̐ Anvayasthaḷa," *Bhārata Itihāsa Saṃśodhaka Maṃḍaḷa Quarterly* 20 [1939]: 57–71) and the "Anvayasthaḷa" published by H. N. Nene in *Bhārata Itihāsa Saṃśodhaka Maṃḍaḷa Quarterly* 17 (1936): 55–59, in addition to "Itihāsa."
23. Nene, "Anvayasthaḷa," p. 58. Cf. Kolte, introduction to *Līḷācaritra,* p. 66–67.
24. It is not really clear whether the reconstructions "Itihāsa" describes are of the *Līḷācaritra* only, or of the biographies of all the incarnations of Parameśvara.
25. Nene, "Anvayasthaḷa," p. 58. *tayā hari bāsāce taḷegāṃvakara datto bāsa teṃhī hīraṃbāpāṭha pradhāna karuni paraśarāma bāsa rāmeśvara bāsa āṇikahī ācārye tayācīṃ vāsanā[n]tarem̐ ekavaṭuni purvārdhacarītrem̐, uttarārdhacaritrem̐, . . . ṛddhipuracaritrem̐ . . . anvayīṃ lāvīlīṃ. sakaḷacaritrācīyā ādi ṭāṃcilīyā.*
26. Ibid.
27. = Gopāḷapaṇḍit. Raeside, "A Bibliographical Index," p. 506.
28. Kolte, introduction to *Śrī Govindaprabhu Caritra,* p. 17.

29. Bāïdevbās was not at the head of the line long enough to count as a full generation. Ibid.
30. Ibid.
31. See note 25.
32. Deshpande, p. 52. *anobācī sīkṣyeṃ hīrāṃbīkā te hī ano bāsāpāsūni līḷā ghokīlīyā hotīyā. maga hīrāïsāpāsūni tyācā sīkṣyī harī bāsī ghokīlīyā hotīyā. maga harī bāsī jayā jayā bhīkṣukāsi līḷācā ghoka hotā tayā tayā mānaleṃyā tiyā līḷā pūsīlīyā. tyā tyā vāsanā āna hīrāïsāpāsūni ghokīlā jo ghoka aiseṃ yāceṃ anvayī lāvūni pustaka keleṃ to hīrāṃbā pāṭha.*
33. Introduction to *Śrī Govindaprabhu Caritra,* p. 54–55.
34. "A Bibliographical Index," p. 481.
35. Ibid., p. 506.

THE WORLD OF GUNḌAM RĀÜḶ

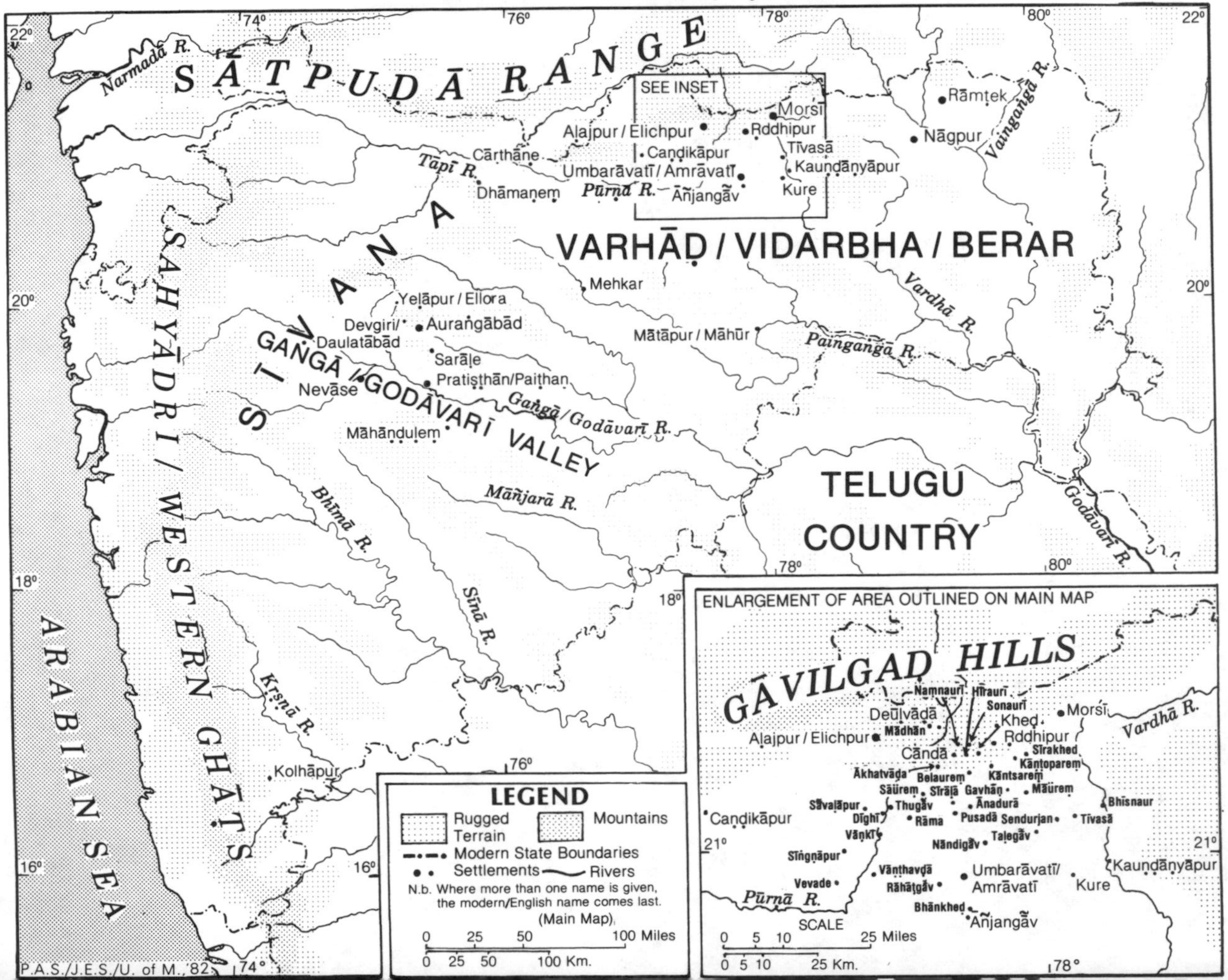

The Deeds of God in Ṛddhipur

Homage to Śrī Pareśa.[1]

1. He takes on an incarnation near Ṛddhipur.[1]

He[2] took on a womb incarnation[3] in the house of a Kāṇva Brāhman[4] in Kāṇṭsareṃ (according to some, in Kāṇṭopareṃ; according to others, in Māürerṃ),[5] a few miles[6] from Ṛddhipur. His father was Anant Nāyak. His mother was Nemāïseṃ.

The Gosāvī's mother had had many children; none of them had survived. She was very distressed about it. Finally the Gosāvī[7] was born as her last child. He was named Guṇḍo.[8]

After about a year, his mother and father died, so he was raised by his mother's brother and sister.[9]

Seven years later,[10] his thread ceremony[11] was performed. He was given the topknot and the thread, and a loincloth. The *paḷasulā* ritual[12] was performed. In this way, four days passed. On the fourth day, the priest said, "Go begging, Guṇḍo. Use the words, 'Om, give me alms, good woman.' "[13]

He would say, "Give me alms," but he would not say "Om."

With this, his thread ceremony was completed. Then they took him to Ṛddhipur.

2. He lives in Ṛddhipur.[1]

Bopa Upādhyāya's[2] [teacher] was Rāma Upādhyāya; his [teacher] was Tīka Upādhyāya. The Gosāvī was sent to study with Bopa Upādhyāya. He began to study the Vedas.

The Gosāvī was extraordinarily talented.[3] What the Gosāvī learned in a day, no one else could learn in a month. What the Gosāvī learned in a month, no one else could learn in a year. He would point out the teacher's mistakes as well as the students'. The [teacher] would say, "Guṇḍo is not ordinary. He must be an incarnation of Īśvara.[4] We don't hear him studying. We don't hear him memorizing. We hear him reciting a whole chapter at once." (According to some, [the teacher said,] "We don't hear him reciting. We don't hear him reading. We hear him memorizing it all at once. This Guṇḍo is not ordinary. He must be an incarnation of Īśvara, or he must be an incarnation of a deity.")[5]

Bopa Upādhyāya would speak this way, and the Gosāvī would laugh and say very softly, "Drop dead![6] It's true, I tell you."

To the students he would say, "More than others."[7]

3. His power becomes evident.

All the students would go to get grass for the teacher's calves. Each of them would get two bundles. They would put them on their heads and carry them back.

The Gosāvī's bundle went along in the air [over his head]. The students saw this. They came to the teacher and told him about it.

The teacher said, "This Guṇḍo is not ordinary. He must be an incarnation of Īśvara, or he must be an incarnation of a deity."[1] Then he said to his wife, "Don't give this Guṇḍo any heavy work."

(According to some, the teacher clasped the Gosāvī's holy feet [and said], "I'm a sinner, Lord. I don't know [who you are]. So please tell me, Lord." And the Gosāvī laughed,[2] but he would not explain.)

4. His light is seen.[1]

One day the Gosāvī had fallen asleep among the students. Light was streaming from his holy body. The students saw it, and they were afraid. They came to the teacher and told him, "Teacher, light is coming from Guṇḍo's head. He is talking to himself. He is saying, 'Why have you come? Why have you gone?' "

The teacher said, "No one knows who this Guṇḍo is. He is an incarnation of Īśvara."

5. He eats with children.

The Gosāvī would come along when children were eating. The Gosāvī would eat with them, and the children would cry out in protest. Their mother would say, "Why are you crying? Let him eat." Then she would portion out [the food, and say], "Rāüḷ,[1] you eat this [serving]; the children will eat these."

They would say, "Mother! The Rāüḷ won't eat his own serving. He'll only eat ours."

She would say, "Rāüḷ, why do you pass up your own share and eat the children's share?"

Still he would eat only the children's share. So she would tell them, "Let the Rāüḷ go ahead and eat. I'll give you some more later."

They would put their plates on their heads, and then he would eat standing up. In this way, he would have a meal of their servings; his own serving he would make into *prasād.*[2]

She would add some more to that serving, and they would eat it.

6. Sādheṃ[1] takes *prasād.*

One day when the Gosāvī was eating at a Kuṇbī[2] house, Sādheṃ came over. She prostrated herself and took *prasād.* The housewife said, "What has come over this Brāhman's widow that she's eating our Kuṇbī food?"

Sādheṃ said, "What's this, my friend? Why are you abusing me? I've only taken the Rāüḷ's *prasād.*"

"So what? It's the Rāüḷ's *prasād,* but the food is ours!"

And the Gosāvī laughed. Then he gave her more *prasād.*

7. He covers a child with a double water bag.[1]

A certain housewife set off to get water. There was no one [else], old or young, in her house. Just then, the Gosāvī came along. She said, "Rāüḷ, take my child for a moment while I get a load of water."

So the Gosāvī took him and played with him for a while. Then he got a double water bag down from its peg. He laid him down to sleep on one of its halves, and he covered him with the other half. And the Gosāvī left.

The woman returned. She set down her water pot. She entered the house, looked in the cradle, and saw no sign [of her child]. She looked on the bed, but he wasn't there either. Then she asked her women friends in the neighborhood, "Did the Rāüḷ leave my child with you?"

"No, he didn't give him to us," [they all said]. Then her neighbor friends added, "How could you put your child into the hands of the Rāüḷ? The Rāüḷ is mad. The Rāüḷ is possessed. What will you do when he throws him into a small well, or when he throws him into a big well?"

At that, she went running into the house. Just then the [top] half of the double water bag stirred. She looked, and she saw her child. He was motionless.

And immediately she cried out, "Oh, mother, what will I do? Oh, mother, what will I do?" and she lifted the child and looked at him. He was sleeping happily.

Then she said, "Look at that! The Rāüḷ has taken good care of my child. The Rāüḷ is our Mother. The Rāüḷ is our Father." And she was happy.

8. He brings a dead child to life.[1]

The Gosāvī used to play with someone's child. It died. It was taken and buried in a pathway, at the northeast corner of the Vājeśvara temple.[2]

The Gosāvī arrived then at its house. [Its mother] saw the Gosāvī and began to cry. Then she said, "Rāüḷ, the child you used to play with died today," and everyone began to cry. And the Rāüḷ felt compassion.

Then the Gosāvī said, "Oh, drop dead! Bring it here! Bring it here, I tell you."

"What can I bring now, Rāüḷ," she said.

"Oh, drop dead!" [he replied]. "It should be brought, I say. . . . It should not be brought, I say. . . . Yes, it must be brought, I tell you!" and he went trotting off.

He went to the place, cleared away the stones, and dug. Then he pulled out [the baby], brushed it, wiped it, and began looking at it blissfully. Then he put it on his hip and brought it back.

[Its mother] saw them, and shut the door. "Take it away! Take it away, Rāüḷ! Take the corpse back!" [she said].

Next door to them lived an old woman. He took [the child] and put it into her arms. "Rāüḷ," she said, "what am I to do? I am a hundred years old."

So the Gosāvī put her nipple into its mouth. Milk rushed into her breast. It began to suck noisily.

At this point, [the mother] opened her door. She looked, and saw what was happening.

The Gosāvī left.

She began to ask for [her child]. The old woman said, "Why wouldn't you take him when he was offered to you? And why should I give him to you now?"

With that, [the mother] set off to make a complaint to the village headmen. The headmen said, "The Rāüḷ gave him to her; the child is hers. You may love the child, but you may not have him. Now you must live near him."

So she began to live near him, and she gave him a bed and a mattress. She gave him a cow.

Eventually he lived to be a hundred years old. He became a skilled cowherd. His name was Dāmodhar. For the rest of his life, he had no fevers. He used to tell the devotees about the divine deed which he had experienced.

9. He lays a child down to sleep in a heap of cotton.[1]

A certain housewife said, "Rāüḷ, would you take my child for a moment, while I go get a potful of water?" She put her child into the Gosāvī's arms. The Gosāvī played with the child for a while.

There was a heap of cotton in a wide, shallow basket. He laid the child down to sleep in it, and the heap closed back over [the child]. Then the Gosāvī left.

The woman returned. She put down the water pot and entered the house. She began to look for her child. She looked in the cradle. She looked on the bed. She looked in the nooks and crannies. She didn't see it anywhere. Then she asked her women friends in the neighborhood, "Did the Rāüḷ hand my child to you?"

"No, he didn't," they said. "The Rāüḷ is mad. The Rāüḷ is possessed. What will you do when he throws it into a small well, or into a big well, or when he throws it into a grain cellar?"

As she was searching this way, the heap [of cotton] stirred. The child was sleeping happily in the basket. "Look at that!" she said. "The Rāüḷ is our Mother. The Rāüḷ is our Father. How well the Rāüḷ has taken care of my child!" And she became happy.

10. He and the children keep warm.

The Gosāvī would build a fire. Each of the children would bring some fuel, and then [the Gosāvī] would throw it all on at once. They would say, "Rāüḷ, throw on just a little," and they would go back and bring [more] fuel. Again the Gosāvī would throw it all on at once.

The fire would flare up, and he would laugh. Again they would bring some, and say, "Rāüḷ! Rāüḷ, throw on just a little bit." They would say it again, but again the Gosāvī would do the same as before.

Finally he would scatter [the fire] and leave.

11. He plays with Māḷī women[1] from another village.

Māḷī women from a neighboring village used to come [to Ṛddhipur], bringing eggplants, carrots, vegetables, flowers, sweet marjoram, and southernwood. They would sit against a wall to the north of the rest house and sell their wares.

The Gosāvī would go there and play with them. He would take a basket in his holy hand and take out grain for barter. He would put in vegetables; he would put in carrots. "This is too little; this is too much," [he would say]. Where there was too little, he would put in more. Where there was too much, he would take some away.

The women would say, "Rāüḷ, why are you taking away what you just put in?"

And the Gosāvī would laugh.

12. He hides behind the Vināyaka[1] image.

The children used to play hide-and-seek. The Gosāvī would come along. He would play with the children, hiding himself.

The Gosāvī would hide behind the Vināyaka image. The children would look all around, but they would not see him. And they would cry out, "Guṇḍo!"

And right there he would say "Boo!" and stand up. And all the children would be amazed. They would play again, and again the Gosāvī would do the same thing.

The Gosāvī would play this way. Then he would leave.

13. He plays with tamarind seeds.[1]

The children used to play with tamarind seeds on the pedestal of the Vināyaka image. The Gosāvī would come along. He would agree to play.

They would roughen one side of the tamarind seeds. They would throw one down. It would fall exactly the way the Gosāvī said. In this way, he won all the tamarind seeds.

The children would say, "All the roughened seeds fall the Gosāvī's way. None fall our way. Come on," they would say, "let's get some more tamarind seeds. Then let's roughen them on one side."

And they would get some more tamarind seeds. They would roughen them on one side. They would play again, and all the roughened seeds would fall the way the Gosāvī said. In this way, he won all the tamarind seeds. Then, as he was leaving, he would say, "Whee! Whee!" and scatter [the seeds]. And the children would tussle for them.

And the Gosāvī would laugh. Then he would leave.

14. He whirls his holy hand.[1]

Māhādāïseṃ[2] said, "Show me, Lord Gosāvī, how you used to whirl your holy hand when you were young." In the Rājamaḍh,[3] near the bathing area, he began to whirl his holy hand around in a circle.

He got a cramp.[4] Then the Gosāvī said, "Oh, drop dead! The Cripple[5] told you, I say," and he struck the ground and laughed.

The people of the village told the Gosāvī [Cakradhar; he told Ābāïseṃ;[6] and] Ābāïseṃ told Māhādāïseṃ.

15. He stays in a dung heap.

Until he was twelve years old, the Gosāvī stayed in Tīka Upādhyāya's heap of dried dung cakes. One day the Gosāvī had fallen asleep[1] in the dung heap. By the middle of the night, light from his holy body had reached up to the heavens. Tīka Upādhyāya's wife saw it. She said to Tīka Upādhyāya, "Get up! Get up! Someone mad or possessed has been left here. He has started a fire."

The teacher came running outside. He saw the light coming from the Gosāvī's holy face, and he prostrated himself. He went up close. He placed his head on the holy feet. Then he made a request: "Lord, please sleep on the raised platform."

The Gosāvī got up onto the platform. Then they gave him a pack-saddle to sleep on, and the Gosāvī went to sleep.[1] The teacher went into the house.

16. He puts a sitting-cloth into a water jar.[1]

The teacher had two daughters, Gāvitrī and Sāvitrī.[2] Gāvitrī was having her menstrual period. She was sitting and eating on the Gosāvī's platform. Her mother said, "Hey! Don't eat on the Gosāvī's platform! Don't sit there!"

"What's wrong with it?" she said. "The homeless have gotten a home. The women of the house [and] the Gosāvī have gotten the verandah."

At this point, the Gosāvī came along. "Hey! Get up! Get up!" [he said]. "Oh, drop dead! Go away, I tell you!" She didn't budge.

So the Gosāvī threw a handful of dust onto the cloth she was sitting on, and he slapped her. He took the cloth and put it into a water jar.

At this point the teacher arrived. [His wife] told him, "Gāvitrī was sitting on the Rāüḷ's platform to eat. I said, 'Hey, get up! Get up!' but she didn't budge. Then the Rāüḷ got here. He threw a handful of dust onto her sitting-cloth. He slapped her. He took the cloth and put it into the water jar. He polluted the water jar."

The teacher said, "A large vessel cannot be polluted. Ladle out the water and burn some rotten grass [in it]."

It was full of water. That night the teacher saw one of the initiated boys taking a bath [in the water]. The teacher said, "Why are you doing this?"

"The Rāüḷ put a sitting-cloth into the water jar, so this has become very holy water," [replied the boy]. "So this is where I came."

Then the teacher had that same water put to everyday use. In this way the Gosāvī did away with [the teacher's] error. [The Gosāvī] was very compassionate.

17. He takes things outdoors.

One day the Gosāvī began to take things outdoors. People said, "Who knows what omen the Rāūḷ sees today." He clasped a low stool to his belly; he set it outside. He clasped a small cot to his belly; he carried it outside. He brought a square stool and set it too outside. He took plates, dishes, and metal water pots and carried them outside.

Then a fire started. It burned the whole village. What the Gosāvī had carried out was saved.

18. He mounts a "horse."[1]

One day the Gosāvī mounted a "horse." Then the Gosāvī said, "Oh, drop dead! Get moving! Get moving, I tell you!" and he beat it with a switch.

The village headmen said, "What you can't get moving will never move. What is there that you can't get moving?"

And the Gosāvī laughed and got down from the "horse." Then the Gosāvī left.

19. Ghāṭe Haribhaṭ[1] forgets.

One day the Gosāvī was mounted on a "horse." Ghāṭe Haribhaṭ came along. He was wearing a halter, with the rope thrown loosely about his shoulders. In his hands was a small earthen bowl; in the bowl were the ashes of a piece of cow dung.

He began to offer incense to the Gosāvī. Then the Gosāvī said, "Oh, drop dead! Go away! Go away, I tell you! Drop dead! Drop dead! Go away! Go to Sīṅgṇāpur,[2] I tell you!"

Immediately he set off for Sīṅgṇāpur. Then the Gosāvī left.

20. He drinks water at Keśav Nāyak's water stand.[1]

One day the Gosāvī went to Keśav Nāyak's[2] water stand. A child had been placed there to guard it. [The Gosāvī] glared at him with his holy eyes and made as if to slap him. He was frightened, and he stepped away.

The Gosāvī opened the spout of the water stand. He put it into his holy mouth. He began to drink the water. "Enough! Enough, I say!" he said, gesturing with his holy hand.

The child said, "Yes, yes. That must be enough now," and laughed at him from a distance.

In this way he emptied two water jars. Then he sat down between the two water jars. He put one of his holy feet into one of the water jars; he put the other holy foot into the other water jar.[3] The Gosāvī played this way for a while. Then he left.

21. He plays touch-the-post.

The Gosāvī went to the Sāmānyeśvara[1] temple. Children were playing there. The Gosāvī agreed to play. The children would say, "Rāüḷ, don't touch this post," and the Gosāvī would touch that very post.

In this way he gave his contact[2] to all the posts, except for one in the northwest corner. There the Gosāvī sat down. The children brought wood-apple fruits and broke them open. The Gosāvī made them into *prasād.* Then he left.

22. He criticizes an ascetic.

The Gosāvī was playing near Bhadra[1] when he saw an ascetic eating his [supposedly] meager meal. And the Gosāvī said, "Syrup, cooked pulse, a dish of oil, a dish of buttermilk, rice with ghee, and salt.[2] [Food from] this house, [food from] that house. Death to it all!"

The Gosāvī criticized him this way. He started to leave. Then the Gosāvī left.

23. He drinks water at the Māṅgs' water stand.[1]

The Gosāvī went to the Māṅgs'[2] water stand. A child was seated there. The Gosāvī took in his holy hand one of the two animal horns[3] that had been placed there, and he ran after the child. [The child] ran away.

[The Gosāvī] took the drinking pitcher in his holy hand, and he drank. He emptied all the water of the water jar. The Gosāvī washed his holy hands and holy face in the water left in the bottom of the jar. He washed his holy feet right in the water jar. Then the Gosāvī left.

24. He uproots and replants a grapevine.[1]

The Gosāvī went to Aḷajpur. At a certain Brāhman's house, there was a grapevine. The Gosāvī uprooted it. The [Brāhman] said, "Hey, Rāüḷ! Why did you pull up a fruit-bearing, blooming plant?"

On the third day, the Gosāvī brought it back. Then he dug in the ground with a stick. He planted the roots. He poured on three handfuls of water from the water jar.

The [Brāhman] said, "Rāüḷ, it's dry and withered. How will it take root now?"

Then the Gosāvī went off. Three days later it sprouted bunches of fruits and flowers. And the [Brāhman] was amazed. He said, "The Rāüḷ is our Mother. The Rāüḷ is our Father. The Rāüḷ is Īśvara. There is nothing the Rāüḷ cannot do." He began to praise him this way.

Then the Gosāvī left.

25. He plays with milkmaids on the Bailaur road.[1]

All the milkmaids used to gather at the foot of a banyan tree. The Gosāvī would go there. He would taste all their curds, milk, ghee, butter, and buttermilk. Those who let him have a taste would sell theirs as soon as they set out. Those who did not let him have a taste would go through the whole village without selling anything.

The others would say to them, "See! The reason you don't sell anything is that you don't let the Gosāvī taste it. Take it to the Rāüḷ now, and it will sell."

So they would approach the Gosāvī. They would give him a taste, and then it would sell. Then the Gosāvī would say, "Oh, drop dead! This is sweet, I tell you," and he would laugh.

This is how he would play.

26. He plays with milkmaids on the Kheḍ road.

Milkmaids would ask other milkmaids, "Why are you late today?"

"The Rāüḷ was playing with us. He was slow about tasting our curds, milk, ghee, and butter. He was playing around. That's why we're late."

Those from the village would say, "It was with *us* the Rāüḷ was playing."[1] Others would say, "It was with *us* the Rāüḷ was playing." All the milkmaids talked together this way.

Some would not let him have a taste. Theirs would remain unsold. When [their curds] were moved, they would turn watery. They would get slushy. The women would go through the whole village this way, without selling anything.

The others would say, "See! If you would let the Rāüḷ have a taste, it would sell. Let the Rāüḷ taste it even now, and it will sell."

So [such a] woman would take [her wares] to the Rāüḷ. The Rāüḷ would take a taste [and say], "Oh, drop dead! It's sweet, I tell you! Go now, I tell you." And she would set off. She would sell it for a high price. Then she would leave.

27. Śrīprabhu[1] plays by escaping from the children at the Keśava temple.

A student had gone into the village at a time when children were playing at Keśava's[2] temple. The Gosāvī went into the temple, and the children quickly shut the door. They began to shout, "We've shut the Rāüḷ in!"

They were shouting this when the student came along. "Why are you shouting?" he asked.

"We've got the Rāüḷ shut up inside."

He said, "I've just come from the marketplace. The Rāüḷ is there, playing his games."

They opened the door and looked. He was not inside. Then they looked in the sanctuary. He wasn't there either. And they were amazed, astonished, and dumbfounded.

28. He plays with Telī women[1] in the marketplace.

Ṛddhipur was a market town. Telī women would be selling oil [there]. They would get no time off. Their unweaned babies would be in their cradles at home. Some of the women would have their babies with them. They would be crying. The Rāüḷ would be there playing with them.

One of the women would say, "Rāüḷ, will you bring my baby from the house and give it to me? I'll pour a ladleful of oil on your head."

At the same time, another woman would say, "Rāüḷ, will you put my baby into its cradle? I'll pour a ladleful of oil on your head."

Thus, he would take one woman's [child] and put it into its cradle, and he would get another woman's and give it to her. The women would pour ladlefuls of oil over his holy head.

[The oil] would go up somewhere; no one knew what became of it. And the women would be astonished. Up above, beings with direct knowledge and beings having the knowledge of particulars[2] would take it.

In this way, he would give them all his contact.[3] Then he would leave.

29. He says, "It's *lā̃k bhākrī.*"[1]

A Telī woman's child was eating *bhākrī* bread[2] made of *lā̃k* grain.[3] The Gosāvī came there. He grabbed the *bhākrī* from [the child's] hands. The Gosāvī began to eat it.

"Rāüḷ! Rāüḷ!" the Telī woman said. "This is Telīs' *bhākrī.*"

"Oh, drop dead!" said the Gosāvī. "It's not Telīs', I tell you. This is *lā̃k bhākrī.*" And he took a bite in his holy mouth. Then he left.

30. He eats at a house where a Śrāddha ceremony[1] is being performed.

An old woman had a smallish house. Brāhmans were seated inside. The Gosāvī was seated outside. The Gosāvī said, "Hey, bring some golden rice! Bring it here! Bring it here, I tell you!"

"I'm bringing it, Rāüḷ, I'm bringing it," [said the woman]. The Brāhmans made the declaration of purpose;[2] then she served the Gosāvī.

She served him panic-seed rice.[3] "Rāüḷ, I'm very poor," she said. "I don't have any rice."

"Oh, drop dead! This is golden rice, I tell you."

Thus the Gosāvī had a proper meal. Then he left.

31. Deities come holding small oil lamps.

On the eleventh day[1] of each fortnight, people used to keep vigil in the rest house. One night at midnight the Gosāvī was coming from Devāḷe tank. On both sides of him were deities holding small oil lamps. Light was streaming from his holy body. He stopped near the "horses,"[2] to the north of them.

At that point, a Brāhman came outside. When he saw, he went inside and shouted, "Hey, listen! Why are you keeping vigil? Come see what is happening to the Rāüḷ!"

They all came out to see, [though] one of them wouldn't come. Then they all prostrated themselves right there. They were very amazed.

Then the Gosāvī went by the High Lane to the second lane north of the rest house.

32. His light is seen in the marketplace.[1]

A three-legged cot had been left behind in the marketplace to the east of the rest house. The Gosāvī had fallen asleep on it. Light from his holy body streamed up to the sky. It lit up the whole village.

Thinking that a fire had started, the village watchmen came running. But they saw no fire. They looked and saw the Rāüḷ asleep. They said to one another, "See! The Rāüḷ is asleep," and they prostrated themselves.

Gradually the light descended and entered the holy body. They were astonished.

Then the Gosāvī left.

33. A thorn is extracted in the Haṭakeśvara[1] temple.

One day the Gosāvī got a thorn in his holy foot. It made the Gosāvī limp. He wouldn't let anyone take it out. The village headmen said to the children, "You watch the Rāüḷ. Grab hold of him as soon as he's asleep."

Soon after that, the Gosāvī went to the Haṭakeśvara temple. When the boys saw that he had fallen asleep, they held him down as they had been told. The barber was sent for. He took out the thorn.

After that he stopped limping. He walked all right.

34. He talks to himself about the High Lane and the Low Lane.

The Gosāvī used to sit on his thinking rock[1] and say to himself, "Oh, I should go to the High Lane. . . . I should go to the Low Lane. . . . I must go to the Rich Men's Lane, I say." And he would run pitter-pattering off. He would go there.

35. He receives an offering of clothes on the Śrāvaṇī day.[1]

Once a year Keśav Nāyak would honor the Gosāvī on an auspicious day. On the full-moon day, Keśav Nāyak sent out some children, saying, "Today you go get the Rāüḷ."

"All right," they agreed.

They approached the Gosāvī. "Rāüḷ, today Keśav Nāyak is having an auspicious ceremony," they said, and they took hold of his holy hand. "Come on. The Brāhmans are in their places. They've made a fire pit. They've raised a canopy. They're making oblations in the fire."

They surrounded him and brought him there. Keśav Nāyak came up to him. He prostrated himself; he touched the holy feet. Then he prepared a seat. The Gosāvī sat on the seat. His holy feet were washed. Then he was offered a set of threads for a sacred thread. A mark was put on his forehead. Sandalwood paste and consecrated rice were applied over it. He was offered a fine silk garment.

Right away he took off the clothes he was wearing. Keśav Nāyak said to the children, "Shred these clothes on a rock, and then bury them." So they shredded them and buried them.

Then the Gosāvī left.

36. He bathes at Sūtak well.[1]

The Gosāvī used to go to Sūtak well. He would keep half his clothes on and wash the other half. These he would spread out to dry, and then he would bathe. Then he would put on the clean clothes and wash the others. He would spread them out to dry. Then he would do the Saṃdhyā rites.[2] He would put a mark on his forehead. Then he would leave.

37. He asks for something to eat.

To the west of the Dheḍ's[1] house was a Brāhman's house.[2] The Gosāvī went there and grabbed hold of the end of the housewife's sari. Then the Gosāvī said, "Oh, drop dead! Give me something to eat! Give me something to eat, I tell you!"

"Rāüḷ," she replied, "let me do my chores. Then I'll give you something to eat."

She would go out to the water jars. The Gosāvī would go with her, clutching the end of her sari. They would go back into the house, and again he would say, "Give me something to eat."

She would reply, "Wait, Rāüḷ. I'll do this work, and then I'll serve you something."

She went to the door again. The Gosāvī went along, clutching the end of her sari. She brought in some fuel. The Gosāvī returned with her, clutching the end of her sari. "Now give me something to eat," [he said].

She replied, "Rāüḷ, let me do the sweeping. Then I'll serve you something."

He kept holding on to the end of her sari. She swept out the inside of the house. Then she scrubbed a metal plate with ashes. She washed it good and clean. She set down a stand and placed the plate on it. She spread out [a cloth] to sit on. "Rāüḷ," [she said], "let go of the end of my sari now, and sit down. Then I'll serve you something."

The Gosāvī let go of the end of her sari. He sat on the seat. She served him. The Gosāvī ate a proper meal; then he said, "Drop dead! That's right, now, I tell you!" Then she gave him pan to chew. Then the Gosāvī left.

38. He serves milk to daughters-in-law.

Vīṭhalu Joisī[1] had two daughters-in-law. He had cows which were giving milk; they gave a great deal of milk. His house was right next door to Emāïseṃ's. The mother-in-law's name was Elhāïseṃ. She used to have milk with her meal and serve buttermilk to her daughters-in-law. And they would be wishing [for milk].

At that point, the Gosāvī would come along. The women would be eating their evening meal. They would be cooling milk in a shallow pan. He would serve the daughters-in-law the milk with a small clay pot. Bending over their plates, they would protest, "Rāüḷ! Rāüḷ! That's supposed to be made into buttermilk in the morning." But they would be protesting falsely. Inside themselves they would be happy.

The Gosāvī would say, "Drop dead! Don't shout!" and act angry. And they would drink it in silence. He would serve buttermilk to their mother-in-law, and he would leave.

In the morning when they churned [the milk], it would turn to buttermilk, and they would get exactly the usual amount of butter.

39. He pours cold water into hot.[1]

One day a woman who was all alone was bathing her baby. She was hoping to herself, "If the Gosāvī comes along, he'll pour some cold water in with the hot."

At that point, the Gosāvī came along. He took a copper water pot in his holy hand. He poured cool water from the water jar into the hot water.

After some time, she said, "That's enough. That's enough, Rāüḷ." Then she bathed her baby. She laid it in its cradle and put it to sleep.

Then the Gosāvī left.

40. He does chores in all the houses.

The Gosāvī would go to someone's house. One of the women would say, "Rāüḷ, would you bring me that stool over there?" He would bring her the stool. He would fill another's copper water pot. He would help wash another's earthen water pot. He would help another pound with a pestle.

He would serve a meal to one; he would ask for a meal from another. He would talk to one; he would slap another. He would sleep on their beds.

In all the houses, the Gosāvī would help with the chores this way, and then he would leave.

41. He predicts deaths.[1]

A member of some household would be about to die. The Gosāvī would go to the house. He would prepare a bier in the courtyard. The people would say, "Rāüḷ, we can't tell what inauspicious sign you see."

Then someone in their household would die. The Gosāvī would accompany him to the burning ground, stay until the skull cracked, and then bathe fully clothed at Sūtak well[2] or Sīndak well.[3]

Then, simply draping his wet clothes over his head, he would go to the house of the next person who was to die. He would go and sit in a corner. The people would say, "Rāüḷ, we can't tell what inauspicious sign you see."

In two or three days someone in their household would die, and the Gosāvī would do those same things.

42. He circumambulates a pipal tree.

There was a pipal tree in the northeast corner of the Kaḷaṅkeśvara[1] temple compound. The Gosāvī used to go there. He would circumambulate the pipal tree. Wherever there was a pit or a hole, he would touch it with his holy hand. In this way he would give his contact[2] to the pipal tree.

Then the Gosāvī would leave.

43. A cat goes into a trance.[1]

A cat was sitting in a corner where two temples met. (According to some, it was sitting on top of the Kaḷaṅkeśvara temple.) The Gosāvī looked at it, and it went into a trance. For three days it kept sitting there in trance.

Then on the third day, the Gosāvī went there, looked at it, and said, "Go away! Go away! Go away, I tell you!" And its trance was broken and it left.

Then the Gosāvī left.

44. He bursts a prostitute's cyst.

A prostitute from Aḷajpur was going on pilgrimage to Rāmṭek.[1] She stopped in Ṛddhipur, at the Nagareśvara[2] temple. All her companions went into the marketplace. Left all alone, she fell asleep, lying on her stomach. She had a cyst on her back.

At that time, the Gosāvī came there. He placed his holy foot on her back and, pounding, burst the cyst. The Gosāvī squeezed out the bloody pus. He took away the pain that she had had.

Then she said, "The Rāüḷ is our Mother. The Rāüḷ is our Father. The Rāüḷ has taken away my pain."

Then the Gosāvī left. Her companions returned. They asked her, "How did this happen?"

"The Rāüḷ came here," she said. "He burst my cyst. He took away the pain. The Rāüḷ is our Mother. The Rāüḷ is our Father. The Rāüḷ has taken care of me."

"You go on with the Rāmṭek pilgrimage," she added. "I'm not coming." And she returned to Aḷajpur.

45. How he ate the prostitute's food.

The same prostitute came to Ṛddhipur from Aḷajpur, bringing foods from the snack stall. Śrīprabhu Gosāvī had just washed his dhoti[1] at Rām well and Lakṣmaṇ well. The Gosāvī was going northwards, toward the foot of a pipal tree, when she arrived.

She met the Gosāvī on the Indur road. She prostrated herself, then she made her offering. The Gosāvī accepted it. He ate right there. He rinsed his mouth and chewed pan.

Then he took a rounded stone in each of his holy hands and said, "Drop dead! Go away, I tell you!" He chased after her. She left from right there. He would not let her enter the village at all.

Then the Gosāvī left.

46. He plays in Māṅgs' houses.

The Gosāvī would go to the Mahārs'[1] quarter.[2] He would lift storage pots down from their stack and say, "Oh, drop dead! What's in here?"

The housewife would say, "What can there be here, Rāūḷ? Why must you take them down?"

He would do the same thing in Māṅgs' houses. When he saw some kind of food, he would taste it and say, "Oh, drop dead! It's sweet, I tell you."

The Gosāvī would act this way; then he would leave.[3]

47. The village headmen make an ordinance.

The village headmen said, "The Rāūḷ goes around among the houses of Māṅgs and Mahārs, and right afterwards he goes into the houses of consecrated Brāhmans. In this way, the Rāūḷ has caused general pollution. Put [the Māṅgs' and Mahārs'] houses outside the village. Then the Rāūḷ won't go to them."[1]

Thus they had houses built outside the city. The original Mahār quarter was razed. But the Gosāvī would go to the new one, too, [saying], "Oh, I shouldn't go, I say. . . . I should go, I say. . . . No, I must not go, I tell you." In this way, he would amuse himself, going from house to house.

48. He answers the Māṅgs' plea.[1]

One day the Māṅgs pleaded, "Rāūḷ, we are dying for lack of water. What can we do, Lord?" The Rāūḷ felt compassion.

Then the Gosāvī said, "Drop dead, I tell you!" and he went there. "You should dig here, I say. . . . You shouldn't dig, I say. . . . Yes, you must dig here, I tell you." And he pointed with his holy big toe.

They dug there, and they struck an unlimited supply of water. So they said, "The Rāūḷ is our Mother. The Rāūḷ is our Father. By the grace of the Rāūḷ we have water to drink."

49. He plays with butchers.[1]

The Gosāvī used to go to butchers' houses. He would sit in their shops. They would have prepared portions [of meat]. He would increase a portion that was too small, and reduce one that was too large. Where there was bone he would put meat, and where there was meat he would put bone. He would make the portions equal. Then he would say, "Drop dead! Now it's right, I tell you." In this way he would get his holy hands dirty.

The teacher saw this. He came to the market [because] there was a Śrāddha ceremony at his house, and he saw what was going on. So he said to himself, "Let me go home and take precautions. Otherwise the Rāüḷ will go just as he is and wash his holy hands in a water jar."

So he set off. When he got to the house he saw that the Rāüḷ was washing his holy hands in the water jar. So he said, "How much can I watch the Rāüḷ? Is there any place that's free of the Rāüḷ?"

In this way, the Gosāvī destroyed his error.[2]

50. He eats a snack at Upāsane's house.

One day the Gosāvī went to Upāsane's house. [Upāsane and his wife] were both asleep. Upāsane saw the Gosāvī and said, "Get up! Get up! The Rāüḷ has come. Bring something for a snack."

She got up. She got out a plate. She put on the plate bits of gram-flour and sesame-seed sweet balls, and added *cār* seeds,[1] *goḍaṃbī* seeds,[2] and sugar. She offered this to the Gosāvī.

And the Gosāvī said, "Drop dead! This is right, now, I tell you." He was laughing and eating at the same time. Then he gave them both *prasād*. Then the Gosāvī rinsed his mouth and chewed pan.

Then the Gosāvī left.

51. He sleeps at Upāsane's house.

Upāsane and his wife were both asleep when the Gosāvī came along. The Gosāvī went to sleep between them, and Upāsane said to his wife, "Get up! Get up! The Rāüḷ has fallen asleep. Set up another bed."

She got up. She prepared another bed. The two of them fell asleep on it.

The Gosāvī woke up. He rinsed his mouth. After he had taken water, the Gosāvī said, "Oh, drop dead! Bring me some condiments, I tell you. Oh, give me them! Give me them! Give me them, I tell you!"

Afterwards they offered him pan. Then the Gosāvī said, "That's right, now, I tell you." And he left.

52. He sleeps in tailors' houses.[1]

The Gosāvī used to go to tailors' houses. They would untie their bundles of cloth. They would spread a cloth beneath the Gosāvī. They would drape other cloths over him. Then they would wash his holy feet. They would offer him a snack, they would offer him pan, and then the Gosāvī would fall asleep.

The Gosāvī would go in this way to all the tailors' houses. The price they got for their clothes would double.

53. He eats snacks in grocers' houses.[1]

The Gosāvī used to go to grocers' houses. He would sit in their shops. He would take the scales in his holy hand. He would put on the scales a two-seer[2] weight, a two-and-a-half-seer weight, a seer weight, a quarter-seer weight, a five-seer weight. He would weigh their wares. He would mix together dried dates and coconut, peppercorns and cloves, cardamoms and betel nuts. What belonged in one place he would put in another.

He would play this way for a while. Then the grocers would bring water. They would wash his holy hands. They would wash his holy feet. Then they would offer him fruit and snacks. The Gosāvī would eat them. Then he would rinse his mouth, and they would give him pan.

They would have good sales, and their profits would double.

The Gosāvī would go in this way to all the grocers' houses.

54. He plays with silver coins at Upāsane's house.[1]

Upāsane and his wife were counting their silver coins[2] when the Gosāvī came along. They saw the Gosāvī coming, and the wife set herself to hiding the coins.

"Don't hide them," said Upāsane.

"If the Rāül sees them," she said, "he will spill them."

At that point the Gosāvī entered. The two of them stepped back. The Gosāvī squatted down. He began to play with the silver coins, describing them as he went through them: "This one is bent. This one is cracked. This one is light. This one is filed down. This one is good. This one is counterfeit. This one is genuine. This one is flat."

The Gosāvī played this way for a while, then he left. So they went back to counting their coins.

55. He eats a Brāhman's food at Devāḷe tank.[1]

A Brāhman from Kheḍ had come to the market, bringing his food with him. "The Rāüḷ pollutes everything in this place," he said, "so I should eat my food right here, and then go into the village." He went to Devāḷe tank. "I'll bathe here," he said, and tied his food to the branch of a pipal tree. After putting it up there, he set about taking his bath.

The Gosāvī came along. He took down the food. As he was eating it, [the Brāhman] saw him and said, "The Rāüḷ is our Mother. The Rāüḷ is our Father. The Rāüḷ is Īśvara. There is no place where the Rāüḷ is not." Then he approached him and touched his holy feet. He ate his own food as *prasād*.[2]

Then the Gosāvī said, "Drop dead! That's right, now, I tell you." Then the Gosāvī left.

56. He pays respect to ritual and to Brahman.[1]

One day the Gosāvī went out past the washing place to have a bowel movement. When he had had his bowel movement, he took a clod of earth in his holy hand and went to Devāḷe tank. To the east of the embankment he cleaned himself with the mud. Then he sipped water from the palm of his hand. He took water in his hand, breathed on it, and sprinkled it on the ground. He performed the ritual properly.

Then, going to the south of a tamarind tree, tucking his dhoti to one side, he urinated standing up.[2]

At that time some Brāhmans were sitting there. They saw him and said, "Look! All this time he has paid respect to ritual. Now he is paying respect to Brahman.[3] Brahman is unchangeable, Brahman is invariable, Brahman is devoid of all qualities—such is Brahman." They began to speak this way.

Then the Gosāvī left.

57. He brings a dead calf to life.[1]

Some people's calf died. They brought it and put it near the "horse"[2] at the foot of the Low Lane. At that time the Gosāvī came along. They said to the Gosāvī, "O Lord, now what are our children going to do, without milk? We had one cow. Her calf has died."

The Gosāvī went up to it and sprinkled it with grass, and it came to life. It went lowing to the house. They were delighted because their calf had come to life.

Their house was in the High Lane, right next door to the water carrier's house.

(According to some, the Gosāvī came in the evening, when the cow came home. The people whose calf it was pleaded, "Rāüḷ, our calf has died. Now what are we going to do, without buttermilk?"

The Gosāvī answered their plea, and immediately went and grabbed it by the tail. "You get up!" he said. "Get up! Get up, I tell you!"

It got up. It went to the house. It began to suck at the cow. Then the people said, "The Rāüḷ is our Mother. The Rāüḷ is our Father. There is nothing the Rāüḷ cannot do." And they were amazed and astonished.)

58. He uproots and replants a gourd vine.[1]

There was a *kohaḷī*-gourd[2] vine growing over a certain Brāhman's house. The Gosāvī uprooted it. As he carried it off, brushing it along the ground, their daughter Dhāï ran after him. "Oh, Rāüḷ!" [she said].

"Why did you pull up a fruit-bearing, blooming plant?" At that, the Gosāvī grabbed her, too, by her foot.

Her mother shouted, "Rāüḷ! Rāüḷ! Let go of Dhāï! Take the *kohaḷī* vine."

The Gosāvī took both [Dhāï and the vine], and threw them into the grain cellar. He left.

Then they pulled her out. Her mother asked, "Dhāï, are you hurt?"

"No," she replied. "I'm not. The Rāüḷ is our Mother. The Rāüḷ is our Father. I was completely happy the whole time the Rāüḷ brushed me along the ground."

On the third day after that, the Gosāvī pulled the *kohaḷī* vine out of the grain cellar. Then he dug in the ground with a stick. He planted the roots in the earth. He poured on three handfuls of water from the water jar.

They said, "Rāüḷ, it's dry and withered. How will it take root now?"

The Gosāvī left. Early the next morning, when they looked at it, it had sprouted clusters of fruits. Then they said, "Look! Look! The Rāüḷ is our Mother. The Rāüḷ is our Father. The Rāüḷ is Īśvara. There is nothing the Rāüḷ cannot do."

Their house was just north of Upāsane's house; in between was an open space.

59. He acts afraid[1] of a dog.

The Gosāvī was playing outside the small door to the south of the Uncamaḍh.[2] Ābāïseṃ went there. She asked the Gosāvī to come with her. As she was bringing him along, there was a dog in their path. The Gosāvī saw it and got frightened. "Help!" [he said]. "Help! It's a dog! A dog, I tell you! Drop dead! It will bite, I tell you. It's a dog, I tell you."

Ābāïseṃ said, "Hey, there, dog! Our Gosāvī is afraid of you. Go away!"

"Oh, the dog will bite, I tell you. . . . It's not going to bite, I tell you. . . . It's a dog, I tell you."

The dog went away. Then the Gosāvī moved on.

60. He startles cows.

He used to hide behind the two "horses"[1] at the eastern gate. Cows would come in from outside [the village], and he would jump up, shouting, "Ho!" The cows would start and run away.

Then he would mount a "horse." He would touch it with his holy hand.

This is how he would play.

61. He repairs a water jar.

The Gosāvī broke a water jar which Vīsa Nāyak had gotten. [Vīsa Nāyak's] wife said, "Oh, Rāüḷ! Why did you break the new water jar? Now what will we do, with no water?"

So the Gosāvī joined the two pieces together. He mixed mud with water and smeared it on.

"Will it hold, Rāüḷ?" [she asked].

Then the Gosāvī left.

Later it broke in another place, but it didn't break in that place.

62. He gives a Brāhman directions.

There was a banyan tree to the west of the Bhairava[1] temple. South of the banyan tree was a tank. The Gosāvī was walking back and forth along the embankment of the tank.

A Brāhman came along. He asked the way to Deūḷvāḍā: "Patron,[2] which road will take me to Deūḷvāḍā?"

The Gosāvī said, "Drop dead! Take the upper road! The upper road, I tell you!"

The man left. Then the Gosāvī left.

63. He acts angry.[1]

To anyone he was angry with, the Gosāvī used to say, "Oh, drop dead! You should be whipped with a wet switch, I tell you. You should be beaten with a wet switch, I tell you. You should stoop over, I tell you!"

64. He gets up on a raised seat.

During the Śimagā festival,[1] a raised seat would be constructed in front of the Paraśurāma[2] temple. The Gosāvī would get up on it. Dancers would be dancing. They would sprinkle him with syringes. The Gosāvī would say, "Oh, drop dead! Go away, I tell you!"

With that, he would get up on another raised seat. And they would sprinkle him with syringes. He would act angry, saying, "Oh, drop dead! Go away, I tell you!"

Again they would sprinkle him with syringes. The syringes would spurt out liquid. He would say, "Yes! That's the way! That's the way!" and laugh.

Then the Gosāvī would leave.

65. He plays with Paraśurāma.[1]

The Paraśurāma temple was an important temple for making offerings.[2] The deity had been worshipped by being covered with an arrangement of flowers.

The Gosāvī went in. He squatted down to the south of the deity. He stuck his holy hand sideways into the flower arrangement. Then he said, "Oh, drop dead! You're here, I say!" and he touched [the deity] with his holy hand. Still, not a single flower fell off.

(According to some, he stood to the east of the deity. Then, bending forward, he stuck his holy hand in and touched it.)

He played this way; then he left.

66. He is offered a garment.

Dādos[1] had gone to the Telugu country.[2] He brought back from there two metal cups and a garment. He gave one of the metal cups to our Gosāvī;[3] the other he kept for himself. He brought the garment to Ṛddhipur.

When he arrived, Śrīprabhu Gosāvī was sitting on the verandah, to the left as you enter. They met there. [Dādos] prostrated himself. He touched the holy feet. He offered the red garment which he had brought. Then he left.

67. He eats a meal at Keśav Nāyak's house.

Keśav Nāyak had a house and fields in a neighboring village. The Gosāvī went there. He ate a proper meal.

Then the Gosāvī returned to Ṛddhipur.

68. He sweeps out a cattle shed.[1]

One day the Gosāvī was sweeping out Keśav Nāyak's cattle shed. "Rāüḷ! Rāüḷ!" [Keśav Nāyak] said. "Why are you doing this? I don't know what omen you see, Rāüḷ."

That evening the cowherd came. "The bulls have strayed off," he said. "They're gone."

[Keśav Nāyak] said, "The omen the Rāüḷ saw has come true."

He did not even go to look for them. The bulls were lost forever.

69. He predicts that Nemāḷ Pāṇḍīyā will lose his eyes.

Nemāḷ Pāṇḍīyā was from Aḷajpur. He was Dhānubāī's[1] husband. He came to Ṛddhipur to have *darśan* of the Gosāvī.

The Gosāvī was sitting inside on his cot. There [Nemāḷ Pāṇḍīyā] had *darśan*.[2] He prostrated himself. He touched the holy feet. He sat down in front of [the Gosāvī].

The Gosāvī said, "Oh, drop dead! Go away, I tell you! You'll lose your nose, I tell you. You'll lose your ears, I tell you. You'll lose your eyes, I tell you."

Nemāḷ Pāṇḍīyā said, "O Lord, these eyes have seen the Gosāvī. Let anything happen to them now."

Soon afterwards there was a raid. The king of Devgiri[3] took him prisoner and carried him off. His eyes were plucked out. If he had asked the Gosāvī, they would have been spared.

70. He accepts a woman's jewelry in time of war.[1]

A dispute had arisen between a certain village and Ṛddhipur (according to some, between Kheḍ and Ṛddhipur). The [enemies] came to take [Ṛddhipur] village. They plundered everything. Some people hid their belongings in grain cellars for safekeeping.

A certain woman took off her gold jewelry. She put it into the Gosāvī's lap. "Rāüḷ," she said, "keep this with you," and she gave it to him. The Gosāvī took it and left.

The two armies had met in the field at the southern embankment of Devāḷe tank. The Gosāvī went in between the two armies. And the people who had come from the neighboring village said, "The Rāüḷ has come. Now we must come to terms with you."

So they made peace with one another. Those people went to their village. The others [the ones from Ṛddhipur] went to their homes.

Then the woman began to inquire among her women friends in the neighborhood. She started saying, "I gave my gold jewelry to the Rāüḷ."

They said, "Oh, no! The Rāüḷ is mad. The Rāüḷ is possessed. He'll throw it into a well. Why did you put it in the Rāüḷ's hands?"

She replied, "Why would the Rāüḷ do such a thing? Besides, if that's what he does, then he does it. So what? If so, the Rāüḷ himself will give me more."

At that point, the Gosāvī came along. "Oh, drop dead!" he said. "Take it! Take it, I tell you!" and he got it out of the fold of his garment and gave it to her.

"Look at this! Look at this!" [she said]. "The Rāüḷ is our Mother. The Rāüḷ is our Father. The Rāüḷ has guarded his child's life savings."

71. He eats at one of a series of meals.[1]

One day the Gosāvī went to Deūḷvāḍā. All the ascetics invited to a series of meals sat down inside. Then all the ascetics were served. Then the Gosāvī was served.

At that time, the sky was a little cloudy. The Gosāvī looked at the sky and said, "Oh, drop dead! It's coming, I tell you. Yes, it's really coming, I tell you."

At that, the rain came. The whole monastery was filled with water. The leaf plates began to float on the water. So the [ascetics] sat outside, up on the verandah.

No rain fell on the Gosāvī or on the woman serving him. The Gosāvī kept on eating. She kept on serving him. But not a drop of water touched them.

This astonished all the ascetics. So they prostrated themselves. They smeared their bodies with the *prasād* of the Gosāvī's leftovers. They praised him. They expressed their remorse. Then the Gosāvī left.

Afterwards, when they cleared away the Gosāvī's leaf plate, another leaf plate sprang up beneath it. Seven leaf plates sprang up this way.

72. He takes care of a woman in confinement.[1]

A certain woman was alone, all alone, with neither older nor younger people in her house. She gave birth to a child. There was no one to take care of her during her confinement. She wished, "The Rāüḷ is our Mother. The Rāüḷ is our Father. If the Rāüḷ comes, he'll take care of me now that I've had my baby."

At that time, the Gosāvī came along. He took care of her needs during her confinement. He served her her meals. He bathed her. When her husband would sit [near her], the Gosāvī would hold the end of his garment between them and say, "Oh, drop dead! Get back, I tell you!" He would drive him away. "Oh, drop dead! She's given birth, I tell you." He would take her plate [of coals] and touch it to all the pots in the stack of storage pots. Then he would leave.

The Gosāvī did this for twelve days. Then he left.[2]

73. A Māṅg goes into a trance.[1]

The Gosāvī was going along the Dābh well road when he met a certain Māṅg. The man prostrated himself fully. And the Gosāvī, placing his holy foot on the man's back, moved on.

The man lay there for three days in a trance. Cows, water buffaloes, and calves walked over him. On the third day he got up.

Then he began to act like Īśvara.[2]

The people said, "This Māṅg has polluted the entire village." So they tied him to a pipal tree in the wilderness.

At that time, a moneylender from Aḷajpur was on his way to Rāmṭek.[3] A vision came to him in a dream, saying, "I am Rāma. I've been tied to a pipal tree in the wilderness."

So at daybreak the man went and found him tied there. He released him. He bought him a house and a field. He put two women there to take care of him.

His Rāmṭek pilgrimage was fulfilled right there. Later he went to see Rāma just for fun.

74. He touches a rock with his holy foot.

During the Gosāvī's solitary period,[1] he would play with a certain rock as he was coming and going on the road. He would touch it with his holy foot and say, "This is here today, I tell you. Yes, it is, I tell you." He would play this way; then he would leave.

Later, after the Gosāvī had accepted leadership,[1] he would seat himself in his palanquin. "Come on! Swing it! Swing it!" he would say, and the devotees would get out the palanquin. Then he would sit in the palanquin and go out. When he reached that place, he would stick out his holy foot. He would hang it down. Then he would touch his trembling, ankleted, holy foot to the rock. Often he would touch only his big toe to it. He would play this way; then he would leave.

75. He meets an official.[1]

The Gosāvī was playing at Āp well. He saw an official coming, and he went over to the foot of a banyan tree. When the official arrived, seated in his palanquin, the Gosāvī was playing, holding on to the banyan tree's aerial roots. Ahead of [the official], his cavalrymen and foot soldiers stopped. The official said, "Hey, there! Keep moving! Why have you stopped?"

They replied, "We can't move. The Rāüḷ is playing up ahead. He has taken away our ability to move or think."

And the official jumped down from the palanquin and prostrated himself. Then he went up close and touched the holy feet. Then he offered his hospitality. The Gosāvī accepted the offer. So a tent was set up right there. A seat was prepared for him. He was offered a cloth to wear while bathing. Then he had a massage and a bath. His worship service was done. He had a meal. He chewed pan. He was given clothes.

[The official] prostrated himself. He touched the holy feet. Then he went to his own village.

The Gosāvī went to Ṛddhipur.

76. He plays with his reflection.[1]

One day the Gosāvī went to Āp well. He squatted on a slab of rock at Āp well. He washed his holy face. He washed his holy hands. He washed his holy feet. And he saw his image in the water. And the Gosāvī said, "Hey! That's me! He's talking, I tell you. He's saying things, I tell you. He's acting, I tell you. He's posturing, I tell you."

And he would stick out his holy foot. He would pull it back again. He would put it forward again. When he looked in, he would see his reflection and laugh.

He would play this way; then he would leave.

77. He takes Dharamāḷī's water and food.[1]

Dharamāḷī used to put his food into a cavity in a tree or rock. The Gosāvī would take it out and eat it. So he would hide it again. The Gosāvī would take it from that place, too, and eat it. So he would bury it. From there, too, [the Gosāvī] would dig it out and eat it.

So he said to himself, "There is no place without the Rāüḷ. Is there any place the Rāüḷ doesn't know?" So he adopted a rule: "First I'll give a meal to the Rāüḷ; then I'll eat." He would not eat until the Gosāvī came. When the Gosāvī came, he would give the Gosāvī a meal, and then he would have *prasād.*

He followed this rule for as long as he lived.

78. He talks to himself about the water buffaloes and their baths at Darbhāḷe tank.

The Gosāvī went to Darbhāḷe tank. He sat on its western embankment. Water buffaloes were lolling inside it. Some of them had moon marks on their foreheads. Some did not. So the Gosāvī said, "This pandit has a forehead mark; this pandit doesn't have one."

Of one who submerged herself he would say, "This one has bathed with his clothes[1] on. . . . This one hasn't."

Of those who submerged themselves he would say, "This pandit is taking a bath from his neck[1] down. This one is good. . . . This one is not good, I tell you. . . . This one is a wreck, I tell you."

The Gosāvī would talk to himself this way. Then he would leave.

79. He plays among cowherds.

[The Gosāvī played in a similar way with some cowherds. He said,][1] "Hey, this is a learned cowherd. Hey, this is a Brāhman cowherd. Hey, this is a celibate cowherd. Hey, this one is just a Śūdra,[2] I tell you."

Then the Gosāvī was ready to leave. The cowherds said, "Rāüḷ! Rāüḷ! Eat some rice and curds before you go." So they chose the finest kinds of food and gave the Gosāvī a meal. Then they ate. Then the Gosāvī left.

80. Umāïseṃ[1] combs his holy hair.

The Gosāvī used to go to Dābh well. There he went to Umāïseṃ's house. She set up a small cot for him to sit on. The Gosāvī sat down on it.

Umāïseṃ would comb his holy hair. She would see a louse. She would hand it to the Gosāvī. He would slap it.

The Gosāvī would throw the lice away, or he would put them elsewhere in his hair. (According to some, he would put them back on his holy head.)

Then Umāïseṃ would wash her hands. She would prepare a plateful of food. She would give the Gosāvī a meal. Then the Gosāvī would leave.

81. He predicts the death by snakebite of Tīka Upādhyāya's wife.[1]

Sitting on Tīka Upādhyāya's[2] verandah, the Gosāvī said, "Oh, it will come just like this, I tell you. And it will bite her just like this, I tell you. Oh, she'll die, I tell you. . . . She won't die, I tell you. . . . Yes, she'll surely die, I tell you."

At that time, a snake appeared. It bit Tīka Upādhyāya's wife. She died. Because she had been an evil woman,[3] the Gosāvī did not even accompany her to the burning ground.

82. He takes food at Tīka Upādhyāya's son-in-law's Śrāddha.

They were performing a Śrāddha for the husband of Tīka Upādhyāya's daughter Sāvitrī. [Tīka Upādhyāya] invited all the Brāhmans to the Śrāddha. He had all the vegetables and other food cooked. He placed them on a platform. He shut the door. He stationed Sāvitrī at the door and went to take his bath. He told her, "If the Rāüḷ comes, don't let the Rāüḷ make leavings of the food." He gave her these instructions and left.

At that point, the Gosāvī came along. He slapped her and pushed her aside. He opened the door. He got onto the platform. He took out the food. He tasted all of it. Then he left.

Tīka Upādhyāya returned. She told Tīka Upādhyāya everything that had happened: "The Rāüḷ came. He slapped me. He opened the door. He got onto the platform. He made leavings of all the food."

So he replied, "Now we'll go to a holy place and do the Śrāddha at the holy place. At least the Rāüḷ won't be able to get his hands on it."

Then the Brāhmans who had been invited to the Śrāddha were called. They were fed. [Tīka Upādhyāya] himself did not eat.

That night his ancestors appeared to him in a dream. "Why didn't you eat anything?" [they asked.] "The Rāūḷ took out the vegetables and the other cooked food. That pleased all three—your father, your grandfather, and your great-grandfather.

So Tīka Upādhyāya got up. He told all the Brāhmans, and then he began to praise [the Gosāvī]: "The Rāūḷ is our Mother. The Rāūḷ is our Father. What is there that the Rāūḷ cannot do?" Then he took a bath and ate the meal. The purpose of his ritual was achieved.[1]

83. He predicts Tīka Upādhyāya's death.

One day the Gosāvī made a bier of sticks in Tīka Upādhyāya's courtyard. He made a triangular sling.[1] The Upādhyāya's daughter said, "Rāūḷ, what inauspicious sign of this sort do you see?"

Soon afterwards, Tīka Upādhyāya got a fever. He died. The Gosāvī slammed a low stool down across the threshold. He arranged a little stand in front of it. Then the Gosāvī said, "Drop dead! Serve me my meal! Serve it to me, I tell you!"

"Rāūḷ," she said, "let the corpse be taken out. Then I'll serve it to you."

"Bring it here! Bring it here! Bring it here, I tell you."

"Rāūḷ!" she said. "Let the corpse be taken out. How can you eat rice when someone has died?"

He refused to let the corpse be taken out. The others said, "Why don't you serve the Rāūḷ, since he's asking you to?" So she took curds out of their sling. She mixed some rice with them. She set this on the little stand. Then the Gosāvī ate his meal of curds and rice, and rinsed his mouth. Then he let them take out [the corpse].

The Gosāvī accompanied him to the cremation ground, and stayed until the skull cracked. Then he bathed fully clothed at Sīndak well. Then he left.

84. To Rāmdev's question he answers, "At Kānaḍī Bhālugā̃v."[1]

One day Rāmdev asked, "Lord, where can I meet our Gosāvī?"[2]

The Gosāvī said, "Oh, drop dead! At Kānaḍī Bhālugā̃v."

If he had left right away, he would have met the Gosāvī. But he stayed on there.

85. He meets Bhaṭ[1] and Māhādāïseṃ.

One day there was no fuel in their lodging, so Bhaṭ and Māhādāïseṃ went toward Dābh well to gather dried cow dung. At the same time, the Gosāvī went toward the Five Pipals. He met Bhaṭ and Māhādāïseṃ at the southwest corner of the Pipals.

They prostrated themselves. They touched his holy feet. Then the

Gosāvī said, "Oh! [You're] Cāṅgdev Rāūḷ's![2] Oh, go! Go! Go to Dābh well. Look at Darbheśvara."[3]

"Yes, Lord," they said, and went to Dābh well. They looked at Darbheśvara. Then they returned.

(Some say they met him when she brought Bhaṭ from Bhānkheḍ.)[4]

86. He tells that a shawl piece was taken by a thief.[1]

Māhādāïseṃ spread out a piece of a two-piece shawl to dry. Someone—no one knows who—carried it away. She began to look for it.

The Gosāvī was sitting against the wall, to the left as you enter. The Gosāvī said, "Oh, drop dead! A thief took the shawl piece, I tell you."

"Lord," replied Māhādāïseṃ, "Gosāvī! How could you let him take it?"

And the Gosāvī laughed.

87. He accepts Māhādāïseṃ's ministrations.[1]

The Gosāvī had a stomach-ache. "Oh," [he said], it hurts here, I tell you. Oh, it hurts, I tell you." So Māhādāïseṃ warmed her hand over a lamp and placed it on his navel. He let her do so, and said, "Yes, right here! Oooh! Right here! Oooh! Ah, it's warm!"

Then Māhādāïseṃ said, "Gosāvī, if warming agrees with you, I'll prepare a pan of hot coals." So Māhādāïseṃ prepared a pan of hot coals. Then Māhādāïseṃ warmed a rolled-up piece of cloth on it, and put that on his stomach. And he took it and said, "Ah, it's warm!"

And he would say, "Yes, right here! Oooh! Right here! Oooh!" and pull the covers over his holy face. He would pull them back again and ask for some water. Māhādāïseṃ would give it to him.

After she warmed him this way, he got better.

88. He eats Māhādāïseṃ's *dhīḍareṃ.*[1]

One day Māhādāïseṃ asked the Gosāvī, "Lord, Gosāvī, I'll give you a *dhīḍareṃ* today. Don't go out to play, Gosāvī."

The Gosāvī accepted her offer. He was delighted, and said, "Oh, drop dead! She'll give me a *dhīḍareṃ,* I tell you!" He didn't go out at all to play. "Oh," he said, "she'll give me a *dhīḍareṃ,* I tell you. I should eat it. . . . I shouldn't eat it, I tell you."

Then Māhādāïseṃ prepared a *dhīḍareṃ* and put it onto a plate. She prepared a seat. The Gosāvī sat in the seat, and Māhādāïseṃ offered him the *dhīḍareṃ.* She poured ghee into a metal cup.

Then the Gosāvī looked at the *dhīḍareṃ.* And he said, "Hey, this isn't a *dhīḍareṃ,* I tell you. This is an *āhītā,*[1] I tell you. Come on! Bring me a *dhīḍareṃ!* Bring me one, I tell you!" And he acted angry.

"Lord," said Māhādāïseṃ, "in the Gaṅgā[2] Valley, where I come from, they call it a *dhīḍareṃ*. Here in your Varhāḍ[3] they call it an *āhītā*."

"Oh, bring me a *dhīḍareṃ*," he said. "Bring me one! Bring me one, I tell you!" And he acted angry.

Māhādāïseṃ began to think, and suddenly she got an idea. So she put some fine wheat flour into milk. She mixed it up. She sponged some ghee onto the earthen griddle. She poured [the batter] onto it in a phallic shape. (According to some, she poured it in the shape of a conch.) On top she sprinkled powdered cardamom, black pepper, and cloves. When one side was done, she turned it over and took it off. She put it onto his plate.

It looked different to him, and he said, "This is what I want. Now it's right, I tell you. Oh, it's good, I tell you." So Māhādāïseṃ, delighted, served him more.

In this way, the Gosāvī accepted the meal.

89. He eats Māhādāïseṃ's nectar balls.

One day Māhādāïseṃ asked the Gosāvī, "Lord, Gosāvī, I'll give you nectar balls today. Don't go out to play, Gosāvī." The Gosāvī agreed.

So the Gosāvī didn't go out at all. And the Gosāvī was delighted and said, "Oh, she'll give me nectar balls, I tell you! Oh, I should eat the nectar balls, I tell you. . . . I shouldn't eat them, I tell you. . . . Yes, I must eat them, I tell you."

The Gosāvī sat down then on a cot. Then Māhādāïseṃ prepared the nectar balls and put them on a plate. She filled a metal cup with ghee and set it down. She served him the nectar balls on the plate.

The Gosāvī went over to the plate. He sat in his place. The Gosāvī rested his merciful gaze on the plate and said, "Oh, drop dead! Heat it! Heat it, I tell you!"

"But, Lord," replied Māhādāïseṃ, "the ghee is freshly made, Lord. It's been strained through a thick woolen cloth, Lord."

"Heat it! Heat it, I tell you," he said, acting angry. And Māhādāïseṃ was frightened. She went to take the cup. And the Gosāvī said, "Oh, why? Why are you afraid? Oh, heat this! This!" And the Gosāvī pointed with his holy hand.

And suddenly, Māhādāïseṃ understood. She prepared a pan of hot coals. She placed a new bowl on top of the pan of coals. Over that she put a clean plantain leaf. She heated the nectar balls on this and put them on his plate.

Then the Gosāvī [said], "This is what I want. Now it's right, I tell you. Oh, they slip! Oh, they slide! Oh, they slither! Oh, drop dead! It's sweet nectar, I tell you! It's jaggery, I tell you."

In this way, the Gosāvī had his meal.

90. Māhādāïseṃ draws designs with colored powder.

Māhādāïseṃ used to sweep the lanes and open spaces along which the Gosāvī would go out to play. She would sprinkle them with cow-dung wash. Inside the northern doorway, she would draw with powder a multicolored garland of vines. She would fill it in thickly in front. She would draw a thick cluster of lotuses.

The Gosāvī would go out. When he had finished playing, he would return. He would place his holy foot so as to avoid the colored designs. But soon he would come to the thick part of the design.

Then Māhādāïseṃ said, "Go ahead, now, Lord, by your divinity." Sometimes Bhaṭ would say it. And the Gosāvī would laugh. Then he would place his holy foot on it and go ahead.

He did this every day for as long as Māhādāïseṃ was there.

91. He has a bath at Ṭoṅkaṇe's house.

The Gosāvī began to think out loud. He began to say to himself, "Oh, I should bathe on Saturday, I say. . . . Oh, I should bathe on Wednesday, I say."

Hearing this, Māhādāïseṃ picked up a metal cup full of oil. Without asking his permission, she poured it on the Gosāvī's holy head. And the Gosāvī acted angry.[1] The Gosāvī kicked the cup with his holy foot and went out.

Māhādāïseṃ followed him out. She met Dādos at the Main Gate. Dādos said, "Rupai![2] Rupai! You're doing wrong. You're doing things contrary to Śrīprabhu's will. You're doing things that will send you to hell. Why are you here? To go to hell?"

Māhādāïseṃ said, "Please be quiet, Dādo. Don't make things worse. It's bad enough that the Gosāvī doesn't care about me. And if you get angry, that just adds to it."

The Gosāvī went straight to Ṭoṅkaṇe's compound. He squatted against the wall of the verandah, to the left as you enter.

Māhādāïseṃ went after him. She stood submissively near the lion-faced stone block[3] on the right-hand side. The oil began to trickle down from the Gosāvī's holy head. He wiped it on the wall with his holy hand. Māhādāïseṃ asked him, "Our Gosāvī[4] does what [we] say, Lord. He accepts [our] offers. He lets [us] serve him. So, Lord, please let me wipe it for you."

"Oh, come here! Come here, I tell you! Wipe it, I tell you!"

Māhādāïseṃ went over to him. She tucked the folds of her sari back between her legs. She began to smear the oil around on his holy head. Ṭoṅkaṇe's wife Sonāïseṃ brought a metal cup full of oil. Then she brought a thick cloth, and Māhādāïseṃ said, "Lord, let me prepare a seat for you." Then Māhādāïseṃ prepared a seat and he sat down on it. Then Sonāïseṃ said, "Mother,[5] a tubful of water is heating. Here's the cleansing mixture, Mother."

Māhādāïseṃ poured the oil onto his holy head. She poured it into his eyes. She poured it into his ears. Then the Gosāvī gave her each of his holy hands twice [to anoint]. He gave her each of his holy feet twice. That made Māhādāïseṃ blissfully happy.

Then the Gosāvī said, "Oh, drop dead! That's right now, I tell you." With that, his massage was finished.

Then Māhādāïseṃ said to Bhaṭ, "Nāgdev, go start a fire under the other tub." Bhaṭ went. As he started a fire under the tub, Māhādāïseṃ gave [the Gosāvī] his massage. As [the Gosāvī] finished bathing with the tubful of water that Sonāïseṃ had put on to heat, [Māhādāïseṃ] said to Bhaṭ, "Nāgdev, bring the other tub."

So Bhaṭ went to get it. The tub had been heated all the way to the top. Bhaṭ couldn't carry it, so he came back and said, "Rupai, that tub is very hot."

Māhādāïseṃ said, "Nāgdev, you pour the water over him. I'll go." So Māhādāïseṃ went. She pulled the burning fuel out of the stove. She put out the flames. She smeared a cloth ring with mud. She brought [the tub with this], carrying it on the palms of her hands. The water in this tub was poured over him: that made two tubfuls of water in all.

And so his bath was completed. Afterwards Māhādāïseṃ offered him a silk garment stiff with yellow starch. Then the Gosāvī gave the cloth he had worn while bathing to Sonāïseṃ, who was as if barren because none of her children survived. The Gosāvī said, "Oh, take it! Take it, I tell you," and pushed it toward her with the big toe of his left holy foot.

Later Māhādāïseṃ started asking her for it: "Give me the cloth."

She replied, "What do you mean? Our Rāüḷ gave me the cloth. Why should I give it away?"

That very day she conceived a child. After nine months she gave birth to a son. The Gosāvī went there. He kept saying of the umbilical cord, "Oh, it's an umbilical cord, I tell you. . . . Oh, it's a snake, I tell you. . . . Oh, it's an umbilical cord, I tell you." Then he cut the umbilical cord.

Then the Gosāvī went to the grain cellar. "Oh, you should use up seven loads [of grain],[6] I tell you," he said. "You should use up five loads, I tell you. You should feed Rīdhaureṃ,[7] I tell you. You should feed Belaureṃ, I tell you. You should feed four villages, I tell you. . . . You should not feed them, I tell you. . . . Yes, they must be fed, I tell you!" And he pointed at the grain cellar with his holy foot.

Then they held the naming ceremony.[8] They fed Rīdhaureṃ and Belaureṃ. They fed four villages. All the people ate, but Sonāïseṃ wouldn't eat anything.

Her family said, "Why aren't you eating?"

She said, "When the Rāūḷ comes, I'll eat in the same row with him."

"Come on!" they said. "The Rāūḷ is mad. The Rāūḷ is possessed. He'll never come. You eat something or your milk will turn bitter."

"No, I won't eat."

At that point, the Gosāvī arrived. Then they gave the Gosāvī a plate at the head of the row. All the others, beginning with Sonāïseṃ, ate in the Gosāvī's row.

The son lived for a hundred years. He never had a fever. He didn't get coughs or colds. He suffered from no diseases. Later, after the Gosāvī was gone, he used to tell the devotees about the divine deed which he had experienced.

92. He says that a sweet ball has too little jaggery.

Māhādāïseṃ made some sweet balls. She had set them out for a while to dry. She had set them out to the west of the Uñcamaḍh, in front of the kitchen. That evening, the Gosāvī came there. And the Gosāvī said, "Oh, this sweet ball has enough jaggery. . . . This one hasn't nearly enough. . . . Oh, this one has gotten hard. . . . This one's gotten crumbly. . . . This one isn't good . . . ," and he touched them with his holy hand.

He played this way; then he left.

93. He says that a shawl piece was taken by a thief.[1]

Ābāïseṃ and Dāïṃbā[2] came from Paiṭhaṇ.[3] They had been sent by the Gosāvī to Śrīprabhu.[4]

Ābāïseṃ had spread out a piece of a two-piece shawl to dry. The Gosāvī was sitting on the verandah, to the left as you enter. Someone—no one knows who—carried off the shawl piece. Ābāïseṃ began to look for it. She couldn't find it anywhere.

At that point, the Gosāvī said, "Hey! A thief carried off your shawl piece."

"Lord!" said Ābāïseṃ. "How could you let him take it?"

And the Gosāvī laughed.

94. Dāïṃbā is prescribed a rule of silence.

Earlier our Gosāvī[1] had said, "Bhojā,[2] Ṛddhipur is Kāśī.[3] There can be no desire, anger, or sensuality there. One cannot talk with anyone who does violence or speaks abuse. There you should keep silent." So [Dāïṃbā] was silent.

One day, when the Gosāvī was standing to the south of the ceremonial platform, Dāïṃbā arrived. He prostrated himself to the Gosāvī. He touched his holy feet. He kept silent there.

[Sometime later,] he got sores in his mouth. So Ābāïseṃ would boil some rice gruel. He would rinse his mouth with it.

One day, as [Dāïṃbā] rinsed his mouth, the Gosāvī was sitting inside, in the Rājamaḍh. There was no one to give him a massage. So the Gosāvī said, "Hey, there! Will you help out?"

"Lord," said Dāïṃbā, "how could I not help out?"

At that, Ābāïseṃ said, "Lord! He talked!" And the sores in his mouth went away.

Then he began to give the Gosāvī his massage. Then [the Gosāvī] had his bath.

95. He gives a Brāhman a gift of gold.[1]

One day the Gosāvī was amusing himself in Niṣkalaṅka's[2] temple when a certain Brāhman came along. He wished him well, and then said, "Patron,[3] my daughter has reached the age for marriage. I have nothing with which to marry her off. So I need some money."

The Gosāvī replied, "Oh, drop dead!" and he went to the north of the temple. He dug in the ground with the big toe of his holy foot. Then the Gosāvī said, "Oh, take it! Take it! Take it, I tell you!" and, filling his cupped hands twice, he put [gold] into the lap of the man's garment. Then he said, "Oh, drop dead! Go away, I tell you!" and he pushed him away.

The man started to go. Then the Gosāvī left.

96. He tells a donkey to bray.[1]

A donkey had dropped dead outside the monastery, at its southwest corner, to the south of the Kamaleśvara[2] temple in the courtyard. The Gosāvī went there. The Gosāvī touched it with his holy hand. Then the Gosāvī said, "Hey! Get up! Get up! Bray! Bray! Bray, I tell you!"

And it got up. It went off braying. And the Gosāvī laughed.

97. He meets Mhāïṃbhaṭ, who offers him jaggery.[1]

Mhāïṃbhaṭ[2] came from Sarāḷe on the Bhāvaī fourteenth.[3] He gave a Brāhman the double silk shawl he was wearing, and took the man's coarse blanket for himself.

In seventeen days, he arrived at Ṛddhipur. On the way, at Sīrāḷā, he sold one piece of a two-piece shawl for eight copper coins. He bought a basket there for one copper coin; he bought seven copper coins' worth of jaggery.

Finally he got to Ṛddhipur. At that time, Śrīprabhu Gosāvī was staying in Tīka Upādhyāya's compound. He was walking back and

forth in the yard, saying, "Oh, drop dead! Mhāïṃyā will come, I tell
you. He will bring jaggery, I tell you. I should eat the jaggery, I tell
you. . . . I shouldn't eat it, I tell you. . . . Yes, I must eat it, I tell
you."

With that, the Gosāvī went onto the verandah. He sat down on a
raised seat and began to look at his holy belly. He was drawing lines
with the finger of his holy hand.

He had begun to act this way when Mhāïṃbhaṭ entered [Ṛddhipur]
by the southern gate. As he entered the gate, he met a Māṅg. Mhāïṃbhaṭ asked him, "Where is Śrīprabhu living?"

The Māṅg said, "He was playing here a minute ago. He just went
to Tīka Upādhyāya's compound."

The man left the village. Mhāïṃbhaṭ went into the village. When
the man's back was turned, Mhāïṃbhaṭ did a full prostration. Then he
came to Tīka Upādhyāya's compound. He had darśan of Śrīprabhu
Gosāvī. He gave him the basket of jaggery. He offered him a gold-
worked shawl. Then he prostrated himself. He touched the holy feet.
Then the Gosāvī said, "Drop dead! That's right, now, I tell you," and
he took some jaggery in his holy hand. He put it into his holy mouth.
He began to eat it. "Oh, drop dead! It's sweet, I tell you," he said, and
put a lump of jaggery into his holy mouth with his other holy hand.
And he began to eat it. He ate the jaggery in such a way that it trickled
out of his holy mouth, got into his beard, and dripped onto his belly.
He gave Mhāïṃbhaṭ prasād.

Ābāïseṃ was eating at the time. She rinsed her mouth quickly. She
came outside. "Lord! Stop! You'll get a stomach-ache," said Ābāïseṃ,
and took the basket inside. Then she brought him some water. She
poured it out for the Gosāvī to rinse his mouth. She washed his holy
belly.

Then Ābāïseṃ asked, "Where have you come from, Bhaṭ?"[4]

Mhāïṃbhaṭ said, "I've come from Saṛāḷe."

Then Ābāïseṃ said, "Where is our Gosāvī[5] living?"

Then Ābāïseṃ washed his feet. She prepared a plate of food for
him inside. "Come in, Bhaṭ," [she said]. "There's a plate of food prepared for you inside."

Then Mhāïṃbhaṭ ate his meal. He rinsed his mouth. Then
Mhāïṃbhaṭ prostrated himself to Ābāïseṃ. "Please let me clear away
the pile of ashes in the stove," [he asked].

From then on, Mhāïṃbhaṭ served the Gosāvī.

98. He plays with the Vāṅkī gate.

The Gosāvī used to get up early in the morning. He would go
trotting out. He would stop at the Vāṅkī gate. It would be closed. He
would pull up the bar planted in the ground. He would roll back the

gate. Its wheel would squeak. And he would go behind the gate and say, "Oh, drop dead! You're shouting, I tell you!" and roll it back again. And the wheel would sound again. "Oh, drop dead! Don't shout!" he would say, and kick it with his holy foot.

He would laugh. He would play with the "horse"[1] at the gate. He would pat it on the back of its neck. Then he would leave.

99. He meets Narasiṃha Daraṇā.

Rām Daraṇā's[1] son Narasiṃha Daraṇā came to Ṛddhipur. The Gosāvī was playing touch-the-post.[2] When [Narasiṃha]'s tent had been set up, to the east of the Rāmnāth[3] temple, he saw the Gosāvī. So he broke through the crowd of his guards. They formed a cordon around him as he met [the Gosāvī] to the northeast of the Rāmnāth temple. He took [the Gosāvī] to his tent. There he prostrated himself. He touched the holy feet. Then the Gosāvī removed the jeweled girdle from [Narasiṃha]'s waist. (According to some, he removed his bracelet.) And he gestured at him.

[Narasiṃha] placed his head on the holy feet. "Lord, if this is in your holy hands, what more can I hope for?" Then the Gosāvī laughed and put down the girdle.

Then [Narasiṃha] gave him a cloth to wear while bathing. He had a massage and a bath. He was worshipped well. He was offered a three-piece silk shawl. (According to some, he wasn't.) Then he had a meal. He rinsed his mouth and chewed pan. Then he left.

100. He breaks off a thorn at Koḷ well.

One day the Gosāvī's plate was filled with food. He sat down in front of his plate. And immediately he got up from his place. He started running. The devotees ran after him.

Near the Koḷ well gate there was a gum arabic tree. He broke one of its thorns with his holy hand. Then he said, "Drop dead! This isn't it, I tell you. . . . Yes, it is, I tell you!" and he broke it off completely and turned back.

Then the Gosāvī returned. When he got back, he ate his meal.

101. He abuses his buttocks when he farts.

The Gosāvī went out by the eastern gate. When he was near the Paraśurāma temple, to the northeast of it, he farted.

And the Gosāvī said, "Die, buttocks! Die! Why are you shouting?" and he slapped his buttocks and laughed.

Then he left.

102. He breaks a pot installed by followers of the Veda.[1]

One day the village headmen installed a pot in the Uñcamaḍh for the Navacaṇḍī festival.[2] They sowed nine kinds of grain between two pillars on the verandah, to the right as you enter. They tied up a string of flowers. They placed a garland. They left a child on guard, and they themselves went away.

The Gosāvī returned from his wanderings. Seeing these things, the Gosāvī acted angry.[3] He went up to them. He kicked down the pot with his holy foot. Then he ruined the string of flowers and everything else, and he slapped the child.

It went crying to tell the village headmen. Then the headmen came and abused the devotees. "Our Rāüḷ isn't like this. These people came from Sīvana.[4] They ruined our Rāüḷ." In such terms the village headmen abused the devotees.

103. He accepts Dāmurt's invitation.[1]

One day Bhaṭ and Mhāïṃbhaṭ went to Deūḷvāḍā to talk to Dāmurt. Bhaṭ and Mhāïṃbhaṭ said to Dāmurt, "Dāmurt, the Gosāvī wants to come to your village."

Dāmurt said, "That's my good fortune."

So Dāmurt came to get the Gosāvī. He set out with palanquin bearers, cavaliers, and attendants to get the Gosāvī. The Gosāvī's body was covered with sandalwood paste. A pearl was placed on his forehead, above a streak of musk. He was wearing bracelets and anklets and gold-worked clothes.

Then Ābāïseṃ entreated the Gosāvī, "Lord, please go. The village headmen are abusing the devotees, Lord."

The Gosāvī agreed to her request. Then the devotees joined hands around him. The Gosāvī looked back and forth. Startled, he very slowly impressed his holy feet on the ground. "The village is in revolt! The village is in revolt, I tell you!" said the Gosāvī.

Ābāïseṃ said, "Oh, no, Lord. It isn't. Dāmurt has come to take you away, Lord."

The devotees were saying, "Now see how the Gosāvī sits in a palanquin!" The devotees began to be afraid.

He met Dāmurt, then, outside, at the foot of the steps. [Dāmurt] prostrated himself. He touched the holy feet. Then [the Gosāvī] seated himself in the palanquin. He held on to the rope. As he was sitting down in the palanquin, Dāmurt said, "Hey there! Now blow the horns!"

Then the palanquin bearers said, "We've seen many great men, but none of those great men knows how to sit like this one."

Then the horns blew, and the Gosāvī left for Deūḷvāḍā.

104. He travels to Deūḷvāḍā.

The Gosāvī was going along the road, sitting in the palanquin. The horns were blowing. Dāmurt was running ahead, his sword and shield in his hands. To the west of the tank the Gosāvī said, "Oh, drop dead! Sit on the horse! Sit on it! Sit on it, I tell you!" and stopped the palanquin. So [Dāmurt] sat on the "horse."[1]

After that [the Gosāvī] moved on. At Mādhān he got down from the palanquin to the east of the village and went into a deity's temple. He played with the deity, then got back into the palanquin and went on.

105. The women of the town wave trays of lights[1] before him.

Then they decorated the town. A festoon was hung in the gateway. Decorated thrones were set up in the marketplace, in the lanes, and in the open spaces. On every house were decorated poles, doorway festoons, banners, and streamers.

The Gosāvī arrived. The village headmen went to meet him outside the gate, to the east of the river. The headmen had *darśan* of him at the southern branch of a banyan tree.

At the gate, prostitutes[2] waved trays of lights before him. In the marketplace, the women of the town waved trays of lights before him. Then Dāmurt's wife waved a tray of lights before him in front of the temple. Inside the courtyard, near the doorway, Brāhman women waved trays of lights before him.

After that, he stayed six months in the Pratimaṭh.[3]

106. He stays in the Pratimaṭh.

Then the Gosāvī sat down on the verandah, to the left as you enter. The wives of the temple priests came there to wave trays of lights before him. Then Ābāïseṃ prepared a meal. Then the Gosāvī had a massage and a bath. His worship service was performed indoors. He ate his meal. Everyone ate in the same row.[1]

107. When he watches a dance, he points out a dancing-girl's mistake.

The Gosāvī sat in the court of the Narasiṃha[1] temple. There was a dance being done. The dancer missed a beat as she danced. No one knew she had, but the Gosāvī noticed. So he said, "Oh, drop dead! She made a mistake, I tell you. She made a mistake right here."

She said, "Lord, I did make a mistake. No one knows the standard for judging my art, Lord, but you knew it, Lord Gosāvī. My good fortune is on the rise, since the Gosāvī has criticized my art." Then she left.

108. Dāmurt praises him.

The Gosāvī was sitting on the verandah, to the left as you enter (according to some, inside), when Dāmurt came. He had *darśan* of the Gosāvī. Then he prostrated himself. He touched the holy feet. Then he knelt before the Gosāvī and began to praise him. "Lord Gosāvī, it is my good fortune that you have come here. Today my good deeds have come to fruition."

He praised him this way, then sat silent.

109. How he hit Dāmurt with a coconut. Bhaṭ and Mhāïṃbhaṭ comfort [Dāmurt].

Then the Gosāvī dismissed Dāmurt. But he sat without saying a word. Then the Gosāvī said, "Oh, drop dead! Go away, I tell you."

He dismissed him once. He dismissed him a second time. He dismissed him a third time. But he didn't budge.

In front of the Gosāvī were the coconuts which he had received as gifts. The Gosāvī took a coconut in his holy hand. Then, acting angry, the Gosāvī said, "Drop dead! Get up! Get up, I tell you!" and he hit Dāmurt with the coconut.

[Dāmurt] got up; he went home.

The devotees said, "When he was there[1] he acted that way, and look how the Gosāvī has begun to act here too." They began to be frightened.

Then the Gosāvī had his massage and bath. His worship was done, and he had his meal. Then he went to sleep.

Then Bhaṭ and Mhāïṃbhaṭ went to see about [Dāmurt]. Since Bhaṭ and Mhāïṃbhaṭ had come, Dāmurt got up. He spread out something to sit on, and they sat down. Then Bhaṭ said, "How is your forehead, Dāmurt?"

"It's fine," he said. "Didn't the Rāüḷ just come to see about me? He touched my forehead with his holy hand. Then he said, 'Oh, drop dead! That hurt, I tell you.' The Gosāvī took my pain completely away. He touched my head with his holy hand and said, 'You're in pain, I say.' "

So Bhaṭ and Mhāïṃbhaṭ were very happy.[2] Then Bhaṭ said, "The Gosāvī had his massage and his bath. His worship was done, he had his meal, and he went to sleep. When we got the chance, we came here."

Then Dāmurt said, "Bhaṭ, when a person is repeatedly dismissed by any great man, he should not stay on into the evening. And when the Gosāvī dismissed me, I wouldn't go. He dismissed me once. He dismissed me a second time. He dismissed me a third time. But I wouldn't budge. So the Gosāvī punished me: he did away with my fault."

110. He eats the girls' food in the kitchen.[1]

They had invited unmarried girls for the Navacaṇḍī[2] festival [meal]. The Gosāvī went [to the kitchen]. He tasted the cooked food that was there; in this way, he made *prasād* of all of it. Then he ate a proper meal.

Later they put garlands on [the girls]. They put red powder on their foreheads and vermilion in the part of their hair. Then the Gosāvī said, "Oh, drop dead! This one is a bride![3] Oh, this one really is a bride, I tell you!" After he had played this way for a while, he left.

111. He tastes Narasiṃha's plateful of food offerings.

Narasiṃha used to receive seven plates of food offerings. The Gosāvī would stand on the low curved wall edging the steps, to the right as you enter. He would sample all seven plates of food before they would go to Narasiṃha.

Then one day [the priest] sneaked them past the Gosāvī. That night, Narasiṃha appeared to [the priest] in a dream. In the dream he said, "The Rāūḷ didn't have a single taste of my food offerings today, so I went hungry."[1]

Early the next morning, [the priest] filled the plates with food offerings. He brought them to the Gosāvī and asked the Gosāvī [to sample them]. But the Gosāvī would not do it. He would not take a single taste.

112. He plays with Narasiṃha.[1]

One day the Gosāvī went up to Narasiṃha and touched him with his holy hand. Then he kept putting his fingers into Narasiṃha's mouth and saying, "Oh, he'll bite, I tell you. . . . He doesn't bite, I tell you! Oh, he'll laugh. . . . He doesn't laugh, I tell you! Oh, he'll talk, I tell you. . . . He doesn't talk, I tell you!"

The Gosāvī played this way for a while. Then he left.

113. He calls the tiger goddess a lion goddess.

One day the Gosāvī went to Vāghīkā's[1] temple and touched Vāghīkā with his holy hand. The Gosāvī gave her a [new] name, [saying], "Oh, this is Vāghīkā. Is she a lion goddess, or a tiger goddess? Oh, drop dead! She's really a tiger goddess, I tell you."

The Gosāvī played this way. Then the Gosāvī left.

114. He purifies himself after he defecates.

One day the Gosāvī went to the west of the river to defecate. When he had finished defecating, he picked up some mud. Then he went to the riverbank. He cleansed himself properly.

Then the Brāhmans said, "Hey! The way we've cleaned ourselves for so long is useless. The way the Rāüḷ cleaned himself now is right."[1]

Then he left.

115. He accepts the invitation of Keśav Nāyak and Vīṭhal Nāyak.[1]

Then Keśav Nāyak and Vīṭhal Nāyak received word from the capital[2] that calamities were striking Ṛddhipur in the Rāüḷ's absence. Some people had fevers. Some had coughs. Some were breaking out with ulcers and boils. Some had leprosy. Some had the itch. Some were moaning with ghost possession. Some were dying. Everyone was in great misery.

Keśav Nāyak and Vīṭhal Nāyak heard this. They sent a message [to the headmen of Ṛddhipur]: "How is it that there are monasteries and pavilions and temples in the village, and yet the Rāüḷ has no place to stay? You should bring the Rāüḷ back and give him his own place to stay. The village is being plundered and looted. It's being devoured. People have fevers. People have itches. People are dying. Without the Rāüḷ, we're having terrible calamities."

So the headmen came to Deüḷvāḍā. They met [the Gosāvī] in the Pratimaṭh, and fell before him.

The Gosāvī started going inside and out. He was delighted, and he was saying, "I'll go now, I tell you. . . . I won't go, I tell you. . . . Yes, I'll surely go, I tell you!"

Mhāïṃbhaṭ said, "Will you sell us a monastery or a small temple? You must make it our property."

"All right," [they agreed].

So Mhāïṃbhaṭ gave them sixty quadruple silver coins.[3] Mhāïṃbhaṭ made a copper plate.[4]

Then the Gosāvī went there.

116. The doors are closed.[1]

Then all four main doors were closed. So they would go in and out through the small doors to do whatever they had to do. The Gosāvī set out the same way, through a back door, and started running along the road to Ṛddhipur.

Bhaṭ started running behind him. He stopped near a banyan tree on the far side of the river. Bhaṭ fell at his feet, [saying], "Lord Gosāvī! Please don't go to Ṛddhipur, Lord."

The Gosāvī agreed to his request, saying, "Oh, Harimā,[2] get up. Get up, I tell you."

Then the Gosāvī returned.

117. He agrees to Dāmurt's request.

Then Dāmurt asked the Gosāvī, "Please stay to celebrate the Southernwood festival.[1] Then you may leave, Gosāvī."

The Gosāvī agreed to his request. So on the festival day, Dāmurt took the Gosāvī and the devotees to his compound. Then he gave the Gosāvī a cloth to wear while bathing. Then [the Gosāvī] had a massage and a bath. Southernwood was offered to him. Clothes were given to him. He was worshipped well. All the devotees offered him clothes.

Then he ate his meal. He rinsed his mouth. Pan was offered to him. He went to sleep right there. Later he woke up.

To the east, facing north, was a stable. To the west of the stable was a small well. He looked down it.

118. He eats the girls' food in the kitchen.[1]

Unmarried girls had been invited for the Navacaṇḍī festival [meal]. The Gosāvī went [to the kitchen]. He tasted the cooked food that was there, and said, "Oh, drop dead! This is sweet. This isn't. This needs salt. This is salty. This is like honey. This is sweet and sour. This is right, I tell you." And he would eat it.

Then he ate a proper meal. Afterwards the girls had their meal.

119. He agrees to Kamaḷā Rāṇī's[1] request.

Then [one morning],[2] the Gosāvī woke up. He was standing to the west of the small well when Kamaḷā Rāṇī came along. She prostrated herself to the Gosāvī. She touched his holy feet. "Lord Gosāvī," she said, "please stay today. I'll perform full-moon observances for a day in your honor, Gosāvī. Please don't leave today, on the full-moon day."[3]

The Gosāvī replied, "Oh, drop dead! Serve it to me! Serve it to me! Serve it to me, I tell you!"

She said, "Lord Gosāvī, since you say so, I'll serve it to you."

And the Gosāvī laughed. He agreed to her request.

Then she brought good materials for worship. She brought the very finest foods. She worshipped the Gosāvī well. Then he ate the meal.

Then, on the first day after the full moon, the Gosāvī returned to Ṛddhipur.

120. He stays in a tent. He stays in the Rājamaḍh[1] for fear of a snake.[2]

Then Mhāīṃbhaṭ bought the monastery, but the Gosāvī was not inclined to stay there. So he stayed in a tent.

Then one day a snake appeared there, attracted by the fragrance of the flowers.[3] The devotees saw it, and cut pairs of sticks with which to catch it. The devotees said, "It will fall onto his holy body as we're catching it," so they took hold of his cot on all four sides, lifted it up, and took it outside.

The Gosāvī said, "Oh, drop dead! Heave ho!" as they put him in the Rājamaḍh. He stayed there.

Then the devotees drove out the snake.

121. He says, "It's daybreak."

One day the Gosāvī was sleeping on his cot. The Gosāvī woke up before dawn. And the Gosāvī said, "Hey, it's daybreak! It's daybreak!"

Ābāïseṃ said, "Yes, Lord. It's daybreak for the servant of God, Lord."

At that, Māhādāïseṃ and Umāïseṃ[1] said, "What is this? Is she the only one who has a claim to God? May only she serve him, and must we do nothing?" And they went in to take care of him.

Then the Gosāvī said, "Oh. . . . Oh. . . . Has the Cripple[2] died?"

Ābāïseṃ said, "No, Lord. I'm not dead. God gave me a God.[3] Rupai[4] and Umai[5] have taken him away."

Then the Gosāvī said, "Oh, come here! Come here! Come here, I tell you! Māhādī's[6] feet turn out. She's the grass of the grass."

So Ābāïseṃ began to take care of him alone.

122. He has them get clothes for Ābāïseṃ.

Māhādāïseṃ had gotten a garment for the Gosāvī. It had become old. Ābāïseṃ was wearing that garment one day, at the time of the worship service. When Māhādāïseṃ saw it, she said, "What is this? Why is she wearing my garment? It could serve as a foot-rest for our Gosāvī's[1] holy feet. Or it could be used as a cover for the handmill or the grindstone or the pestle. It could be made into rags for wiping the floor."

So Ābāïseṃ took off the garment, and they completed the Gosāvī's worship service. Then the Gosāvī said, "Oh, go to Cāndā,[2] I tell you. Go to Pāṭaṇ,[2] I tell you. Go to Pusadā,[2] I tell you. Put on a lamp-blacked garment, I tell you. Get one that's betel-colored, I tell you. Get one worth seven silver coins,[3] I tell you. Get one worth five silver coins, I tell you. Get two for one silver coin, I tell you." In those days clothes were cheap.

So Mhāīṃbhaṭ went to the marketplace. For two silver coins he got two garments, as red as the red powder for forehead marks. He brought them and placed them before the Gosāvī. Then the Gosāvī held up the ends of the garments and said, "Here, put them on. Put them on, I tell you!"

Ābāïseṃ said, "Oh, Lord, what do I need clothes for? The Gosāvī is my only shawl, and the Gosāvī is my only sheet."

The Gosāvī said, "Oh, put them on. Put them on, I tell you!"

So Ābāïseṃ put them on. Then the Gosāvī said, "Oh, the Cripple[4] looks like the mother of the bridegroom, I tell you."

Then Bhaṭ said, "You may have no salt to eat your tamarinds with, but you'll say, 'I got clothes for my mother.' And Śrīprabhu got clothes for Ābāïseṃ, and Ābāïseṃ is Śrīprabhu's servant."[5]

Bhaṭ extolled the greatness of the Gosāvī in such terms. Afterwards, Mhāïṃbhaṭ, Māhādāïseṃ, and Umāïseṃ were very sad.

123. He serves Ābāïseṃ sugar.

One day Ābāïseṃ was sitting against a pillar in the monastery, eating. The Gosāvī was asleep on his cot. In the northeast corner was a large earthen pot full of sugar.

Śrīprabhu Gosāvī got up from his cot. He scooped out a handful of sugar and put it onto Ābāïseṃ's plate.

And Ābāïseṃ cried out, "Mhāïṃbhaṭ! Run here! Run here!"

The Gosāvī said, "Oh, drop dead! Why are you shouting? Why? Eat it! Eat it! It's sweet, I tell you."

At that point, Mhāïṃbhaṭ arrived. No one knows where[1] the Gosāvī was sitting. And Mhāïṃbhaṭ remained silent.

124. He says, "Give away loot."[1]

One day the Gosāvī said to Ābāïseṃ, "Oh, drop dead! Give away loot!" He began to act this way.

Mhāïṃbhaṭ did not understand, so Mhāïṃbhaṭ said, "Ābāï, what does 'loot' mean?"

Ābāïseṃ said, "Mhāïṃbhaṭ, it's King Gosāvī's gift-giving."

Mhāïṃbhaṭ said, "What's needed?"

"A sari and blouse for the potter['s wife]," said Ābāïseṃ. "Give the potter a two-piece shawl." (According to some, "Cover the pile of pots with a two-piece shawl.")

So Mhāïṃbhaṭ did so. He had a pile of pots brought to the monastery. Then he let people take them. (According to some, he let people take them right there [at the potter's].)

If someone took more than one pot, the Gosāvī would say of him, "Oh, drop dead! He's a thief! A thief! He's taking another of your [pots]!" And the person would give it up, and the Gosāvī would laugh.

In this way he let the whole pile of pots be taken—by the village headmen, by the grocers, by the merchants, by the poor, and by the rich. But it was one pot per person: no one was permitted another.

125. He has them sprinkle *dovai*[1] during the Bhāvaī festival.[2]

On the day of the Bhāvaī festival, the Gosāvī said to Ābāïseṃ, "Oh, drop dead! Go on! Sprinkle at the Bhāvaī festival, I tell you. . . . Don't sprinkle, I tell you. . . . Yes, you must sprinkle, I tell you. Get water pots, I tell you. Make a turmeric mixture, I tell you. Build a platform of dough balls, I tell you. Erect a canopy of crêpes, I tell you. Cook dough balls and crêpes, I tell you."

So Ābāïseṃ got some water pots. She made a turmeric mixture. She cooked dough balls and crêpes. Then she set out with them.

The Gosāvī said, "Oh, drop dead! Take a double blanket as a cover. Take one! Take one, I tell you!"

So Ābāïseṃ took a double blanket as a cover. Then she left. She made a canopy. She built a platform of dough balls. She erected a canopy of crêpes. She sprinkled the turmeric mixture to celebrate the Bhāvaī festival. She broke [some of the] water pots. Then Ābāïseṃ said, "Mhāïṃbhaṭ, put the basket of water pots away. We'll be able to put them to use."

But then the Gosāvī said, "Oh, drop dead! Break them all, I tell you!" So they broke them all.

Then the Gosāvī said, "Oh, here! Here! Sprinkle *dovai!* Sprinkle it, I tell you!"

Ābāïseṃ did not understand this at all. So she asked Sādheṃ, "Elho, what does '*dovai*' mean?"

Sādheṃ answered, " '*Dovai*' means grass." So Ābāïseṃ started sprinkling grass around.

Then the Gosāvī said, "Oh, drop dead! That's not it, I tell you! Sprinkle the yellow kind! The yellow kind!"

So Ābāïseṃ sprinkled the turmeric mixture and yellow grass.

Then he returned to the monastery.

126. He looks after Ābāïseṃ.

Ābāïseṃ's oldest son, Sāraṅgpāṇibhaṭ, died. Her stomach was constantly burning from her suffering because of that. Even though she had the presence of two Gods,[1] her stomach would not be calmed.

One day she was asleep on a raised platform. The Gosāvī came there. And the Gosāvī said, "Oh, drop dead! Your stomach is burning, I tell you," and he reached out his holy hand and touched her. "Oh, it's burning, I tell you. . . . It's not burning, I tell you. . . . Oh, now it's really burning, I tell you."

Ābāïseṃ said, "No, Lord, it's not burning now."

From then on her stomach stopped burning. Her suffering went away.

127. He gives her the name "Cripple."

Ābāïseṃ had broken her arm. Then one day she was asleep on a raised platform. The Gosāvī came there. The Gosāvī held her broken arm in his holy hand. He began to play, [saying], "Oh, she's a cripple, I tell you! Oh, her arm is broken, I tell you. Oh, I should break this [other] arm, I tell you. . . . I shouldn't break it, I tell you."

Ābāïseṃ said, "No, Lord! Please don't break it! I use it to serve you, Gosāvī."

The Gosāvī said, "Oh, drop dead! It won't get broken, I tell you." Then he kept silent.

128. Bhaṭ offers him water at Ābāïseṃ's request.

One day Ābāïseṃ was sitting eating. The Gosāvī was asleep on his cot. He woke up and asked for some water.

Ābāïseṃ said, "Go, Nāgdev, will you? Give the Gosāvī some water."

"All right," he said, and got some water. At that time, the sight of [the Gosāvī's] unfathomable holy body could not be borne. So [Bhaṭ] sat behind a post and from there offered him a metal cup of water.

The Gosāvī refused to accept it. Then Ābāïseṃ said, "Come on, Lord! Please take it." And then the Gosāvī accepted the water.

129. He scrubs someone's back.[1]

A certain woman was all alone. When she was bathing, she would say to herself, "If the Rāüḷ comes along, he'll scrub my back."

At that, the Gosāvī would come along. He would scrub her back. When he finished scrubbing her back, he would thump her on the back [and say], "Drop dead! That's enough, I tell you."

So she would say it was enough. Then the Gosāvī would leave.

130. He drinks the water of Jāṇāḷe tank.

The water of Jāṇāḷe tank was soft. Māhādāïseṃ used to bring it from there early in the morning, carrying it in two full water pots slung from a bamboo pole across her shoulders. They would use it in serving the Gosāvī. She would do this every day.

At some point the devotees said, "That's too far away." So Mhāïṃbhaṭ tested all the water in the village. The water of Jāṇāḷe tank proved [even] softer than that of Karaḍ well.

The water used to get disturbed by the cattle, so she would go before dawn. She would fill two copper pots and bring them slung from a pole across her shoulders. They kept using the water of Jāṇāḷe tank.

131. He saves Māhādāï[1] when she is bitten by a snake.

One day Māhādāïseṃ got up one watch[2] into the night. She took the copper water pots and went out. She filled the copper pots, hung them from both ends of the bamboo pole, lifted them, and set off. As she did this, a snake bit her. But she kept going, carrying the two pots slung from the pole across her shoulders.

She set down her load in the main courtyard, and fell down in a faint.

The Gosāvī was sitting on his cot at the time. Ābāïseṃ cried out to him, "Oh, Lord! Rupai,[1] the maid-servant of Devakī,[3] has been bitten by a snake."

The Gosāvī went straight to the main courtyard. He looked at her: the poison was extracted.

Then she got up. She prostrated herself to the Gosāvī. She touched his holy feet. Then the Gosāvī said, "Oh, drop dead! I wonder, did the snake bite Māhādī?[1] Or did Māhādī bite the snake,[4] I say."

132. Umāïseṃ is reprimanded.

One day the Gosāvī went to get something from the stack of storage pots. The stove was full of burning hot coals. The [end of the] Gosāvī's shawl fell into the stove. Umāïseṃ held it up.

Ābāïseṃ said, "Why did you hold it up? Are there too few of the Gosāvī's servant girls to hold it up?"

Then she kept silent.[1]

133. How he comforted Umāïseṃ.

One day Umāïseṃ was husking rice. The Gosāvī broke the top of a jug on her head, and Umāïseṃ began to cry. Umāïseṃ said, "Why did he hit me? What have I done to him? I don't hurt or break anything of his." And she began to cry.

Ābāïseṃ said, "Be quiet, Umāï. The Gosāvī has destroyed your karma."[1]

Then the Gosāvī came over. He touched her with his holy hand. Then he said, "Oh, I've hurt you, I say. There, now. Be quiet. Be quiet! Be quiet, I tell you!"

Ābāïseṃ said, "Umāï, the Gosāvī is consoling you. Prostrate yourself to him."

Umāïseṃ said, "What is this? I'm the one who was hit. And *I* should be prostrating myself? Have I stolen his metal cup or something?"

Then Umāïseṃ prostrated herself to the Gosāvī.

He left.

134. He says, "Take the rice-and-split-pulse and *purī*-bread[1] vow to Vājā."[2]

One day the Gosāvī had trouble urinating. He crossed the threshold seven times.[3] He had a child throw stones. Then the Gosāvī said, "Oh, take a vow! Take a vow, I tell you!"

Ābāïseṃ said, "What vow should I take, Lord?"

"Oh, take the rice-and-split-pulse and *purī*-bread vow to Vājā."

So Ābāïseṃ said, "Vājā, let our Gosāvī's urine flow, and I'll give you rice-and-split-pulse and *purīs*."

Then the Gosāvī urinated. Ābāïseṃ made the rice-and-split-pulse and the *purīs*.

(According to some, he had her make it right in the monastery. According to others, the Gosāvī went [to Vājā's temple]. He urinated right there.)

Then the Gosāvī ate that meal [of rice-and-split-pulse and *purīs*] with his devotees looking on. Then the Gosāvī rinsed his mouth and chewed pan. Then he returned to the monastery.

135. "The seed[1] of the lineage of Kurus and Pāṇḍavas."[2]

One day Mhāïṃbhaṭ was commenting on the Gītā.[3] He was composing verses himself, and explaining them himself. He himself was raising problems. He himself was resolving them.

He was composing the verse, "The seed of the lineage of Kurus and Pāṇḍavas" when the Gosāvī came along. When Mhāïṃbhaṭ said, "The seed of the lineage of Kurus and Pāṇḍavas," the Gosāvī said, "Oh, drop dead! The seed of the extinction of the Kuru and Pāṇḍava lineage."

Then he sat down on his cot.

136. He tells a Brāhman a line of scripture.

A certain Brāhman was reciting a line from the scriptures: "Dhanañjayā, Dhanañjayā."[1]

The Gosāvī said, "Oh, drop dead! It's 'Nāgujayā, Nāgujayā.' "[2] The Gosāvī told him this line.

Then the Gosāvī left.

137. He says, "A decapitated head . . . ," and so on.[1]

One day [the Gosāvī said], "Oh, drop dead! A decapitated head, a shard of pottery. Mix with the dust, I tell you! Don't mix with it, I tell you!"

After this, when the Gosāvī would get angry, he would curse this way.

138. He accompanies Sobhāgeṃ to the burning ground when she dies.[1]

Sobhāgeṃ[2] died. Bhaṭ said, "We should bury her."[3]

Dāïṃbā said, "We should burn her. I gave the Gosāvī my word." Then, taking refuge on the roof of the monastery, he began to cry, "My Sobhāgeṃ! My dear Sobhāgeṃ! My potful of *sobhāgeṃ*.

Bhaṭ said, "If you burn her, we won't help carry her out."

Dāïṃbā said, "Don't take her out. I'll get the village Brāhmans and I'll have them carry her out."

So Dāïṃbā went. He said to the Brāhmans, "My mother has died. Bhaṭ says we should bury her. I say we should burn her. So come on." And the Brāhmans came. They made a bier.

Then the Gosāvī got up from his cot. He spit out the pan that was in his holy mouth. He put on a silk cloak with a hood that covered his face.

Ābāïseṃ said, "Crush pan and put it into her mouth." So they crushed pan and put it into her mouth. Then they put her onto the bier.

"Oh, drop dead! She's dead, but she still chews pan, I tell you!" Then the Gosāvī set off with her to the burning ground. All the devotees set off after him.

Dāïṃbā patted himself on the back. "Here am I—Bhojā![4] The Gosāvī said that he would do [for Sobhāgeṃ] what must be done for our father and brothers. The Gosāvī has made it come true."[5]

Then they put the ball of rice into her mouth as they lifted her onto the pyre. They poured out a stream of water. They broke the water pot at her feet.[6]

The Gosāvī stayed until her skull cracked. He bathed fully clothed, with his double silk shawl on. Then he returned to the monastery in his wet dhoti.

139. He gives a Brāhman a meal.

The Gosāvī was sitting to the left as you enter when a certain Brāhman arrived. The Brāhman said, "Patron,[1] give me a meal."

The Gosāvī said, "Oh, drop dead! Go on! Go to the kitchen, I tell you."

So he went to the kitchen. Ābāïseṃ spread something for him to sit on. She washed his feet. She put a mark on his forehead. She prepared a plate for him. He ate. She gave him pan to chew.

He approached the Gosāvī and said, "Greetings! Blessings on my long-lived patron!"

And the Gosāvī slapped him.

"What is this, Patron? Why are you hitting me, when you have just given me a meal?"

Then the devotees said, "That's the Rāüḷ for you."

So he prostrated himself and left.

140. He criticizes a female Mahātmā[1] for not wearing women's clothes.[2]

Nāgā Rāüḷ's wife[3] arrived, dressed in men's clothes. The devotees saw her, and she asked the devotees, "What is the Rāüḷ doing?"

The devotees said, "The Rāüḷ can't see anyone now. He's asleep."

"How can he not have time for me?" she said, and forced her way in.

And the Gosāvī woke up. He acted angry: "Oh, drop dead! You miserable hag! You're buck-toothed! Buck-toothed, I tell you! Oh, drop dead! Take off [those clothes]! Take them off! Take them off, I tell you!"

So she went and took them off. Then the Gosāvī said, "That's right, now. That's the way I want it."

141. He criticizes singing.

A Mahātmā and his wife came along, bringing a stringed instrument[1] with them. They plucked at the string and began to sing a song.

As they began to sing, the Mahātmā sang in one mode,[2] his wife sang in another mode, and they played the instrument in a third mode.

And the Gosāvī said, "Die, you miserable wretches!"

And they kept silent.

Then the Gosāvī left.

142. He climbs a rose-apple tree in an orchard.

One day as the Gosāvī and the village children were playing, they ended up underneath a rose-apple tree in an orchard. Then the Gosāvī touched the rose-apple tree with his holy hand, and he climbed up it. He gave contact[1] with himself to all the branches and boughs. He put unripe rose-apple fruits into his holy mouth.

And the Gosāvī would say, "Oh, it's sweet, I tell you. . . . No, it isn't, I tell you!" as he bit them and spit them out.

Then the Gosāvī left.

143. He plays at the Paraśurāma fair.[1]

On Sundays there was a fair in front of the Paraśurāma temple. The Gosāvī would go to the fair. He would give all the people contact[2] with himself. He would sample all their wares: curds, milk, ghee, [flowers at] the flower stall, [pots at] the potter's stall, betel leaves, and betel nuts.

Their profits would double.

144. He watches the cowherds' contest.

One evening the cowherds wrapped on silk turbans. Some wrapped on thick woolen turbans. Some anointed themselves with sandalwood paste. Others anointed themselves with blue paste.

They took *kubā*-wood[1] crooks, entered the arena, and whirled them around. At the same time, they said, "We will give milk to the calves and the children." They would not name anyone else.

Then the Gosāvī went in among them, onto the threshing floor. Then the Gosāvī said, "Drop dead! This one's right, I tell you. This one isn't, I tell you." He would take a crook in his holy hand. He would whirl it around his holy head. He grabbed some of them by the tucks of their dhotis.

The Gosāvī played this way for a while.

145. He abuses a Mahātmā for wearing women's clothes.[1]

One day a certain Mahātmā[2] arrived, dressed in women's clothes. He asked Bhaṭ, "What is the Rāüḷ doing?"

"The Rāüḷ is eating his meal," [replied Bhaṭ]. And with that, the man started inside.

At that point, the Gosāvī came outside. Then the Gosāvī said, "Oh, drop dead! Go away, you miserable wretch! You're practically toothless! Oh, drop dead! Go on! Take them off! Take them off, I tell you!"

So he took off the clothes. He put on men's clothes. Then the Gosāvī said, "That's right, now. That's the way I want it, I tell you."

Then the man left.

146. The difference between two batches of *poḷī*-bread[1] brought in by Ekāïseṃ.

One day Ekāïseṃ said to Bhaṭ, "Nāgdev, I'd like the Gosāvī to eat my food."

Bhaṭ said, "[Telling me] is not the way to make it happen."

So she said to Ābāïseṃ, "Ābāï, I'd like the Gosāvī to eat my food."
Ābāïseṃ said, "Mhāïṃbhaṭ takes care of that."
So she said to Mhāïṃbhaṭ, "Mhāïṃbhaṭ, I'd like the Gosāvī to eat my food."
Mhāïṃbhaṭ said, "Bhaṭ takes care of that."
So she had Demāïseṃ[2] make two *poḷī*-breads of granulated wheat flour. Then she put them on a plate for him, in the temple hall. She put them on it stacked one on top of the other.
Then the Gosāvī approached the plate. He sat in his seat. Then he looked at the plate, and picked up the two *poḷī*s. He turned them over and examined them. "Oh, drop dead!" [he said]. These aren't right, I tell you!" And he threw them outside. (According to some, he threw them outside the temple courtyard.)
Ābāïseṃ said, "What is this? What have you done?" and everyone began to question Demāïseṃ.
Then Demāïseṃ told them. Then, while more *poḷī*s were being made, the Gosāvī stayed seated in his place.
Then the *poḷī*s were finished. They were put on his plate. The Gosāvī examined them closely. Then the Gosāvī said, "Oh, drop dead! These are right, I tell you." Then he ate them, rinsed his mouth, and chewed pan.[3]

147. He makes fun of hard bread by calling it a piece of wood.

One day the wheat flour would not knead right. The *poḷī*-bread came out hard and tough. Then a plate was prepared for the Gosāvī. The Gosāvī sat in his place. Then he took the *poḷī*s in his holy hand. The Gosāvī examined them closely and said, "Oh, drop dead! It's a lump of dirt! A lump of dirt! Oh, it's a piece of wood! A piece of wood, I tell you!"
After this, the Gosāvī sat silently in his place. Ābāïseṃ said, "Another time I'll make them right, Lord! Beat your servant girl, thrash me, Lord, but please don't throw them out, Gosāvī. Please eat them now!"
The Gosāvī agreed to her request. Then he ate them. He rinsed his mouth and chewed pan.

148. He makes fun of dry vegetables by calling them *darbha*-grass.[1] (Some say, dry vegetables. According to others, grass.)

The Gosāvī was eating his meal when he found a blade of grass in his vegetables. The Gosāvī held it in his holy hand. And the Gosāvī said, "Oh, it's *darbha*-grass, it's *darbha*-grass!" And the Gosāvī held it in the prescribed way, and sat silently.

Then Ābāïseṃ said, "Please drop it now, Lord. Another time I'll clean the food better, Lord! Beat your servant girl, thrash me, Lord, but please eat your meal now."

So he removed the grass from his fingers and threw it away. Then the Gosāvī ate his meal. Then he rinsed his mouth and chewed pan.

149. He asks for a yam.

A yam had been received as an offering to the Gosāvī. The Gosāvī had a stomach-ache. So Ābāïseṃ wouldn't let him eat any of it, because it was sweet. Ābāïseṃ hid the yam in a haystack, and then she prepared the Gosāvī's plate.

Then the Gosāvī sat in his place. "Oh, drop dead!" he said. "Serve me the yam, I tell you!"

Ābāïseṃ said, "The yam is all gone, Lord. There isn't any now."

The Gosāvī said, "Oh, drop dead! It's in the haystack, I tell you!"

So Ābāïseṃ served it to him. Then the Gosāvī ate his meal.

150. He asks for the sorghum cakes promised in a vow.

One day a woman said, "Let me have a good sorghum crop. Let a heap of it come to my house. Then I'll make sorghum cakes for the Rāüḷ."

She had a good sorghum crop. A heap of it came to her house. But she forgot to do [what she'd promised].

And one day when the Gosāvī had gone out, the woman was coming toward him from the opposite direction. They met at a corner near his thinking rock.[1] And the Gosāvī twisted the end of her garment[2] and said, "Oh, drop dead! Give me the sorghum cakes you promised in your vow, I tell you!"

She said, "I'll give them to you, Rāüḷ! I forgot to, Rāüḷ."

Then she made the sorghum cakes. She brought them to the monastery.

(According to some, Umāïseṃ husked some sorghum the next day. Then she ground it and made sorghum cakes. Then the Gosāvī ate the sorghum cakes.)

Afterwards, on another day, she prepared his plate.[3] The Gosāvī sat in his place. Then the Gosāvī said, "Oh, drop dead! Serve me sorghum cakes! Serve me them, I tell you!"

She said, "There aren't any sorghum cakes, Lord."

"Oh, yes, there are. There are, I tell you!"

There were a couple left. She put them on his plate. Then the Gosāvī ate his meal. (According to some, the devotees brought them from the woman's house.)

151. He asks for the *tūr*-pulse[1] pods which had been given to the washerwoman.

There were some stale *tūr*-pulse pods which Ābāïseṃ gave to the washerwoman. Afterwards, she prepared the Gosāvī's plate. When the Gosāvī had sat in his place, he said, "Oh, drop dead! Serve me the *tūr*-pods! Oh, bring me the *tūr*-pods! Bring the *tūr*-pods, I tell you!"

So she brought *tūr*-pods from Keśav Nāyak's house and put them on his plate. The Gosāvī examined them closely.

Then the Gosāvī said, "Oh, drop dead! Bring those same ones, I tell you!"

So Ābāïseṃ brought the same *tūr*-pods from the washerwoman's house. Then the Gosāvī examined them closely and said, "That's right, now. That's the way I want it, I tell you."

Then he ate his meal, rinsed his mouth, and chewed pan.

152. He calls "adulteress" a woman waving a tray of lights[1] before him during the Dīvāḷī festival.

On the first day of the fortnight, the Gosāvī sat on his cot. The women of the town got together and brought plates full of materials for worship. They came to the monastery and waved trays of lights before the Gosāvī. Mhāïṃbhaṭ put blouses on their trays. When [the blouses] ran out, he put on the price [of a blouse].

To one of the women waving a tray of lights before him, the Gosāvī said, "Oh, you're an adulteress! An adulteress, I tell you!"

She got embarrassed and ran away.

Later Mhāïṃbhaṭ sent the price [of a blouse] to her house.

153. Pendhī is called a beautiful woman.

Pendhī was a Brāhman's wife. She was wearing a garment of coarse white cloth and a blouse with cuffed sleeves. Her head was like a heap of pots. Her teeth were blackish. At her wrists were strands of tin. On her feet were toe rings of bell metal. On her hand was a pearl ring. She was as black as soot.

She had gone to get water. When she returned with her water pot, her neighbor said to her, "Hey! Have you gone to wave a tray of lights before the Rāüḷ?"

"No, I haven't," she said.

"Well, go, then. The Rāüḷ will give you a blouse, or he'll give you the price of a blouse."

And she was delighted. She put down her water pot and went into the house. She smoothed her hair with oil from the lamp. She surrounded her eyes with soot from the griddle. She covered her whole forehead with red powder. She lit an oil lamp and put it on a plate. She added a fistful of sorghum. Then she set out.

When Pendhī arrived, the Gosāvī was still sitting on his cot, and all the devotees were sitting around him. When the devotees saw her, they laughed and said, "Here comes Pendhī, Lord, a beautiful woman!"

She arrived. All the devotees moved to one side. She stood before the Gosāvī. She waved her plate around in front of him. Then she said, "Give me a blouse, Rāūḷ, or give me the price of a blouse," and she began to wave her plate around in front of him.

Then the Gosāvī looked at her. And the Gosāvī looked at Mhāīṃbhaṭ and said, "Oh, drop dead! Give her both! Give her them, I tell you!"

Mhāīṃbhaṭ gave her a blouse and six copper coins. Then she left.

154. He gives a Bharāḍī[1] an offering on the first day of the fortnight.

On the first day of the fortnight, the Gosāvī was sitting on a "horse"[2] in front of the rest house. The Bharāḍī performed on the first day of the fortnight. On his head was a peacock-feather cap. He wore yellowish clothes. He had a turban on his head and blue paste on his body. There were clapsticks in his hand. He was clapping them loudly.

The Gosāvī heard his performance. He heard the song,

> On a tall verandah, Sāmāïseṃ was churning.
> Chains of gold formed the rings of her churn.

Mhāīṃbhaṭ gave the man a silk garment as *prasād.*[3] Then the Gosāvī left.

155. He describes the arrangements for marital prestations.[1]

The Gosāvī said, "When a widow makes a second marriage, she should first be given a white silk garment. Then she should be given a red one.[2] First she should be served two *poḷī*-breads, then she should be served four. First she should be served oil and sorghum, then she should be served ghee and rice.

"If the woman has been deserted, she should first be given a red silk garment to wear. First she should be served four *poḷī*s, then she should be served two. First she should be served ghee and rice, then she should be served oil and sorghum.

"Her bed should be set next to [her husband's]. Otherwise she'll set [the village] on fire.[3]

"Then, whether she gets along or not, the bride price for a widow [should be paid] in cash."

Later, Mhāīṃbhaṭ asked the village headmen, and they corroborated everything exactly.

156. He says that his daughter and son-in-law are coming.

One day the Gosāvī was walking back and forth in the main courtyard. The Gosāvī said, "Oh, drop dead! My daughter and son-in-law will come, I tell you. . . . She isn't coming, I tell you. . . . Yes, she'll surely come, I tell you! My daughter must be anointed, I tell you. She must be bathed, I tell you. She must be given a sari and blouse, I tell you. She must be served a good meal, I tell you. My son-in-law must be given a two-piece shawl, I tell you."

* * *

At that time, there was in Sā̃vaḷāpur a certain Brāhman's daughter-in-law. She had no mother or father. She had no brothers or sisters. They harassed her badly in her in-laws' house.

One day, her husband beat her and abused her: "Go away, you most unlucky of unlucky ones!"

She set out angrily. Her husband asked her, "Where are you going?"

"I am going to my maternal home," she replied.

"Where is your maternal home?"

"Isn't it in Ṛddhipur?"

He said, "Who is there?"

"The Rāüḷ is there," she said, and set off. And he set off bchind her.

* * *

Mhāïṃbhaṭ said, "What daughter does the Gosāvī have who will come today?"

Then she came. The Gosāvī embraced his daughter. She clung to the Gosāvī's neck and began to cry. Then his son-in-law embraced him.

Then Ābāïseṃ anointed her. She gave her a bath. She fed her a meal.

She was there for five days. Then Mhāïṃbhaṭ gave her a sari and a blouse. He gave the son-in-law a two-piece shawl. Then she left.

She returned one day, bringing a basketful of *dhīḍareṃ*s[1] and a pitcherful of ghee. She placed them before the Gosāvī.

The Gosāvī was sitting on his cot. The Gosāvī would break up a *dhīḍareṃ,* dip it in the pitcher, and eat it.

Then Ābāïseṃ took the basket away. The Gosāvī said, "Oh, drop dead! They're sweet, I tell you! Oh, why are you taking them away?"

"That's enough, now, Lord," said Ābāïseṃ.

Then he washed his holy mouth with his holy hand. He rinsed his mouth and chewed pan.

She returned to her village.

157. He eats Vesa Paṇḍit's[1] daughter's *āvaḷā*-fruit.[2]

One day Vesa Paṇḍit's wife came with their daughter for *darśan* of the Gosāvī. She prostrated herself to the Gosāvī. She touched his holy feet. Her daughter, who was with her, had an *āvaḷā*-fruit in her mouth. The Gosāvī saw it.

"Oh, give it to me! Give it to me, I tell you!" the Gosāvī said. "Oh, give me the *āvaḷā!* Give it to me, I tell you! Oh, give me the *āvaḷā!* Give it to me, I tell you!"

Her mother said to her, "Come on! Give the Rāüḷ what he is asking for!"

So she took the *āvaḷā* out of her cheek. She was naked. She wiped it on her buttocks and gave it to him. The Gosāvī ate it.

158. He looks at his holy face in a water jar.[1]

One day the Gosāvī went up to Tīka Upādhyāya's water jar. The jar was full of water. The Gosāvī looked into it and saw his reflection. And he laughed and said, "Oh, drop dead! You're me, I tell you!"

He made faces. Whenever he saw his reflection, he would laugh. Then he played for a while. Then he left.

159. How he swam with the children.

The Gosāvī used to go with the village children to the open well. The children would leave their turbans at the side and go into the water. The Gosāvī would go in with his clothes on.

Then they would swim. He would let the children hold onto his waist. And the Gosāvī would dive under, and they would be immersed. And they would shout, "Rāüḷ! We're sinking! We're sinking!" And the Gosāvī would laugh.

He would take hold of a child's waist, and make himself heavy. And the child would sink. Water would go into his nose and his mouth. And the Gosāvī would laugh.

He played this way for a while. Then he left.

160. He plays in the Vanījārs'[1] camp.

To the north of the Paraśurāma[2] temple, near the banyan tree, was the Vanījārs' camp. The Vanījārs would stop there, on both sides of the road. They would set up their three-legged stands.

The Gosāvī would go there. He would go up to the stands. "This is a group of ten," [he would say]. "This is a large group. This is too thin. This is too small. This is too large. This is torn. This is broken."

He would play this way at all the stands. Then he would return to the monastery.

161. He plays with horse traders at Karaṇḍ orchard.

The Karaṇḍ orchard was full of *rāyaṇī*-trees.[1] Horse traders used to stop there, to the north of the orchard, near the Kheḍ road. The Gosāvī would go there as they were branding the horses. And he would say, "This horse is blue; it is worth five hundred [silver? coins]. This one is white with a reddish tint. This one is a bay. This one is a chestnut. This one is dappled.

"This one is a proper horse. This one is an elephant. This one is an ass. Oh, drop dead! There are only these three kinds. There isn't a fourth, I tell you!" And he would touch them with his holy hand.

At that point, the horse traders would come to him. They would prostrate themselves, and then they would ask, "Rāüḷ, please eat here."

The Gosāvī would say, "Oh, drop dead! Bring it here! Bring it here, I tell you!"

So they would bring him bread and ghee. He would eat it. Then he would return to the monastery.

162. Keśav Nāyak's mother offers *tulasī*[1] to his holy feet.

To the north of the rest house was a niche. The Gosāvī used to sit there. Keśav Nāyak's mother used to wash the Gosāvī's holy feet. Then she would offer *tulasī* to his holy feet. Then she would prostrate herself. She would drink the water that had washed his feet, and then she would eat.

Sometimes when he was riding in his palanquin she would stop the palanquin. She would offer *tulasī* to his holy feet.

This was her regular observance.

163. He gives Vesa Nāyak's[1] mother his leftovers as *prasād*.[2]

Vesa Nāyak's[1] mother would not take a meal without first having the Gosāvī's *prasād*. She would come to the monastery. She would prostrate herself to the Gosāvī, and offer *tulasī* to his holy feet. Then she would take his *prasād*, and then she would eat.

One day Ābāïseṃ was giving out the *prasād*. "I won't take *prasād* this way," [said Vesa Nāyak's mother]. "I'll take it when the Rāüḷ gives it to me."

Then the Gosāvī had his meal, and the Gosāvī gave her the *prasād* with his own holy hand. Then she left. She ate. Then the Gosāvī rinsed his mouth and chewed pan.

(According to some, Vesī Paṇḍit's mother came to the monastery. She prostrated herself. Then she herself prepared [him] some food. She washed his holy feet. Then she offered *tulasī* to his holy feet, and the Rāüḷ had his meal. Then the Gosāvī gave her his leftovers as *prasād*.

She ate them. Then, from that day on, she would not take a meal without first having *prasād*.)

164. He agrees to Keśav Nāyak's request.[1]

Keśav Nāyak dug a well, but he couldn't strike water. Then the Gosāvī came along, and Keśav Nāyak said to the Gosāvī, "Rāūḷ, I have dug a well, but I can't strike water. So what should I do, Lord?"

So the Gosāvī hit the ground with his right holy foot, and he said, "Oh, drop dead! Dig here! Dig! Dig, I tell you!"

So he dug there, and he struck a limitless water supply. Then the Gosāvī returned to the monastery.

165. He eats off a leaf plate at the inaugural ceremony for Keśav Nāyak's well.[1]

Keśav Nāyak dug his well. He had done the masonry work inside the well, but he had not built a wall around the top.

The Gosāvī went there. He stood at the southern gate [of the compound]. And the Gosāvī said, "Oh, drop dead! Do the inaugural ceremony! Do it, I tell you!"

Keśav Nāyak said, "The Rāūḷ is telling me to do the inaugural ceremony, even though I have not built a wall around the top. So he must see some omen."

So Keśav Nāyak erected a canopy. Then the Gosāvī ate off a leaf plate under the canopy. He sat facing north, in front of a Lambodara[2] image on a pedestal.

Keśav Nāyak got a fever. He died right away.

166. He accepts Vāma's food.

One day the Gosāvī was going along the Dābh well road. Vāman Nāyak was approaching him from the opposite direction. He met the Gosāvī on the road. He prostrated himself. He touched his holy feet. Then Vāman asked, "Please come to eat, Lord."

The Gosāvī said, "Oh, drop dead! Go on! Serve it to me! Serve it to me! Serve it to me, I tell you! Serve it to me right here on the ground, I tell you!"

Vāma brought the food right there. He made a tent out of his two-piece shawl. Then he washed the holy feet. He made a mark with fragrant paste and consecrated rice [on the Gosāvī's] forehead. Then the Gosāvī ate right there.

(According to some, they were in the village. He ate curds and rice that were hanging in the sling.)

Then [the Gosāvī] returned to the monastery.

167. He accepts a drink of water from Pomāï, the waterwoman.

Pomāïseṃ was from Vāṅkī. She brought a heavy metal plate with her, and came to Ṛddhipur to become a mendicant.[1] She had a regular income in Vāṅkī. So Bhaṭ said, "Pomāïseṃ, if you become a mendicant, you'll lose your regular income; and the sixty silver coins you get are useful for the Gosāvī."

So Pomāïseṃ said, "Then what should I do, Bhaṭ?"

Bhaṭ said, "Become a mendicant's mendicant. Stand at the threshold of the main gate, with a begging bag in your hand. Say the word 'Alms!' there when the mendicants return from begging. They'll give you alms from their begging bags." So that was what she did every day.

Each of the devotees was assigned a regular task. Her task was to serve water. She could not run along with the palanquin: she was too fat.

There was a pipal tree to the east of Odyāḷe tank, south of the Rāmnāth temple. She would sit beneath that pipal tree, with a water bag in her hands and a silver cup in her lap. She would see the palanquin approaching. She would go up to it and pour water into the silver cup. Then she would offer it to the Gosāvī, and then he would move on.

She would get the sixty silver coins of her regular income. They would be put to use in the service of the Gosāvī.

168. He slaps Bhaṭ when they climb down the High Lane.

People's gutters were overflowing. (According to some, there was a light rain falling.) [The High Lane] had turned to mud. It was slippery. The Gosāvī climbed down it holding on to Bhaṭ's hand. When they reached the bottom, he let go of Bhaṭ's hand and slapped him.

Bhaṭ said, "Oh, Lord! Why are you hitting me now, Lord, when you've just climbed down the difficult part?"

And he laughed. Then he returned to the monastery.

169. He swims in Moḷīya well.

One day the Gosāvī went to Moḷīya well. He was washing his holy feet. As he washed his holy feet, his holy body lost its balance. It fell into the water. The holy body would go down into the water and come back up. And Bhaṭ and Mhāïṃbhaṭ circled around the top, but they did not go in.

He went down into the water this way for a while, and then came up again and got out.

Then the Gosāvī said, "Oh, drop dead! If the Cripple[1] were here, she would have jumped in."

Then he returned to the monastery. He began to tell Ābāïseṃ about it: "Oh, drop dead! I just went, and I just fell in. If you had been there you would have jumped in, I tell you."

Ābāïseṃ asked Mhāïṃbhaṭ, "Mhāïṃbhaṭ, what is the Gosāvī talking about?"

Mhāïṃbhaṭ said, "The Gosāvī is saying we are completely selfish." Then Mhāïṃbhaṭ told Ābāïseṃ the whole story. "We didn't jump in. If you had been there, you would have jumped in: that's what he's saying."

Ābāïseṃ said, "What is this, Bhaṭ? This is a bad thing that's happened. His light was almost snuffed out. What would we do if the Gosāvī died?" And she began to lament.

The Gosāvī said, "Oh, be quiet! Be quiet! Why are you lamenting?"

So Ābāïseṃ kept still.

170. He slaps Mhāïṃbhaṭ when he washes his holy feet.

The Gosāvī sat on a raised seat on the southern edge of the open well, in front of the Bandeśvara[1] temple. The Gosāvī's holy feet were covered with mud.

Mhāïṃbhaṭ asked a woman for her water pot. He filled it and brought it over. Then he washed the holy feet. When Mhāïṃbhaṭ finished washing them, [the Gosāvī] slapped him.

"Lord!" said Mhāïṃbhaṭ. "Why are you hitting me, now that I've cleaned your holy feet?"

"Oh," the Gosāvī replied. "Oh, drop dead!" and he laughed. Then he left.

171. He eats Dhāno's cereal.

Dhāno's brother Āpe[1] had gotten weak. The cereal for his diet was cooling in a wooden bowl. The Gosāvī went there. He was eating the cereal when Āpe saw him and shouted, "Dhāno! Dhāno! Run here! Run here! The Rāüḷ has eaten my cereal. I told you the Rāüḷ would come and eat my cereal."

"Why are you shouting?" she said. "Let the Rāüḷ eat it. I'll give you some more later."

Then the Gosāvī finished eating and left. Then she gave [Āpe] some more.

172. Mhāïṃbhaṭ is criticized for paying for tubers.

A Māḷī woman was selling a basketful of *mohāḷu*s. (According to some, *pothī*s.)[1] The Gosāvī went up to her. She peeled *mohāḷu*s and gave them to him. (According to some, she peeled *pothī*s and gave them to him.) And the Gosāvī ate them.

The woman started saying, "Rāüḷ, my mother-in-law will get angry. That's enough, Rāüḷ." Still she kept peeling them and giving them to him. Eventually he ate up the whole basketful of *mohāḷus*.

Then Mhāïṃbhaṭ asked her, "How much do you get for your *mohāḷus*?" (According to some, "for your *pothīs*?")

"They're worth a copper coin,"[2] she said.

Mhāïṃbhaṭ started to give her a copper coin. "Goodness me!" she said. "How nice of you. God knows you; [he knows] you're rich. My Rāüḷ ate the *mohāḷus*. Why are you giving me a copper coin?"

So Mhāïṃbhaṭ held his peace.

173. He scatters a cartload of jaggery.[1]

Someone from a neighboring village had brought a cartload of jaggery to sell. The Gosāvī went up to it. He put his holy hand into the jaggery. And the man grabbed his holy hand without knowing [whose it was].

And the Gosāvī acted angry. He took hold of the cart and heaved it over, then smashed the jaggery with his holy feet. He ground the jaggery into the dirt.

The man stood to the side. Afterwards he went to make a complaint to the village headmen. When he had made his complaint, the headmen said, "Complaints against others are taken to the Rāüḷ, but to whom can we take a complaint against the Rāüḷ? The village belongs to the Rāüḷ; the Rāüḷ can take care of it. If you had let him take some, you would have doubled your profits. But, even now, go and offer some to the Rāüḷ."

So he went. He offered some to the Gosāvī. He collected all the jaggery, sifted it with a winnowing fan, and sold it. His profits doubled.

174. He becomes dispirited.

Sādheṃ was sweeping the yard of her hermitage at Vevade (according to some, Cārṭhāṇe) when some people arrived from Ṛddhipur. Sādheṃ asked them, "Is our Rāüḷ doing well?"

"No," they said. "The Rāüḷ is dispirited. He hasn't eaten for eleven days. The devotees have long faces."

Sādheṃ set off immediately, with nothing but the clothes on her back. She would walk until evening, when she would stop. She had gotten as far as Thugāv̄ this way when she lost her way. She sprained her ankle and couldn't walk. So she went to a Brāhman's house. She said to the woman, "May I stay here, my friend?"

The woman said, "Where will you stay?"

Without saying a word, she lay down on their verandah, wrapping the end of her garment around her.

Soon the woman's husband returned from outside. He asked his wife, "Who is that sleeping [here]?"

"This Brāhman woman," she said. "She went to sleep [here] even though I told her not to."

He asked, "Mother, where are you coming from?"

"My friend, I'm coming from the Gaṅgā[1] Valley."

"Where are you going, Mother?"

"To Ṛddhipur. To the Rāüḷ's place."

Then he went into the house. He filled a water pot with warm water and brought it to her. He washed Sādheṃ's feet. He gave her milk and rice to eat. He gave her a bullock's packsaddle to sleep on. "Sleep here, Mother," he said.

She got up early the next morning. She took her bundle from its peg. Saying, "Govinda[2] ho! Govinda ho!" she sat down on the road. Then she said, "Today I will drink nothing but water that has washed the Gosāvī's feet. I will eat nothing but the *prasād* of the Gosāvī's leftovers." This was the vow she took.

At that point a certain Brāhman came along, mounted on a horse. "Where are you going, Mother?" he asked.

"To Ṛddhipur. To the Rāüḷ's place."

"So why are you sitting down?"

"My friend, I've sprained my ankle. I can't walk."

"Get up on this horse, Mother."

He dismounted. He sat her on the horse. He brought her to the threshold of the main gate and set her down.

Everyone came running, saying, "Elho[3] has come! Elho has come!" They embraced her. "Elho," [they said], "your face looks wilted. First drink some water."

Sādheṃ said, "No. I've given it up. I won't drink anything but water that has washed his feet."

Ābāïseṃ approached the Gosāvī. "Oh, Lord, your maidservant Elho has come. She's thirsty, Lord. She's saying, Lord, 'I won't drink anything but the water that has washed the Gosāvī's feet.' "

The Gosāvī said, "Oh, drop dead! Bring a two-handled tub! Bring it! Bring it! Bring it, I tell you!"

Ābāïseṃ brought a two-handled tub full of water. He put both his holy feet into it. Then Ābāïseṃ washed his holy feet. Then she gave the foot water to Sādheṃ, and Sādheṃ drank her fill. Then it was given to all the devotees.

Then Ābāïseṃ asked, "Elho, are you hungry?"

"No, Mother," said Sādheṃ. "I won't eat anything but the *prasād* of the Gosāvī's leftovers."

The Gosāvī was sitting on his cot. Ābāïseṃ went to him, and Ābāïseṃ said, "Oh, Lord, your maidservant Elho is hungry. She's saying, Lord, 'I won't eat anything but the *prasād* of the Gosāvī's leftovers.' "

The Gosāvī said, "Oh, drop dead! Serve it to me! Serve it to me right here on the ground!"

The Gosāvī had the sort of meal that he usually had every day. Then [Sādheṃ] had a meal of his *prasād.* Then all the devotees had a meal.[4]

Later that day, Ābāïseṃ ate a little rice and buttermilk. If she hadn't taken it, the Gosāvī would have recovered right away. His depression would have gone away.

Later his depression did go away. Then Sādheṃ went and prostrated herself. The Gosāvī embraced her. Then the Gosāvī said, "Oh, you've come, I say."

175. He gives Sādheṃ his molar as *prasād.*[1]

The Gosāvī was sitting on his cot. The Gosāvī's molar was loose. So the Gosāvī put his finger into his holy mouth and pulled out his molar.

Sādheṃ was sitting nearby. The Gosāvī said, "Oh, drop dead! Take it! Take it! Take it, I tell you," and he gave it to Sādheṃ.

176. He gives Sādheṃ his fingernail as *prasād.*[1]

One day the Gosāvī was sitting on his cot. With his holy right hand, the Gosāvī broke off a fingernail of his holy left hand. Then the Gosāvī said, "Oh, drop dead! Take it! Take it! Take it, I tell you!" and he gave it to Sādheṃ.

Sādheṃ wrapped it in a scrap of silk cloth and tied it around her neck.

177. He gives Sādheṃ a piece of betel nut as *prasād.*[1]

The door of the main gate was loose. So it was Sādheṃ's task to hold it. The Gosāvī would say, "Oh, swing me! Swing me!" and the palanquin would set off.

Sādheṃ would be holding[2] the gate. And the Gosāvī would spit out over it the pan in his holy mouth. All the [other] devotees would take it as *prasād.*

One day Sādheṃ thought to herself, "I'm such a sinner that I'm missing the *prasād.* All the [other] devotees are taking *prasād.*"

Knowing her wish, the Gosāvī held a piece of betel nut in his cheek. Then the Gosāvī got to the main gate, and, with his holy hand, took the piece of betel nut from his mouth. Then the Gosāvī said, "Oh, drop dead!" and gave it to Sādheṃ. (According to some, he had held it in the fingers of his holy right hand. He gave it to her.)

178. How he says, "It's a pancake."[1]

The day before, there had been a great feast. Much ghee had been served. Sādheṃ had not been able to eat it [all]. There was [some] left over.

The next day Sādheṃ was eating it. It was the cold season. [The ghee] had congealed on her plate. She was sitting and eating in the northwest corner of the Uñcamaḍh, when the Gosāvī came along.

"Oh," said the Gosāvī. "Oh, drop dead! It's a pancake, I tell you."

"It's not a pancake, Lord," said Sādheṃ. "It's ghee."

The Gosāvī said, "Oh, drop dead! Take it away! Take it away! Take it away, I tell you! You'll get flabby, I tell you."

So Ābāïseṃ took away the ghee. She poured out just a little. [Sādheṃ] ate that.

(According to some, the Gosāvī said, "Oh, drop dead! Take it away! Take it away! Take it away, I tell you! You'll get sick to your stomach, I tell you." So Ābāïseṃ took it away. She left just a little. Then Sādheṃ ate her meal.)

179. Sādheṃ is criticized for singing a folk song.

One day Sādheṃ was pounding grain. She began to sing in praise of the Gosāvī. She sang a folk song: "Govinda[1] is my mother. Govinda is my lady. Govinda wears my baby's garb."

At this, the Gosāvī said, "Die, you! Die, you!"

180. He punishes Sādheṃ.

Ābāïseṃ had made Sādheṃ stand guard. When the Gosāvī came, he used to break up the cooked food and ruin it. He would make *prasād* of it. That is why she had Sādheṃ stand guard.

The Gosāvī came along. He began to make *prasād* [of the food]. Sādheṃ shouted, "Ābāï! Run here! Run here! The Gosāvī is making *prasād*."

The Gosāvī said, "Oh, drop dead! Why are you shouting?" and he ran at her.

She started to run. She was so fat that she couldn't run away. She got caught in the barrier at the gate. She got caught in the bar across the small door to the west.

Her body was exposed. With his holy hand the Gosāvī took hold of her breasts, and immediately he began to put on an act. "Oh, cut them on the slicing blade, I tell you! Fry them, I tell you. Make spice powder of them. Make a rice cake of them, I tell you. Make a salad of them, I tell you. Hang them up, I tell you."

Sādheṃ began to shout, "Ābāï! Run here! Run here!"

When Ābāïseṃ arrived, the Gosāvī let [Sādheṃ] go.

Ābāïseṃ said, "Can there be anything wrong with Īśvara? Does he like this kind of thing?"[1]

Then from that time on, Bhaṭ sewed blouses for the women.

181. Similarly, he threatens Sādheṃ when she takes a bath.

One day Sādheṃ was bathing naked, outside the small door to the west. (According to some, it was in the corner where two monasteries met.) The Gosāvī saw her and ran after her, grabbing a burning faggot from the stove. "Oh, drop dead!" [he said]. "Put on a cloth! Put on a cloth, I tell you!"

Sādheṃ shouted, "Ābāï! Run here! Run here!"

Ābāïseṃ came running. She took the burning faggot from his holy hand.

Ābāïseṃ said, "What has happened to these Brāhman widows? Why don't they wear a cloth while they bathe? Can there be anything wrong with Īśvara? Does he like this kind of thing?"[1]

Then from that time on, they wore a cloth when they bathed.

182. He abuses Sādheṃ by saying her nose will be destroyed.

One day the Gosāvī said to Sādheṃ, "Oh, drop dead! You'll lose your nose, I tell you. . . . No, you won't, I tell you."

And Sādheṃ was frightened. She began to tell Dāïṃbā, "Oh, Dāï, today the Gosāvī said, 'Drop dead! You'll lose your nose, I tell you!' "

Dāïṃbā said, "Sure you'll lose it. Can the word of Brahman[1] be proved wrong?"

And she was frightened all the more. She left immediately. All day long she crammed herself, whimpering, into a corner in someone's house, her arms around her legs and her head on her knees.

At night she returned. Ābāïseṃ asked, "Elho,[2] where were you today?"

So she began to tell Ābāïseṃ: "The Gosāvī told me I would lose my nose. I told Dāï, and Dāï said the same thing: 'Sure you'll lose it. Can the word of Brahman be proved wrong?' After that I was hiding in someone's house."

Ābāïseṃ said, "The Gosāvī was teasing you. Get up! You must be hungry. Take a bath and eat your dinner."

She took a bath and ate her dinner. Her fear subsided.

183. He calls Sādheṃ a black bull[1] from Aḷajpur.

One day the Gosāvī said to Sādheṃ, "Oh, you're a black bull from Aḷajpur, I tell you. Yes, you are, I tell you."

184. He calls Sādheṃ a Māṅg's chicken.[1]

The Gosāvī was sitting on his cot when Sādheṃ came to him. She prostrated herself to the Gosāvī. She touched his holy feet.

The Gosāvī said, "Oh, you're a Māṅg's chicken! Yes, you are a Māṅg's chicken, I tell you."

(According to some, the place was on the Dābh well road, near Vāma's field.)

185. He gives Sādheṃ a lock of his hair.[1]

The Gosāvī was sitting on his cot, and Ābāïseṃ was combing his holy hair. Sādheṃ entered. She prostrated herself to the Gosāvī. She touched his holy feet. She sat down near him.

Ābāïseṃ kept combing his holy hair. She arranged it in a top knot. A lock of hair fell out. The Gosāvī took it in his holy hand and gave it to Sādheṃ. "Oh, drop dead!" the Gosāvī said. "Take it! Take it! Take it, I tell you!" So Sādheṃ took it.

Later she knotted it in a [piece of a] thin sari. She tied it on her arm.

186. He says "Hail!" when he meets Āüseṃ.[1]

One day, when the Gosāvī was sitting on his cot, Āüseṃ arrived from the Gaṅgā[2] Valley. She prostrated herself to the Gosāvī. She touched his holy feet.

The Gosāvī said, "Oh, drop dead! You're a female yogī! A female yogī, I tell you. Oh, hail![3] Hail, I say! I say, 'Hail,' I say."

Āüseṃ said, "O Swami, Lord of the World! [You] say this thing here, and [Cakradhar] says the same thing there. So are you his?" Then Āüseṃ added, "Oh, Lord, with Cakra Swami[4] gone, the banks of the Gaṅgā[2] look burning red."

The Gosāvī said, "Oh, drop dead! It's true. It's true, I tell you."

187. He lets Āüseṃ worship him with colored powder.[1]

One day Āüseṃ said to the Gosāvī, "O Swami, Lord of the World! I will worship you with colored powder, Lord Gosāvī."

The Gosāvī said, "Oh, drop dead! Do it! Do it! Do it, I tell you!"

Then the Gosāvī had his massage and bath. Then she collected the colored powder. She collected black, yellow, green, and red powders. Then she drew a multicolored garland of vines.

She prepared a seat. The Gosāvī sat on the seat. She worshipped him. She prepared a mixture of rice and split pulse. She arranged rows of plates. Waving vegetables, lamp-shaped sweets, fist-shaped sweets, and lumps of rice before the Gosāvī, she gave them to the devotees.

The Gosāvī watched; he tasted [the foods].

Āüseṃ said, "Hail to Cakra Swami! And hail to Guṇḍam Swami[2] as well!"

With this, the worship service was finished. Then [the Gosāvī] ate his meal.

188. He upbraids Āü about her leavings.

One day Āüseṃ cooked some sorghum sweets. She ate half of them herself, and set aside half for the Gosāvī. They were good, so as she was eating she took some more with her left hand. She ate them and rinsed her mouth.

Later, when it was time for the Gosāvī's meal, she put [the sweets] into a dish and brought them to him. The Gosāvī said, "Oh, drop dead! It's leavings! Leavings, I tell you!"

"No, Lord," said Āüseṃ. "It's not leavings. They were good, so I took more with my left hand, Lord."[1]

Then the Gosāvī ate his meal.

189. He demands a filled sweet from Āüseṃ.

Āüseṃ used to bring a filled sweet for the Gosāvī. But one day Mhāïṃbhaṭ told her not to. "Āü, don't bring the filled sweet for the Gosāvī. Afterwards the Gosāvī doesn't eat his regular meal."

"All right. You go away now. Now I won't bring it."

As the Gosāvī was having his massage, he kept looking toward the door and saying, "Oh, drop dead! The female yogī hasn't come!" As he was having his bath, the Gosāvī said, "Oh, drop dead! The female yogī hasn't come!" Then his plate was prepared. When it was time for his meal, he said, "Oh, drop dead!" The Gosāvī said this three times, and then sat silent.

Ābāïseṃ said, "Mhāïṃbhaṭ, Āü hasn't brought the filled sweet, so the Gosāvī won't eat his meal."

So Mhāïṃbhaṭ went to her and said, "Āü, the Gosāvī won't eat his meal. You take him a filled sweet."

"Go away," said Āüseṃ. "Now I won't come."

Then Mhāïṃbhaṭ fell down before her. So she brought the filled sweet. The Gosāvī said, "Oh, drop dead! Has the female yogī come?"

"Yes, I've come." Then Āüseṃ offered the filled sweet to the Gosāvī. Then he ate his meal.

190. Similarly, he asks for sorghum sweets.

The Gosāvī's plate was ready, and the Gosāvī sat in his place. Then the Gosāvī said, "Oh, drop dead! The female yogī is coming, I tell you. She'll bring sorghum sweets, I tell you."

At that point, Āüseṃ arrived, bringing sorghum sweets and filled sweets. She put them on his plate. Then he ate his meal.

For six months, he insisted on eating his meals this way, from her dish.

191. He upbraids Āü for killing a scorpion.[1]

One day the Gosāvī went to Āü's hut. A scorpion had appeared in the hut, and Āü had killed it. She was holding it by the tail to throw it out when the Gosāvī saw her. The Gosāvī said, "Oh, drop dead! You're a female yogī! A female yogī, I tell you! Are yogīs supposed to do such things? Oh, drop dead! Why did you kill it?"

Āüseṃ said, "O Swami, Lord of the World! It would have bitten me, Lord."

The Gosāvī said, "Oh, drop dead! You've bitten it,[2] I tell you! How can it bite you, I say."

And immediately the Gosāvī left.

192. He calls Āü a midwife.[1]

One day Āüseṃ came to the monastery wearing a colored silk garment. She looked good. The Gosāvī said, "Oh, drop dead! You're a midwife! A midwife, I tell you! Oh, drop dead! Take it off! Take it off, I tell you!"

Āüseṃ replied, "Yes, Lord, I'll take it off. Starting today, even if I'm given one, I won't wear it, Lord."

Then Āüseṃ took off the silk garment. Then the Gosāvī said, "Now that's the way I like it, I tell you."

Then she touched his holy feet.

193. He meets Kothaḷobā.[1]

Bhaṭ used to go to Vāṅkī, Dīghī, Thugā̃v, and Deūḷvāḍā to beg. He would get solitude then; he would beg then; he would meditate then.

And Mhāīṃbhaṭ would beg in Taḷegā̃v, Vāṇṭhavḍā, and Kauṇḍāṇyāpur. He would also collect from the money-changers.[2] All the money would be put to use in the service of the Gosāvī.

One day Bhaṭ went to Vāṅkī. There he was sitting in solitude in Sīdhanāth's[3] temple.

Kothaḷobā was serving as Sīdhanāth's priest. He arrived. He placed his clothes in the temple hall and put on a loincloth. He took a water pot, went to the river, filled the water pot, and brought it back. He got cow dung. Then he swept the temple hall from corner to corner and sprinkled cow-dung wash on it. He drew designs with colored powder.

Then he took his clothes and went to the river. He took a bath. He filled a copper water pot and brought water in it. Then he went up to the *liṅga*.[4] He wrapped his turban around his nose and mouth so that he wouldn't breathe on the *liṅga*. Then he poured water on it and arranged flowers over it. Then he prostrated himself and circumambulated the *liṅga*. Then he left.

As he was leaving, Bhaṭ said, "If you would give the true Īśvara this kind of service, you'd get something completely different."

Kothaḷobā replied, "Is there a true Īśvara?"

"Yes, there is," said Bhaṭ.

Then [Kothaḷobā] said, "Where is he?"

And Bhaṭ replied, "Isn't he Śrī Guṇḍam Rāüḷ at Ṛddhipur?"

"Will you take me there?" he said.

"All right."

Bhaṭ set off immediately. When they arrived at Ṛddhipur, the Gosāvī was sitting on his cot. He met [Kothaḷobā]. Kothaḷobā gave him a lime as an offering.

Immediately he became a follower of the Gosāvī. He stayed on.

194. He gives him the name Kothaḷā.

One day the Gosāvī said, "Oh, you're a sack [*kothaḷā*]. A sack, I tell you!" Kothaḷobā's body was large. He was big and fat.

So Kothaḷobā said, "The Gosāvī is making me practice self-restraint. He is telling me how to live."

Mhāïṃbhaṭ said, "You are a lucky man. No one else's luck is as good as yours, if the holy one who speaks so seldom is telling you how to live."

195. He tells Kothaḷobā that he should be whipped.[1]

One day the Gosāvī said to Kothaḷobā, "Oh, drop dead! You should be whipped with a wet switch, I tell you! You should stoop over, I tell you! You should store up seven loads [of grain],[2] I tell you. You should store up five loads, I tell you. Beg alms. Beg, whether you get anything or not. If you don't [get anything], serve yourself a few grains of *lā̃k*."

Then Kothaḷobā said, "Mhāïṃbhaṭ, the Gosāvī is telling me to die."

Mhāïṃbhaṭ said, "You're lucky, blessed, fortunate."[3]

196. During his massage, his holy body is lifted up, and he has it put back down.

One day when Ābāïseṃ wanted to give him a massage, the Gosāvī said, "Oh, drop dead! Kothaḷā! Where's Kothaḷā?"

So Ābāïseṃ said to Kothaḷobā, "The Gosāvī wants you to give him his massage."

Kothaḷobā went right to the well. He washed his hands and feet. When he had finished bathing, he returned.

The Gosāvī sat down on a cushioned seat. Then [Kothaḷobā] took fragrant ointment and applied it to the holy body. He gave him a massage, anointing his holy body, rubbing oil on it, massaging his holy feet, holding him. As he held the holy body, he lifted it up.

And the Gosāvī said, "Hey! Let me go! Let me go! Let me go, I tell you!"

So he set him down on the cushioned seat. And the Gosāvī laughed.

Then he finished the massage.

197. He upbraids Kothaḷobā when he is pounding rice.

One day Kothaḷobā and Mhāïṃbhaṭ's wife, Demāïseṃ,[1] were pounding rice. Their legs were spread one on the other's. Mhāïṃbhaṭ came in from outside, saw them, and became suspicious. He imagined to himself, "If they are like this during the day, what must they be doing at night?"

At that point, the Gosāvī came along. And the Gosāvī said to Kothaḷobā, "Oh, drop dead! Take your leg off her leg! Take it off! Take it off, I tell you!"

So he took his leg off her leg.

198. How he exonerated him.

Then, from that day on, Kothaḷobā wasted away little by little, until he became thin. He didn't eat any food. He didn't drink any water. And so he turned livid.

Seeing this, the Gosāvī began to talk to himself. "Oh, drop dead!" said the Gosāvī. "Kothaḷā is not like that."

Bhaṭ said, "Mhāïṃbhaṭ, the Gosāvī is exonerating Kothaḷobā."

Mhāïṃbhaṭ said, "I didn't know, Lord! I didn't know, Lord!" and prostrated himself to the Gosāvī.

The Gosāvī said, "Oh, drop dead! Do that to Kothaḷā, I tell you!"

So Mhāïṃbhaṭ prostrated himself to Kothaḷā. And his sin[1] was taken away.

199. He pats a woman gathering cow dung.

One day Bhusāres[1] had stopped in the southeast corner in front of the rest house. Their bullocks had been tethered to ropes there. A woman who gathered cow dung had filled her basket there with dung. She tried to lift it, but she couldn't get it up. So she looked around.

At that point, the Gosāvī came along there. She said, "Rāüḷ! Help me lift this, will you?"

So the Gosāvī lifted it and put it on her head. And he patted her on the face.

Then the Gosāvī left.

200. He eats dried plantain[1] at the house of a woman doing a month-long fast.

Maiḷbhaṭ's sister was named Rāṇāïseṃ.[2] She had undertaken a month-long fast. One day the Gosāvī went to her house. The Gosāvī said, "Oh, drop dead! Get up! Get up! Get up, I tell you!"

So she got up. She prostrated herself to the Gosāvī. She touched his holy feet. Then the Gosāvī went to sleep on the bed.

Later, when he woke up, Rāṇāïseṃ poured ghee into a metal cup. She offered him ten dried plantains.

Then the Gosāvī said, "Now this is what I want, I tell you. Oh, bring me them! Bring me them! Bring me them, I tell you." Then the Gosāvī ate them, and rinsed his mouth.

He returned to the monastery.

201. He accepts Maiḷbhaṭ's food.

One day the Gosāvī was sitting on his thinking rock.[1] The Gosāvī said, "Oh, I should go to Nāṃnaurī, I say. . . . I should go to Sonaurī, I say." He began to think out loud this way.

At that point, Maiḷbhaṭ came along. He prostrated himself to the Gosāvī. He touched his holy feet. Then he invited him for a meal.

The Gosāvī accepted the invitation; then he said, "Well, get going! Go on, I tell you! Serve it to me! Serve it to me! Serve it to me, I tell you!" And the Gosāvī left right away.

Maiḷbhaṭ's house shared a fence with the water carrier's house. [The Gosāvī] went there to the house. He sat down. His holy feet were washed, and *tulasī*[2] was offered to them. Then he ate a meal of ghee and rice, and a sour dish made with fried pulse cakes.

The Gosāvī said, "Oh, drop dead! It's good! It's good! Give me more, I tell you."

So they gave him more of the sour dish, as well as crêpes and a spiced dish of *cavaḷā*-beans,[3] with ghee. Finally, he had a serving of milk and rice.

And so he had a proper meal. Then he was offered water to rinse his mouth, and pan to chew. Then the Gosāvī returned to the monastery.

202. He meets Māhādevobā, who brings a citron as an offering.

One day the Gosāvī was walking back and forth in the main courtyard, when Māhādevobā arrived. They met inside the main gate, two arms' lengths from the foot of the inner steps.

[Māhādevobā] presented him with a citron, and then prostrated himself. He touched the holy feet. Then he embraced Bhaṭ and Mhāïṃbhaṭ.

203. He says that one Gaṅgā[1] Valley pilgrim is missing.

Ākoseṃ was Ābāïseṃ's sister. She set off from the capital[2] to go to Rāmṭek.[3] She got to Ṛddhipur. She [and her party] stayed in someone's house.

Māhādev Pāṭhak's[4] wife stayed behind to watch their belongings. All the others came to have *darśan* of the Gosāvī. They had *darśan* of the Gosāvī in the main courtyard. They prostrated themselves. They touched his holy feet. Then the Gosāvī counted them. "One, two, four. . . . One is missing, I tell you." He counted them again. "One, two, four. . . . Oh, one of the Gaṅgā Valley pilgrims is missing, I tell you."

Bhaṭ asked, "Has someone stayed behind at your lodgings?"

Ākoseṃ said, "Māhādev's wife stayed behind."

Bhaṭ said, "Why are you staying so far away? Move over here, the Gosāvī remembers you so well."

"All right." So they moved right there.

The Gosāvī was sitting on his cot when Māhādev's wife came. She had *darśan*. She prostrated herself. She touched his holy feet.

And the Gosāvī said, "Oh, so you've come?"

"Yes, Lord, I've come," she said, and prostrated herself again.

204. He says, "This isn't the right one."

One day the Gosāvī walked back and forth one and a half times, holding Māhādev's hand. Māhādevobā was watching the Gosāvī, afraid to meet his eyes.

Then Māhādevobā said, "Tīpurārībhaṭ![1] Run here! Run here!"

And the Gosāvī looked at him, and said, "Oh, drop dead! This isn't the right one, I tell you." And he let go of him.

Then he took hold of Tīpurārībhaṭ's hand and walked back and forth.

205. He talks about the black man and the white man.

One day the Gosāvī went out to play. Māhādevobā and Lakhudevobā[1] ran with his palanquin, and they got tired. They didn't come for *darśan* of the Gosāvī. So the Gosāvī said, "Oh, drop dead! The black woman's black [son] hasn't come, I tell you." Gāṅgāïseṃ's Lakhudevobā was dark-skinned. "Oh, drop dead! The white woman's white [son] hasn't come, I tell you." Ākoseṃ's Māhādevobā was light-skinned.

The next day they came for *darśan* of the Gosāvī. They prostrated themselves. They touched his holy feet. Then Bhaṭ said, "Māhādev, why didn't you come yesterday for *darśan* of the Gosāvī?"

"Our legs were tired, Nāgdev, from running with the palanquin. That's why we didn't come."

Bhaṭ said, "You shouldn't do that. When you are here, you should come for *darśan* of the Gosāvī."

After that, they came every day for *darśan* of the Gosāvī.

206. He asks for oranges.

Ākoseṃ had brought oranges from the capital.[1] They were all gone. The Gosāvī began to ask for them. "Oh, drop dead!" the Gosāvī said. "Give me oranges, I tell you!"

Ābāïseṃ said, "Lord, the oranges are all gone. There aren't any left, Lord."

"Oh, drop dead! Give me them! Give me them! Give me them, I tell you!" he insisted.

They got two silver coins'[2] worth of oranges from Mehkar, but by then the Gosāvī had changed his mind. So they sold the oranges and put the two silver coins to use in the service of the Gosāvī.

207. He calls a man his son-in-law.[1]

When Ākoseṃ set out from her village to go on pilgrimage to Rāmṭek,[2] her in-laws sent someone to accompany her. Then when they got to Ṛddhipur, the man came along with Ākoseṃ. Ākoseṃ and Bhaṭ said to him, "Tell them in the village that Āko did go to Rāmṭek. [In fact,] she stayed with the Gosāvī because he is Īśvara."

Then they anointed him and gave him a bath. They prepared good food for him. They were putting pressure on him not to tell [the truth]. Ābāïseṃ prepared his plate. She lit lamps on lamp stands. They treated him like a son-in-law.

Then one day the Gosāvī went there. He held the man's head with his holy hand. Then the Gosāvī said, "Oh, you're my son-in-law! My son-in-law, I tell you." This is how the Gosāvī named him.

The man ate his meal.

208. He tells about a stolen bull.

One day a man's bull was lost. He looked everywhere, but he couldn't find it. So he said, "Now I'll go to the Rāüḷ. If the Rāüḷ tells me where the bull is, then he must be Parameśvara."

So he came and prostrated himself. Then he said, "Rāūḷ, my bull is lost. It can't be seen, Lord."

The Gosāvī replied, "Oh, drop dead! Go on! It's sitting behind the Mahārs' quarter,[1] I tell you."

So he went, and found it sitting there. Then he said, "He really is Īśvara."

209. He stops the rain during his bath.

One day the Gosāvī had had his massage. He was taking his bath. A slight drizzle was falling. So the Gosāvī sheltered his holy face with his holy hand and looked up. Then the Gosāvī said, "Oh, drop dead! Stop! Stop! Stop, I tell you!"

And it stopped.

Then his bath was finished, and his [wet] clothes were taken off. The sky cleared, and the sun came out. Then the Gosāvī said, "Now that's the way I like it, I tell you."

Then he took in the mild sunshine for a while. Then he left.

210. He stops the rain when he's going out.

One day when the Gosāvī was going out, it started to rain. The Gosāvī said, "Oh, drop dead! Stop! Stop, I tell you!" and he warded it off with his holy hand and his holy face.

And the rain stopped.

Then the Gosāvī went out.

211. He says to get drenched going out, and to come back dripping.

One day the Gosāvī was going out. The Gosāvī said, "Oh, swing me! Swing me!" and his palanquin set out. "Oh, get drenched going out, and come back dripping."

So all the devotees set off with the palanquin. And it started to rain. All the devotees got wet. All the devotees spread their clothes on the palanquin.

Then the palanquin stopped at the Rāmnāth[1] temple, and a pile of clothes was brought from the monastery. They put them on. Someone was sent back to the monastery with the wet clothes.

Later the Gosāvī came out of the marketplace. All the people said, "The Rāūḷ didn't let his own clothes get a bit wet." Everyone was surprised and astounded by this.

Then he returned to the monastery.

(According to some, Keśav Nāyak had invited him for a meal. The Gosāvī went there. His worship service was done there. He ate a meal there along with his devotees. Then the Gosāvī returned to the monastery.)

212. He meets Ābāïseṃ.

When our Gosāvī[1] was staying in the Gaṇapati monastery,[2] he sent Ābāïseṃ from the Gaṇapati monastery to Ṛddhipur to serve Śrīprabhu.[3]

She arrived in Ṛddhipur. The Gosāvī was staying in Tīka Upādhyāya's compound.[4] She met the Gosāvī there. The Gosāvī said, "Oh, drop dead! So you've come?"

"Yes, Lord. Śrī Cakradhar Rāyā[5] sent me to you." Then she prostrated herself to the Gosāvī. She touched his holy feet.

From then on, she began to serve Śrīprabhu Gosāvī.

213. He meets Lakṣmīndrabhaṭ.[1]

Bhaṭ used to beg in Vāṅkī, Dīghī, and Deūḷvāḍā for the service [of the Gosāvī]. One day Bhaṭ had gone to Deūḷvāḍā. He was sitting in a corner of Narasiṃha's[2] temple. Lakṣmīndrabhaṭ was expounding a *purāṇa.*[3] In expounding the *purāṇa,* Lakṣmīndrabhaṭ evoked its sentiments with originality. Then, full of passion, he said, "There's a soul, but there's no god [for it]."

Bhaṭ replied, "There is a god, but there are no souls [who come to him]."

Lakṣmīndrabhaṭ said, "Isn't this a soul?" and he placed his hand on his chest.

Bhaṭ said, "Isn't that God? He lives in Ṛddhipur," and he raised his hand toward Ṛddhipur.

And immediately Lakṣmīndrabhaṭ got up. Bhaṭ got up also. [Lakṣmīndrabhaṭ] came for *darśan* of Śrīprabhu. He met Śrīprabhu. He prostrated himself. He touched the holy feet. Then Lakṣmīndrabhaṭ became a disciple, and began to stay in the Gosāvī's presence.

Lakṣmīndrabās's[4] wife heard that he had renounced the world. So she said, "He'll practice renunciation only as long as he doesn't see me. See if he doesn't come back now! Now I'll go and get him." Boasting this way to her whole family, she started off.

She adorned herself, took a man with her,[5] and mounted a horse. She arrived this way at the monastery, dismounted at the main gate, and entered.

Then she said, "Why have you done this?"

Lakṣmīndrabhaṭ said, "I did it for the good of my soul."

His wife said, "I've brought along that man over there, the one with the red two-piece shawl and the strong arms. Should I go live with him?"

Lakṣmīndrabhaṭ said, "That will be fine. Bring him here, and I'll put the red paste on your forehead."[6]

When he said this, she cried out, "I've been robbed! I've been robbed!" She threw herself down in the main courtyard. Letting out a sob, she put her head on her legs and began to cry.

Then Mhāïṃbhaṭ comforted her. She was given a bath and a meal. Then Mhāïṃbhaṭ gave her a blouse and a silk garment.

She went to Sīṅgṇāpur.

214. One day, when he is asked to, he makes it rain.

One year the rains went away. There was a bad drought. The devotees would go to beg. At first people gave alms, then they stopped giving alms. Gradually they became very stingy.

Finally the people were in turmoil. So the village headmen said to the devotees, "It's not raining at all. There is a famine. Ask your Rāüḷ to do something about it."

Then one day, when the Gosāvī was sitting on his cot, Ābāïseṃ said to the Gosāvī, "Please, Lord, we need rain. The mendicants are getting no alms. There's a famine. The mendicants are suffering greatly, Lord."

So he agreed to her request. He got up from his cot. He went outside. It was as hot as it is in the months of Caitra and Vaiśākh.[1]

And then he looked at the sky. There was a spot of cloud the size of a finger. And the Gosāvī said, "Oh, drop dead! Come here! Come here, I tell you!"

The cloud spread out. It took form. And the rain fell. It saved the whole earth. There was a time of plenty.

Then the headmen said, "The Rāüḷ is our Mother. The Rāüḷ is our Father. The Rāüḷ is powerful. The Rāüḷ has protected our children and babies."

215. He sorts the measures.

The Gosāvī used to go into the marketplace. He would compare the measures. One which was too small he would break on Gaṇeśa's[1] head. One which was correct he would leave intact.

The bards would sing his praises: "Yes, Lord. Break the false measures, Rāüḷ! Keep the true ones. The Rāüḷ is our Mother. The Rāüḷ is our Father. The Rāüḷ is the helper of the poor. Punish the sinners, Lord. The Rāüḷ is powerful. You tolerate no falsehood, Rāüḷ."

216. He scatters jujubes.[1]

Māḷī women from Hīraurī used to come to Ṛddhipur to sell jujubes. They came one day with their jujubes. The Gosāvī went there and put his holy hand into [one woman's] jujubes. But the woman grabbed it and held it up.

And the Gosāvī acted angry[2] and said, "Oh, drop dead! Go away!" He overturned her basket and smashed [the jujubes] with his holy foot.

Then the Gosāvī pulled out a stick supporting her awning, and ran at her.

She came to the village headmen to make a complaint. The headmen said, "The Rāüḷ is powerful. The village is the Rāüḷ's. Complaints against others can be made to the Rāüḷ, but to whom can a complaint against the Rāüḷ be made? See, if you had let him take some, you would have doubled your profits. Even now, collect them and sell them. Go on!"

So she went, and she collected them. She picked out some good ones, and put them aside for the Rāüḷ. Then she sold the others. Her profits doubled.

At that time, the Gosāvī went there. She invited the Gosāvī over and offered him the jujubes.

Then the Gosāvī said, "Now this is the way I like it, I tell you." Then he ate the jujubes and left.

217. He criticizes a Ṭhākūr's[1] wife's pearls.

One day a certain Ṭhākūr's wife came for *darśan* of the Gosāvī. She came all dressed up. There was a pearl nose ring in her nose.

So the Gosāvī said, "Oh, drop dead! It's a green onion! A green onion, I tell you!"

Then she was embarrassed, so she took off the nose ring and held it in her hand. Then she prostrated herself, touched his holy feet, and left.

218. He asks for a sweet cucumber.

One day the Gosāvī said, "Oh, drop dead! Give me a sweet cucumber, I tell you! Oh, give me a sweet cucumber! Give me one! Give me one, I tell you!" He insisted on it.

Then the Māḷī in Hīraurī had a dream, and he came with some sweet cucumbers. He offered them to the Gosāvī.

Then the Gosāvī said, "Now this is the way I like it, I tell you." He ate them.

219. He asks for ears of wheat.

One day the Gosāvī said, "Oh, drop dead! Give me ears of wheat! Give me them, I tell you!"

Mhāïṃbhaṭ said, "It's the season of Caitra and Vaiśākh.[1] How can we get ears of wheat now, out of season?"

Bhaṭ said, "If there weren't any, the Gosāvī wouldn't ask for them."

So they went to a low place where wheat had been sown, and they brought some from there. They parched them. Then they offered them to the Gosāvī.

Then the Gosāvī said, "Now this is the way I like it, I tell you." And he ate the ears of wheat.

220. Similarly, he asks for mangoes.

One day the Gosāvī said, "Oh, give me some mangoes, I tell you! Oh, give me mangoes! Give me them! Give me them, I tell you!"

Mhāïṃbhaṭ said, "How can we get mangoes out of season?"

Bhaṭ said, "How can there not be any, if the Gosāvī is asking for them? There are some, and so the Gosāvī is asking for them."

It was the month of Bhādrapad.[1] The mango crop of the month of Śrāvaṇ[2] had come. [The mangoes of one tree] had been wrapped in cloth and kept carefully for the king. Thorny branches had been placed at the foot of the tree. Guards were keeping watch in turns.

Bhaṭ, Mhāïṃbhaṭ, Kothaḷobā, and Vāḷukobā[3] went to Aḷajpur. Mhāïṃbhaṭ offered a silver coin[4] per mango, but that was refused. So Bhaṭ checked out the approaches and escape routes. [When the others said,] "What should we do now?" Bhaṭ said, "Tonight when they're asleep, we'll steal some."

They went begging right away. They ate their meal by the river. Then at about midnight they came [to the mango tree]. Bhaṭ knew well the right time for stealing.[5]

Then Bhaṭ carefully lifted away the thorny branches, and Kothaḷobā put his feet on Vāḷukodev's shoulders and climbed into the mango tree. He picked a hundred mangoes. (According to some, he picked a sackful.) They tied the sack shut; then they left.

As they were returning by the back roads, Vāḷukobā jammed his foot on a stump. Finally they got back. They offered the mangoes to the Gosāvī. Then the Gosāvī said, "Now this is the way I like it, I tell you," and he ate them.

Then they said, "Oh, Lord, Vāḷukodev jammed his foot."

The Gosāvī replied, "Oh, tie it! Tie it! Tie my pan to it!" So they tied to it the pan from his holy mouth. The pain went away. He got better.

(According to some, they had [the mangoes] pressed soft. Then Ābāïseṃ made crêpes. She squeezed out the mango pulp. Then she prepared the Gosāvī's plate, and the Gosāvī said, "Now this is the way I like it, I tell you." Then he ate them.)

221. He asks for *āḷakavasā.*[1]

One day the Gosāvī's plate was prepared. He sat in his place. The Gosāvī said, "Oh, give me some *āḷakavasā,*[2] I tell you! Give me some, I tell you!" and he drew back his holy hand and sat silent.

Then Ābāïseṃ said, "Mhāïṃbhaṭ, what does '*āḷakavasā*' mean?"

Mhāïṃbhaṭ said, "It means *taravaṭā*."[2]

At that time, rain had fallen out of season. Some *taravaṭā*-herb had come up behind the monastery. (According to some, on top of the monastery.) They looked with lamps and torches, and found it growing [there]. So they brought it. Then [Ābāïseṃ] boiled it, squeezed it, and cooked it with fried asafoetida. Then she put it onto his plate.

Then the Gosāvī said, "Now this is the way I like it, I tell you." Then he ate his meal. He rinsed his mouth and chewed pan.

222. Similarly, he asks for eggplant.

One day the Gosāvī's plate was prepared. Then he sat in his place. And the Gosāvī said, "Oh, give me eggplant! Oh, give me eggplant, I tell you."

Bhaṭ said, "How can we get eggplant at this time of year? [But] if there weren't any, the Gosāvī wouldn't ask for it."

Mhāïṃbhaṭ said, "When I was out begging, I saw an eggplant on Govindbhaṭ Toḍole's[1] fence."

So they went there. They brought back the eggplant. They cooked it with asafoetida, black pepper, and powdered spices. Then they put it on his plate.

Then the Gosāvī said, "Now this is the way I like it, I tell you." Then he ate his meal, rinsed his mouth, and chewed pan.

223. He accepts Govindbhaṭ's[1] worship.

Every day Govindbhaṭ would make two garlands, and he would offer them to the Gosāvī. This was his regular observance.

224. He accepts marriage.

One day when the devotees had gone out to beg, they saw a Telī woman carrying nuptial crowns for a bridal couple. Māhādāïseṃ said to her, "Oh, Telī woman! Please give our Gosāvī a bridegroom's crown."

So she made another very nice one. She brought it and tied it on the Gosāvī's holy head. Then the Gosāvī shook his holy head, and shook the two pendants [on the crown]. "Oh, drop dead!" [he said]. "Tie a wedding bracelet on me, I tell you. Tie up the piece of betel nut for the bride to find, I tell you. Anoint me with turmeric, I tell you.[1] Sound the horn, I tell you. Let the gutters overflow with ghee, I tell you. Build a platform for the ceremony, I tell you. Erect a canopy, I tell you."

The horns began to sound. They made dough balls and crêpes.

They put rice on to boil. They put twists of wheat dough on to boil. They brought sets of gourds full of ghee.

Then Īśvar Nāyak said, "If the Gosāvī wants to get married, I'll give him my daughter."

The devotees asked the Gosāvī, "Oh, Lord, Īśvar Nāyak will give you his daughter, so you should accept her, Lord."

And the Gosāvī acted angry, and said, "Oh, drop dead, I tell you!" [Then] he kept silent.

Then they cracked open the gourds full of ghee. They gave a feast for all the people.

Then Māhādāïseṃ sang wedding songs. The Gosāvī said, "Oh, drop dead! Sing! Sing, I tell you!"

Māhādāïseṃ said, "What should I sing, Lord?"

The Gosāvī said, "Oh, sing about Kṛṣṇa and Rukmiṇī,[2] I tell you. Sing about how grandly the horns were played, I tell you."

And Māhādāïseṃ was inspired. She immediately began to sing about Rukmiṇī's engagement ceremony.[3] She sang the verse, "Surely he touched her in her soul."[4]

And the Gosāvī said, "Oh, yes! Yes! Surely he touched her in her soul."

Then Ābāïseṃ said, "Oh, Lord, please get up. Eat your evening meal."

The Gosāvī said, "Oh, I've eaten, I tell you."

Ābāïseṃ said, "Where did you eat, Lord?"

The Gosāvī said, "Oh, I've eaten, I tell you. I [ate] in Rukmiṇī's palace."[5]

"That was in the Dvāpara Age, Lord, and this is the Kali Age!"[6]

And the Gosāvī laughed. Then Ābāïseṃ prepared his plate. The Gosāvī sat in his place. Then he turned over the crêpes, the *puri*-bread, the stuffed wheat cakes, the pulse cakes with holes, and those without, examining all of them. Then the Gosāvī said, "Oh, drop dead! There's no *bhākrī*-bread,[7] I tell you!"

Ābāïseṃ said, "Oh, Lord, how can there be *bhākrī* at a wedding?"

Then for four days the Gosāvī listened to the story of Rukmiṇī's engagement ceremony. On the fourth day, they did the final rites of the wedding.[8] Then he lost interest.

In this way, the whole village was fed in celebration of his wedding. [The village of] Belaureṃ was fed. The gutters really did overflow with ghee.

Later, when the wedding party and the devotees had eaten, they suddenly went out in a band.[9]

225. Suddenly he sets out with a band of his followers.[1]

One day the Gosāvī said, "Oh, swing me! Swing me!" and he arranged a band of his followers.

So they brought his palanquin. He mounted the palanquin. All the devotees set out. They made swords out of sticks. Half of them were in front of the palanquin; half were behind.

And so he set out.

226. He stays in Belaureṃ.

Then the Gosāvī went to Belaureṃ. He stayed in the inner courtyard of the fortress. Then he went to the stable. He had a meal of the horses' fodder. Then at night he had his evening meal.

Then, early the next morning, the Gosāvī left.

227. He stays at Ānadurā.[1]

Then the Gosāvī went to Ānadurā. Kāïṃdaraṇā, the Demon-in-Battle, approached the Gosāvī. Then he prostrated himself. He touched the holy feet.

Then [the Gosāvī] stayed in his household shrine. (According to some, he stayed for three nights.) Then he had a massage and a bath. His worship was done. Clothes were offered to him. Then he ate his meal.

Then the Gosāvī said to [Kāïṃdaraṇā], "Oh, drop dead! You are going to lose your eyes, I tell you."

He said, "Oh, Lord, with these eyes I've seen the Gosāvī. Now I don't care whether I lose them or not."

* * *

At about the same time, the king started to give a gift to a bard. The man stretched out his left hand to take it. The king asked, "Hey, you, why don't you give me your right hand?"

The bard said, "My right hand is already too full, with the gift of Kāïṃdaraṇā, the Demon-in-Battle."

And the king was not at all pleased. He was upset with [Kāïṃdaraṇā], so he summoned him. He came. Then the king said, "Hey, you! How dare you be more generous than me? Put out his eyes!"

So they put out his eyes. If he had asked the Gosāvī when he had the chance, they would have been spared.

228. He has his palanquin set down at Sīrāḷā.[1]

Then the Gosāvī went to Sīrāḷā. He had his palanquin set down at the southern embankment of the tank. And immediately he went trotting over to Nāgnāth's[2] temple. He went up to the *liṅga*.[3] He touched the *liṅga* with his holy hand. Then he said, "Oh, drop dead! You're here, I say."

Then he left right away.

229. He stays in the Gopāḷa[1] temple at Pusadā.

Then the Gosāvī went to Gopāḷa's temple at Pusadā. He was sitting in the temple hall when the temple priest's child came with food offerings for Gopāḷa. The Gosāvī said, "Hey, there! Bring them here! Bring them here! Bring them here, I tell you."

He placed them before the Gosāvī. The Gosāvī ate them. [The child] went home.

At home they asked him, "Hey, what happened to the food offerings?"

"God ate them."

"Come on! How could God eat them?"

"God is sitting in the temple hall. God has on bracelets and anklets. He has a pearl forehead mark. He has a beard down to his navel. He has a palanquin with fringe. He is being fanned with a chowry. His devotees are there."

They said, "Does this mean the Rāüḷ has come here?" Immediately they came to see. They saw the Gosāvī. They prostrated themselves. They touched his holy feet. Then they invited the Gosāvī home, and he accepted their invitation. Then they took him to their house.[2]

230. He is worshipped and eats a meal at the temple priest's house.

That night the Gosāvī had a massage and a bath at the temple priest's house. His worship was done, and he ate his meal. He went to sleep on a bed with a mattress.

Then early in the morning he woke up. Then the Gosāvī went to Gopāḷa's temple. All the devotees were with him. The temple priest took the palanquin on his shoulder.

Then [the Gosāvī] sat in the temple hall. Someone brought plantains and sugarcane for the deity. He placed them inside, near Gopāḷa. He prostrated himself and left.

The temple priest brought [the offerings] and placed them near the Gosāvī. Then the Gosāvī said, "Now this is the way I like it, I tell you," and he ate a piece of sugarcane. He made two of the plantains *prasād*. Then the Gosāvī said, "Oh, drop dead! Take it! Take it! Take it, I tell you!" and he gave *prasād* to the temple priest.

Then the Gosāvī left. (According to some, he stayed for three nights.)

231. He has them eat gourds at his maternal uncle's village.[1]

Then the Gosāvī went to his maternal uncle's village. Bitter gourds had grown up on an empty lot there.

And all the devotees were hungry. The Gosāvī looked at the

gourds, and they became like nectar. Then the Gosāvī said, "Oh, drop dead! Eat the gourds, I tell you."

The devotees tried them. They were as sweet as nectar. So they all ate their fill of them. They tasted like bananas.

Then the Gosāvī went up to the empty lot. When he looked at the lot, he was moved. And the Gosāvī said, "This was my mother's brother's house. This was my mother's sister's house. I grew up here. My thread ceremony was performed, and then they took me to Ṛddhipur."

232. He stays in Nāndigā̃v.

Then the Gosāvī went to Nāndigā̃v. A Ṭhākūr approached him, prostrated himself, and touched the holy feet. Then he invited the Gosāvī home, and the Gosāvī accepted his invitation and went inside. Then he stayed for three days in the household shrine.

The Gosāvī was offered a cloth to wear while bathing. Then he had a massage and a bath. His worship was done. Clothes were offered to him. Then he ate his meal. He went to sleep.

He was offered clothes and ate his meals this way for three days, in the houses of three brothers. He stayed just three days. Then he left.

233. He stays in Āñjangā̃v.

Then the Gosāvī went to Āñjangā̃v. All the village headmen approached him. They met him in front of the entrance to the village. They prostrated themselves. They touched his holy feet. Then they invited the Gosāvī in. They took him into the fortress. He stayed in the shrine for three nights.

The Gosāvī was offered a cloth to wear while bathing. Then he had a massage and a bath. Then his worship was done, and he was offered clothes. Then he ate. He had a meal of bananas, crêpes, and sugar. Then he was offered water to rinse his mouth and pan to chew.

234. He meets a Ṭhākūr who gives him a citron as an offering.

Early the next morning, the Gosāvī left. To the west of the village was an orchard. The Gosāvī went there. A certain Ṭhākūr approached from the opposite direction. He was coming along with a citron in his hand.

He had *darśan* of the Gosāvī. He put the citron into the holy hands, then prostrated himself. The Gosāvī said, "Now this is the way I like it, I tell you," and he ate it.

235. He agrees to the bards' request.

The devotees were taking the Gosāvī to the Gaṅgā[1] Valley when they met some bards on a plain to the west of a village. [The bards] prostrated themselves; then they said, "No, Lord, our Varhāḍ[2] deity must not go to the Sīvana[3] country. If these people from Sīvana take you away, Lord, Varhāḍ will be orphaned. The Rāüḷ is our Mother. The Rāüḷ is our Father. Without the Rāüḷ, everything is desolate. We're subject to calamities and afflictions, Lord. Please turn back, Gosāvī."

So the Gosāvī agreed to their request. Then the Gosāvī said, "Oh, turn it around! Turn it around!" and made the palanquin turn back.

236. The village headmen of Umbarāvatī receive him.[1]

Then the Gosāvī went to Umbarāvatī.[2] The village headmen of Umbarāvatī approached him across a stream to the south of the village. The Gosāvī saw them coming, and pulled down a curtain over his palanquin. He refused them *darśan*. He would not accept their invitation. He left.

Then, as the Gosāvī was crossing the river, he reached down from the palanquin, took water with the fingernail of his holy hand, and put it into his holy mouth. (According to some, he touched the water with the big toe of his holy foot.)

Then he left.

237. He stays in Rāhāṭgā̃v.[1]
He goes to Bhānukheḍ.

Then the Gosāvī went directly to Bhānukheḍ. His palanquin went toward the Koḍeśvara[2] temple. At that time, day laborers were bringing faggots from there. They said, "Why are you coming this way to die?" (Or, "to the burning ground?")[3] "There's a tiger sitting up ahead."

At that, the Gosāvī said, "Now it will eat us here, right here, I tell you! . . . It won't eat us, I tell you. . . . Oh, it will surely eat us, I tell you," and he acted frightened. All the devotees began to be afraid.

So he went to the Vaḍajaṃbā[4] temple. He had the palanquin set down at the foot of a banyan tree.

238. He plays with Vaḍajaṃbā.[1]

Then the Gosāvī went to Vaḍajaṃbā's temple. He touched Vaḍajaṃbā with his holy hand. Then the Gosāvī said, "Oh, you're here, I say!"

He played this way for a while; then he left.

239. He has the devotees eat sesame seeds and molasses.

All the devotees were hungry. So the Gosāvī went to a sugarcane mill. Someone had brought a basketful of sesame seeds, [and the Gosāvī] brought a potful of molasses. Then they mixed together the sesame seeds and the molasses, and the Gosāvī distributed it as *prasād.* Each of the devotees took two bites.

And then the Gosāvī said, "Swing me! Swing me!" So the devotees wiped their hands and faces.

They set off right away.

240. He has the palanquin set down at Māḷdharā.
He has the palanquin set down at Tīvasā.
He has the palanquin set down at Sendurjan.[1]
He crosses a stream bed and stays in Bhīsnaur.

Then he left the palanquin behind on a large rock. All the devotees were tired out; they stayed behind. Only Bhaṭ and Māhādāïseṃ set off with the Gosāvī.

Night fell. The Gosāvī crossed a stream bed that was right in their path. Bhaṭ and Māhādāïseṃ crossed it behind the Gosāvī.

He went up to some people's compound. It was the eleventh day of the fortnight.[2] Everyone had gone off to a vigil service, locking the gate behind them.

Bhaṭ opened the gate with his head. Māhādāïseṃ ripped her garment and made a torch of it. She lit a lamp wick. A large potful of water was heating. She washed the Gosāvī's holy feet with it. Then she washed Bhaṭ's feet, and then she washed her own.

Then Bhaṭ went to call the people. He said to them, "Hey! Why are you keeping vigil? The Rāüḷ has come to your house."[2]

So they all came. They prostrated themselves to the Gosāvī. They touched his holy feet. Then the Gosāvī had a massage and a bath. His worship was done. Clothes were offered to him. Then he had a meal.

They set up a bedstead and put a mattress on it. He wouldn't sleep on it. They set out all the beds. He wouldn't sleep on them. Then the Gosāvī said, "Oh, set out this one for me! Set it out!" and he went up to the bed where the children were sleeping. So they made the children get up. Then he went to sleep on that bed. And he said, "This is the way I like it, I tell you."

Bhaṭ said, "How could it not be so, now, Lord, since you made the children get up?"[3]

"Oh, drop dead!" he said, and laughed.

Then Bhaṭ and Māhādāïseṃ took their baths. Māhādāïseṃ said, "Eat your meal, Nāgdev."

Bhaṭ said [to the housewife], "If you'll break your eleventh-day fast, I'll eat."[2]

The housewife said, "All right."

So they both ate.

241. He says, "Oh, you've come!"

Early the next morning, Ābāïseṃ came. Then the Gosāvī said, "Oh, you've come!"

"Yes, Lord, I've come." Then she prostrated herself. She touched his holy feet.

Mhāïṃbhaṭ and Lakṣmīndrabhaṭ were tired. Someone's horse was grazing there. They got hold of it and put a belt on it as a rein. They both mounted it, and came to Bhīsnaur. They let the horse go.

An unseasonable rain had fallen. Their arms and legs were splattered with mud. They had turned white. When he saw them, the Gosāvī said, "Oh, drop dead! You're pigs! Pigs, I tell you!"

"Yes, Lord," they said. "Without the Gosāvī we look like miserable pigs."

That day he ate at the second brother's, on the third day at the third brother's. Thus he ate at three of the brothers'. He did not take food from the fourth.[1]

Then he left.

242. He stays in a hovel in Gavhāṇ.

Then the Gosāvī went to Gavhāṇ. A certain old woman there had a hovel, a very small house. The Gosāvī went there. He sat down on her bed. All the devotees sat around the bed. The old woman sat out under the overhanging eave.

It was raining. The old woman would try to come inside, and [the Gosāvī] would say, "Oh, drop dead! Go back! Back, I tell you."

And the devotees would say, "Do *you* ever have good fortune! Īśvara has come to your house."

The old woman would say, "Even with Īśvara there's mine and thine. His own are sitting around the bed, but I'm not even allowed inside."

The devotees brought pods of *tūr*-pulse.[1] (According to some, they brought pods of *vāl*-pulse.[2]) They boiled large potfuls of them. The devotees shelled the pulse pods and offered them to the Gosāvī. Then all the devotees ate pulse.

It rained continuously this way for three days. The Gosāvī stayed there three nights; then he left.

243. He stays at Ākhatvāḍā. He receives worship and a meal at a Ṭhākūr's[1] house.

Then the Gosāvī went to Ākhatvāḍā. He had the palanquin set down at the Kaḷaṅkeśvara[2] temple. Then he sat in the temple hall.

A certain Ṭhākūr came from the village. He prostrated himself to the Gosāvī. He touched his holy feet. Then he invited the Gosāvī home: "Oh, Lord, please come to my house."

The Gosāvī accepted the invitation, and went there. The man took one of the poles of the palanquin on his shoulder, and carried him to the house. Then he made a seat for him on the bed. Then he washed his holy feet, and gave him a cloth to wear while bathing.

Then [the Gosāvī] had a massage and a bath. Clothes were offered to him. He wrapped them around himself.

Then the Gosāvī sat in his seat. Then a mark was made on his forehead and grains of rice were applied to it. Then his worship was done, he ate his meal, and he rinsed his mouth and chewed pan. Then he went to sleep.

Then, early the next morning, he left.

244. He stays in Sīrakheḍ.

Then the Gosāvī went to Sīrakheḍ. All the village headmen came to receive him. They came playing horns and drums, singing, playing instruments, dancing, impressing their feet on the ground, and clapping clapsticks. They prostrated themselves to the Gosāvī. They touched his holy feet. Then they invited the Gosāvī in.

The Gosāvī accepted their invitation, and they took him into the village. He stayed in Kamaḷ Nāyak's house.

The Gosāvī was offered a cloth to wear while bathing. Then he had a massage and a bath. He was worshipped, and he ate his meal. Then he went to sleep.

He stayed there this way for three nights.

245. He brings a dead woman to life.[1]

Kamaḷ Nāyak's wife had a fever. For seven days she didn't eat; then she died. And everyone began to cry. They prepared a bier outdoors. They took fuel to the burning ground.

During all this, the Gosāvī had sat silent. He laughed. He clapped his hands. Then he went up to her. With his holy hand, he drew back the end of her garment from over her face. Then he said, "Oh, drop dead! Get up! Get up! Get up, I tell you!" and he slapped her on the face with his holy hand.

She jumped up, startled. She prostrated herself. She touched his holy feet. Then the Gosāvī said, "Oh, drop dead! Give me some buttermilk gruel to eat, I tell you."

So she stood up. She washed a plate. Then she served him buttermilk gruel. The Gosāvī ate it. Then he rinsed his mouth and chewed pan.

And all the people were amazed and astonished.

246. How he accepted clothes offerings.

Then she made the best preparations of fine foods: pulse cakes with holes, crêpes, nectar balls, rice milk, stuffed wheat cakes, *puri*-bread, pulse cakes without holes, molasses balls, sugared crêpes, and rice milk. She got him a fine garment. She gave the devotees uncooked food,[1] and they cooked it.

Then she gave the Gosāvī a cloth to wear while bathing. He had a massage and a bath. Then she worshipped him. She offered him the garment.

She asked the devotees, "Which one of you was Meidev of Dīghī?"[2]

The devotees replied, "Don't you recognize him?"

"No, I don't recognize him."

"He's the one sitting over there," they said. "His in-laws are there."

So they hugged him.

Then she prepared the Gosāvī's plate. She served Kothaḷobā in the same row as the Gosāvī. All the other devotees sat in a row in sight of the Gosāvī. Then the Gosāvī ate his meal, and the Gosāvī rinsed his mouth.

Then the Gosāvī said, "Oh, drop dead! Take it! Take it! Take it, I tell you! Oh, eat this! Eat it! It's sweet, I tell you," and he pushed his plate toward Kothaḷobā.

[Kothaḷobā] said, "Yes, Lord. It's special *prasād*," and he took it. He began to eat it, and at the same time, he smirked at the devotees.

The devotees said, "Take your lump of food now—up to your neck!"

Then [Kamaḷ Nāyak] washed the plate and drank [the water with which he had washed it]. His wife collected the grains of rice from beneath it, and ate them.

247. At the request of Īśvar Nāyak, he departs for Ṛddhipur.[1]

Then Īśvar Nāyak went to Sīrakheḍ, when he heard that the Gosāvī had gone there. He met the Gosāvī, and prostrated himself. He touched his holy feet. Then he made a request of the Gosāvī: "Oh, Lord, Gosāvī, please return to Ṛddhipur. It's been a long time, Lord."

So the Gosāvī accepted his request. Then the Gosāvī mounted a horse. (According to some, he sat in his palanquin.) In this way, he traveled to Ṛddhipur.

At Taḷegā̃v he had the palanquin set down on the southern embankment of the tank. Then he went and played with Māṅgjāī.[2]

Then he returned to the monastery.

248. He gives Īśvar Nāyak three names.[1]

One day the Gosāvī said, "Oh, drop dead! You're a big water bag! A big water bag, I tell you!" The Gosāvī said this to him because he drank a lot of water.

"Oh, you're a head! A head, I tell you! Oh, you're a big head, I tell you." This was because his head was big.

The Gosāvī gave him *prasād* names[2] like this.

249. He calls him a gold thief.[1]

One day the Gosāvī said, "Oh, drop dead! You're a gold thief! A gold thief, I tell you!"

Mhāïṃbhaṭ used to seat him in the gold bazaar. As he traded in gold, he would keep a little for himself and give a little to Mhāïṃbhaṭ.

Then Mhāïṃbhaṭ would sit down to trade in gold. He would sit with a ring on his finger, a cap on his head, and a long loose robe on his body. He would beg alms. He would beg right away, in a hurry.[2]

250. He gives Mhāïṃbhaṭ a name.

Then Mhāïṃbhaṭ would come home. He would take off his ring, his robe, and his cap. Then he would put on an untucked dhoti and drape a patchwork of rags over his shoulders. Then he would go out to beg. He would beg right away, in a hurry. This is how he would serve the Gosāvī.

People would say, "This man deals in gold. Why should he eat beggars' food? He must take it and feed it to the Rāüḷ's cows. That's why he's begging. Why would a gold dealer eat such food?" For alms they would give Mhāïṃbhaṭ spoiled food, stale food, food that had gone sour, food that had dried up, pot scrapings, and husks.

Then he would return to the monastery. He would present his begging bag to the Gosāvī to purify with his glance. The Gosāvī would make it *prasād* [by taking] as much as would fit in three of his fingers.

Then [Mhāïṃbhaṭ] would go to the small well. He would sit at the edge of the well. He would mix the food together and eat it. He would drink that muddy water.

At that point, the Gosāvī would go there and say, "Now this is the way I like it, I tell you. There's the fodder,[1] I tell you; there's the horse, I tell you. The fodder makes the horse, I tell you."

This would happen every day.

251. He says, "That's enough" when Īśvar Nāyak is fanning him with a chowry.[1]

Īśvar Nāyak used to fan him with a chowry; this was his regular task. One day he was waving the chowry over the Gosāvī, and at the same time wishing, "It would be nice if the Gosāvī would dismiss me."

Then the Gosāvī said, "Oh, drop dead! That's enough! That's enough! Go away! Go away, I tell you!"

So he stopped. He left.

252. On the Māhāṇḍuḷ road, he says that a *lā̃k* cart is broken down.

Then the Gosāvī went to Māhāṇḍuḷ.[1] To the east of the village, on the edge of the village land, a *lā̃k*-grain cart had broken down. The Gosāvī went there and said, "Oh, the *lā̃k* cart has broken down, I tell you," and he touched it with his holy hand.

The people said, "Yes, Lord, it is broken. So what should we do, Lord?"

The Gosāvī replied, "Oh, drop dead! Put on a new axle, I tell you!"

(According to some, he did this at Māhāṇḍuḷeṃ[1] in the Gaṅgā Valley. Mhāïṃbhaṭ wrote down the date and the day of the week [that those who thought this said]. Then he searched in the Gaṅgā[2] Valley. There was a village Māhāṇḍuḷeṃ. So he asked the people there, "On such-and-such a date, on such-and-such a day of the week, was someone's cart broken down here?"

The people said, "Yes, there was one broken down."

And he was amazed.)[3]

253. He says that the man who was Vāsudevbhaṭ has become grass.

There was a small well in the temple courtyard. White grass had grown up to the east of the well. The Gosāvī went there. Māhādāïseṃ was with him.

And the Gosāvī said, "Oh, the man who was Vāsudevbhaṭ has become grass, I tell you," and he touched the grass with his holy hand. "Oh, it's true. It's true, I tell you. Vāsudevbhaṭ has become grass, I tell you."

Māhādāïseṃ asked, "But, Lord, why has Vāsudevbhaṭ become grass?"

The Gosāvī said, "Oh, drop dead! He killed a bird, I tell you. He became grass because of that sin, I tell you."

And Māhādāïseṃ got goose-bumps.[1]

254. He says, "Sāṇubāï,[1] come here. Bite him."

The Gosāvī used to go to Sāṇubāï's cell. He would hold onto both door jambs with his holy hands, and look inside. Then he would say, "Oh, you're here, I say. . . . You're not here, I say. . . . Yes, you are here, I tell you," and he would enter.

About anyone he was angry with, the Gosāvī would say, "Sāṇubāï, come here! You bite him, I tell you."

Sometimes the Gosāvī would go into her cell. He would touch her with his holy hand and say, "Oh, bite me now, I tell you," and he would laugh. Then he would leave.

255. He says, "She has come from Kolhāpur; she has gone to Mātāpur."[1]

One day the Gosāvī was sitting on his cot. And the Gosāvī said, "Oh, she has come from Kolhāpur; she has gone to Mātāpur, I tell you."

So Ābāïseṃ asked, "Who, Lord? Who has come?"

The Gosāvī said, "The goddess of Kolhāpur has come to serve me. She has gone to Mātāpur, I tell you."

256. He says, "Aren't you Bopā?"

The Gosāvī thumped one of his childhood friends. He said, "What is this, Rāüḷ? Why have you thumped me?"

And the Gosāvī looked at him and said, "Aren't you Bopā? Aren't you, I say. Aren't you Bhoiyā, I say," and laughed.

257. He plays with the cover over his two-piece spread.

There was a lotus in the center of his two-piece spread. The Gosāvī used to play with it. He would scratch at it with the nails of his holy fingers. He would do things like this, play with it this way, and laugh.

Then for fear that it would get torn, Mhāïṃbhaṭ made a leather cover. He tied cords to the four sides of it. He stretched the four of them and tied them onto the cot. So the Gosāvī would scratch it the same way with his holy hand. His nails would make a brushing sound, and he would laugh.

And the Gosāvī would say, "Oh, drop dead! Take it off! Take it off! Take it off, I tell you!"

He would play this way; then he would go to sleep.

258. He plays with his anklet.

The Gosāvī would rinse his mouth, and his worship service would be performed. Then they would place an anklet on his holy foot. The anklet would make a sound. And he would play with it and say, "Oh, drop dead! It's shouting 'Oy, Oy!' " And he would stamp his holy foot on the ground. It would make even more noise.

Then with his holy hand, he would take off the anklet and break it. He would throw it away. Then he would walk back and forth and say, "Now this is the way I like it, I tell you."

So Mhāïṃbhaṭ would make another anklet, bring it, and put it on his holy foot.

And [the Gosāvī] would say, "Oh, drop dead! Why? Why?" He would say these things, and play this way with his anklet.

259. He plays with a chain.

They would place a chain wound with flowers in his holy hands. He would hold it between his holy feet until his worship was over. And he would say, "Oh, drop dead! Why? Why are you putting this on me?" and he would throw it jingling away. And he would leave.

He was not interested in chains.

260. He plays with a reflection.[1]

He would see the sun's reflection in a water jar or a churning pot. He would try to catch it in his holy hand, but the water would get all stirred up and he could no longer see [the reflection]. And he would say, "Oh, drop dead! It's hiding, I tell you!" and he would withdraw his holy hand.

He would look again, and he would see it. Again he would put his holy hand in, and again the water would be stirred up; [the reflection] would not go into his hand. And he would say, "Oh, drop dead! It's gone! It's gone, I tell you!" and he would laugh.

He used to play this way.

261. He pretends that he is cold, with ashes and a lamp.

The Gosāvī used to sit down wherever he would see a pile of ashes. He would hold his hands over the ashes, and say, "Oh, drop dead! I'm cold, I tell you!" and he would warm himself over the ashes.

Someone would ask, "Rāüḷ, why are you doing this?" and the Gosāvī would say, "Oh, drop dead! I'm cold, I tell you!" and laugh. And then he would leave. This is the way he would play.

At night they would light a lamp in the monastery, and he would go up to it, too. He would hold his holy hands over the lamp, rub them, and say, "Ah, it's warm. Ah, it's warm. Oh, drop dead! I'm cold, I tell you."

Ābāïseṃ would say, "Oh, Lord, shall I prepare a pan of hot coals?"

And the Gosāvī would say, "Oh, drop dead!" and laugh. And he would leave. Then he would go to sleep.

262. He accepts Jagaḷ Daraṇā's service.

Then Jagaḷ Daraṇā [would send] for the Gosāvī's use a palanquin, a chowry, a new cot, a two-piece garment, bracelets, chains, a stiff brush, a water tub, a metal dish, a metal plate, a metal bowl, a metal cup, a mirror, a comb, an iron pot, two copper pots, a thick blanket, and two milch cows. 15.[1]

[The cows] gave milk. They stayed until they went dry, and then they were sent back. [Jagaḷ Daraṇā] would send two others which were giving milk. They were tethered near the small well. They were fed pot scrapings and husks.

Four silver coins' worth of flowers were needed for [the Gosāvī's] worship. After he had been worshipped with them, the Gosāvī would go out. He would feed the used flowers to the cows. Then they would be milked. During this, the Gosāvī would act angry[2] with himself.

Then Ābāïseṃ would serve him the milk, and he would have his evening meal.

The daily *prasād* would go to Jagaḷ Daraṇā. He would eat only when the *prasād* came. He had taken a vow that he would not eat a meal until he had had *prasād*.[3]

263. He says "Dhāmaṇeṃ" and "Māüreṃ."

The Gosāvī used to sit on his thinking rock[1] and say to himself, "Shall I go to Dhāmaṇeṃ, or shall I go to Māüreṃ? Oh, shall I go to Nāṇaurī, or shall I go to Sonaurī?"

He would talk to himself this way; then he would go where he wanted to go.

264. He says "Sīrāḷā" and "Pusadā."

Then the Gosāvī walked back and forth, and went trotting over and stood on his thinking rock.[1] Then he began to say to himself, "Shall I go to Rāmā, or shall I go to Sāüreṃ? Shall I go to Sīrāḷā, or shall I go to Pusadā?"

He would talk to himself this way. He would think. Then he would go where he wanted to go.

265. He calls Nāthobā[1] a leg.

One day the Gosāvī had gone to sleep on his cot. A lamp was burning brightly. And Nāthobā sat near the cot for four watches.[2]

The Gosāvī would place his holy hand on [Nāthobā's] head and say, "Oh, you're a leg, a leg [of my cot], I tell you." He would touch him with his holy hand. He would hold him to himself. He would give him pan as *prasād.* Then he would go to sleep.

266. He tells the sun to rise.

It was the cold season. Early one morning the Gosāvī was having his bath. It was cold. He pointed with his holy hand in the direction of sunrise, and said, "Oh, come up! Come up, I tell you!"

The sun rose the distance it travels in one watch.[1] Then the Gosāvī said, "Oh, drop dead! Shine hotly! Shine hotly, I tell you!" And the sun began to burn with fierce rays.

Then the Gosāvī said, "Oh, drop dead! Now it's right, I tell you." Then the cold went away.

Then he had his massage, and he had his bath.

267. He embraces Bhutānandeṃ.[1]

One day the Gosāvī was sitting on his cot, when Bhutānandeṃ came. The Gosāvī got up from his cot and embraced her.

Bhaṭ had gone off to the Vājeśvara temple for solitude. He was sitting in the northwest corner of the temple, giving a sermon, when Bhutānandeṃ went there. She prostrated herself to him several times, but he would not embrace her. Bhutānandeṃ said, "The Gosāvī embraced me. Why won't you embrace me?"

At that, everyone began to laugh: "If he doesn't embrace the Gosāvī, whom will he embrace?"

Then all the devotees came home. The Gosāvī went to the northeast of the lion-faced stone block[2] in the Uñcamaḍh, and met them there. Then Bhutānandeṃ said, "Oh, Lord, please embrace me again. All these people are laughing at me. They won't embrace me, Lord."

The Gosāvī answered, "Oh, drop dead! Come here! Come here! Come here, I tell you!" and he embraced her again.

All the devotees were amazed. Then all the devotees, with Mhāīṃbhaṭ in the lead, embraced her. Then they eased Bhutānandeṃ's weariness. They washed her feet. Then Ābāïseṃ served her a meal, and she ate it and rinsed her mouth.

268. He foresees Keśav Nāyak's fire.[1]

One day the Gosāvī went to Keśav Nāyak's stable, and began to talk to himself. The Gosāvī said, "Oh, this one will escape. This one won't escape, I tell you. Oh, this one is sure to escape, I tell you."

Then a fire broke out. The ones that the Gosāvī had said would escape did escape. All the other horses were burned.

Then Keśav Nāyak said, "It happened just the way the Rāüḷ said it would. If I had let them go right away, the animals would have survived. The Rāüḷ is our Mother. The Rāüḷ is our Father. The Rāüḷ is Īśvara. Nothing differs from the word of the Rāüḷ."

269. He makes Vīṭhal Nāyak's offering of camphor fall to the ground.

Vīṭhal Nāyak was from Taḷegā̃v. One day the Gosāvī was sitting on the curved molding of the Uñcamaḍh steps, to the right as you enter, when Vīṭhal Nāyak arrived. He had *darśan* of the Gosāvī. He prostrated himself. He touched the holy feet. He put camphor into the palm of his hand and held it up in sight [of the Gosāvī]. The Gosāvī struck the palm of his hand, and the camphor fell to the ground.

Then Vīṭhal Nāyak said, "Oh, Lord, I don't know how to serve you." So he put the whole box into [the Gosāvī's] holy hands.

Then the Gosāvī took some with three fingers and put it into his holy mouth. Then he said, "Now this is the way I like it, I tell you."

Then Vīṭhal Nāyak said, "Oh, Lord, I've seen many great men, but I've never seen a great man who would eat camphor this way." Then he prostrated himself to the Gosāvī, touched his holy feet, and left.

270. He accepts Jog Nāyak's[1] clothes offering.

One day the Gosāvī had his massage. He had his bath. The Gosāvī was shown all his clothes, but he would not accept any of them. Then Jog Nāyak remembered, "I have a garment which is kept in a tube.[2] It's priceless. It's lying in the corner with the pots and pans. Would it do?"

So he went, took the garment from its tube, and brought it back. Then he offered it to the Gosāvī. The Gosāvī said, "Now this is the way I like it, I tell you," and he accepted the garment.

Then Bhaṭ said, "Yes, Lord. How could you not [be satisfied] now?"[3]

The Gosāvī said, "Oh, drop dead!" and laughed.

271. He eats Mhāïṃbhaṭ's food at night.

One day Mhāïṃbhaṭ prepared white food for the Gosāvī. He got large amounts of curds, pulse cakes, crêpes, rice, rice milk, porridge, stuffed wheat cakes, and milk and curds to mix with the rice. He made sugar crêpes, and sugar sweet balls and sesame-seed sweet balls. He prepared this food, and stood at the main gate, making a presumptuous wish. He thought, "I'm so lucky. Īśvara is going to accept this [food] of mine."

The Gosāvī had gone out. Night fell, but the Gosāvī still had not returned. Then Bhaṭ said, "Mhāïṃbhaṭ, did you make (according to some, "feel") some wish?"

Mhāïṃbhaṭ said, "Yes, Bhaṭ. I thought to myself, 'Īśvara is going to accept this [food] of mine, so I'm lucky.' "

Bhaṭ said, "Ah, that was a bad way to feel. What is your food compared to Īśvara? Besides, what can a person[1] own? All this is Īśvara's. You're saying you'll attain the eternal absolute by means of noneternal food. Go, now, fall down before the Gosāvī."

So Bhaṭ and Mhāïṃbhaṭ left. At that time, the Gosāvī was sitting at the foot of the banyan tree at Dābh well. There Mhāïṃbhaṭ fell before him. He said he was sorry, and then pleaded, "Oh, Lord, the food is spoiling."

So the Gosāvī went to the monastery. Then he was offered a cloth to wear while bathing, and he had a massage and a bath. Then his worship service was performed, and he ate the meal.

(According to some, the Gosāvī had fallen asleep in the Cācaleśvara[2] temple. [Mhāïṃbhaṭ] pleaded with him there. Then he returned to the monastery.)

272. He ruins Mhāïṃbhaṭ's shawl.

One day [Mhāïṃbhaṭ] got the Gosāvī a blue-black two-piece shawl for sixty silver coins.[1] And he thought to himself, "I have such good fortune. This silk shawl of mine is going to be accepted by Īśvara."

At that time, the Gosāvī had his massage and his bath. Then [Mhāïṃbhaṭ] offered him the shawl and made his wish. And the Gosāvī acted angry.[2] With his holy foot, he rubbed the shawl in the mud of the gutter. He dragged it along with his holy foot. And he kept saying, "You're crumpled! You're sooty and dirty!" and he put it in the mud of the gutter. He rubbed it around in the mud with his holy foot.

Then Bhaṭ said, "Mhāïṃbhaṭ, have you rejoiced about something in your heart?"

Mhāïṃbhaṭ said, "Yes, Bhaṭ."

Bhaṭ said, "Ah, Mhāïṃbhaṭ, you've done wrong. Go on, prostrate yourself."

So he prostrated himself. He said he was sorry, and he touched the holy feet.

Then he washed the shawl, and [the Gosāvī] accepted it.

273. He pours out Mhāīṃbhaṭ's water.[1]

It was Tīpurārībhaṭ's job to draw the water [for the Gosāvī's bath]. One day Mhāīṃbhaṭ drew a tubful of water. The Gosāvī arrived, he sat down on his square stool, and he looked at the water. Then the Gosāvī said, "Oh, drop dead! This isn't right, I tell you. This is Mhāīṃbhaṭ's water, I tell you," and he poured it out.

Then he remained seated in his place while a potful of water heated. Then Tīpurārībhaṭ drew the water.

Then the Gosāvī said, "Now this is the way I like it, I tell you," and he had his bath. He put on his clothes.

The Gosāvī wanted only the person assigned to a task to do it. No one else was allowed to do it.

274. He throws away his sacred thread when it has been washed by Mhāīṃbhaṭ.[1]

One day the Gosāvī had his massage and his bath. Mhāīṃbhaṭ applied cleansing mixture to [the Gosāvī's] sacred thread.[2] He rubbed it clean, washed it well, and placed it in the holy hands.

And the Gosāvī threw it into the mud and rubbed it around. Then he said, "Oh, drop dead! Take it! Take it! Take it, I tell you!"

Then Tīpurārībhaṭ washed it clean and placed it in the Gosāvī's holy hands. Then the Gosāvī said, "Now this is the way I like it, I tell you."

Then he finished his bath and put on his clothes. Then his worship service was performed.

275. He meets Sāraṅg Paṇḍit.[1]

Sāraṅg Paṇḍit set off for Vārāṇasī.[2] He arrived at Ṛddhipur and met the devotees. Sāraṅg Paṇḍit said to the devotees, "Don't point out Śrīprabhu to me. The Gosāvī Śrīprabhu was pointed out to me at Yeḷāpur. I'll recognize him by myself."

"All right," [they agreed].

Then the Gosāvī woke up, and was walking back and forth in the temple courtyard. Sāraṅg Paṇḍit came, and had *darśan* near the lion-faced stone block[3] of the Uñcamaḍh. Then he prostrated himself and touched the holy feet. He offered the following verse:

> Be devoted, my heart, to the Supreme Lord named Guṇḍam.[4]

The Gosāvī answered, "Oh, drop dead! This isn't the one, I tell you!" and Sāraṅg Paṇḍit hung his head.

Then Sāraṅg Paṇḍit invited the Gosāvī for a meal, and the Gosāvī accepted the invitation. Then [Sāraṅg Paṇḍit] brought all the foods and gave them to Ābāïseṃ, and Ābāïseṃ prepared the meal.

Then the Gosāvī was given a cloth to wear while bathing, and he had his massage and his bath. His worship was done. Fine clothes were offered to him. Then incense and a plate of lamps were waved before him,[5] while songs were sung.

Then his plate was prepared. A seat was prepared, and the Gosāvī sat in the seat. Then he ate his meal, along with the devotees. Then he rinsed his mouth and chewed pan.

All of this was done nicely, with affection. So the Gosāvī said, "Now this is the way I like it, I tell you."

276. He says that Ṭhulubāï[1] ate sorghum.

One day the Gosāvī said, "There will be sorghum mash, I tell you. It, too, will fall, I tell you. Oh, the sorghum! She ate the sorghum, I tell you!"

277. He gives Bhaṭ's son a name.

One day the Gosāvī said, "Oh, it's Harimā's[1] Harimā, I tell you."

The Gosāvī saw Vairāgyadev[2] coming, so he said, "Oh, drop dead! Harimā's Harimā has come."

When Vairāgyadev was seven years old, his thread ceremony[3] was performed with him sitting on the Gosāvī's lap. They performed a thread ceremony as [grand as] a wedding, the Gosāvī gave such a festive ceremony for him.

Then when he was twelve years old, Bhaṭ taught him the religion.[4] He became a disciple right away. Then after three and a half years, he went for *darśan* of Parameśvara.[5]

278. He receives worship and a meal at Voḍaṇ Jhaḍap's house.

The Gosāvī used to go to everyone's house, but never would he go to Voḍaṇ Jhaḍap's house. Then one day the Gosāvī went to Voḍaṇ Jhaḍap's house. Bhaṭ and Mhāïṃbhaṭ were with him.

Voḍaṇ Jhaḍap was a Rājput.[1] He was a very fierce man. He was not at home, having gone to Kheḍ.

Then [the Gosāvī] arrived. [Voḍaṇ Jhaḍap's] wife stood in front of the door. The Gosāvī slapped her, pushing her back. Then he went inside. He held the storage pots from the stack to his fat stomach, and lifted them down. He carried them across, and broke them in the central room of the house. The whole time he was panting. He mixed everything together: sesame seeds, rice, wheat, sorghum, *uḍīd*-pulse,[2] and *cavaḷā*-beans.[3]

At this point, they saw Voḍaṇ Jhaḍap approaching, and Bhaṭ and Mhāïṃbhaṭ got frightened. As they went to meet him at the threshold, they thought, "He's a very fierce man. What will happen?" Then, very frightened, Bhaṭ said, "Hello, Voḍaṇ Jhaḍap. The Rāüḷ has come to your house."

"I'm fortunate," he said.

"Your wife stood in front of the door. He slapped her, pushing her back."

"Sinful woman!" he said. "Why did she stand in front of the door when the Gosāvī came? Of course the Rāüḷ hit her."

Bhaṭ said, "He broke all your pots."

"Good," he said. "Now the Gosāvī will give me copper pots."

Then he entered the house. The Gosāvī acted frightened. He tried to leave, but [Voḍaṇ Jhaḍap] said, "Oh, Lord, where are you going now?" and fell before him. He invited the Gosāvī [to stay]. Then he set up a bed and mattress. The Gosāvī sat on it.

Then [Voḍaṇ Jhaḍap] brought wheat flour, rice, *cavaḷā*-beans, ghee, and plantains from the market. He brought copper pots from the brazier's house. (According to some, all the pots in the house were turned to copper. If he had asked for gold ones, they would have become gold.)

Then [Voḍaṇ Jhaḍap] gave Bhaṭ and Mhāïṃbhaṭ the uncooked grain. Then he gave the Gosāvī a cloth to wear while bathing, and [the Gosāvī] had his massage and his bath. Meanwhile, Mhāïṃbhaṭ cooked. Then the Gosāvī was worshipped nicely. Clothes were offered to him. Then his plate was prepared, and he ate his meal. Then Bhaṭ and Mhāïṃbhaṭ ate in sight of the Gosāvī. [Voḍaṇ Jhaḍap] ate in the same line with them.[4] Then the Gosāvī rinsed his mouth and chewed pan.

Then the Gosāvī returned to the monastery.

279. He abuses renouncers by calling them cleaners of harrow blades.[1]

Nyāya Bhāratī[2] came from Vārāṇasī to Kheḍ. With him were five hundred renouncers. Keśav Nāyak approached him to bring him [to Ṛddhipur]. Keśav Nāyak greeted him, and said, "Please come to my village."

He said, "We won't come to your village."

Keśav Nāyak said, "Why won't you come?"

"The Rāüḷ is there. He is polluting everything. If he can be restrained, we'll come."

Keśav Nāyak said, "The Rāüḷ is powerful. The village belongs to the Rāüḷ. How can I have the Rāüḷ restrained? That's how things are."

So he said, "Then we'll think it over before we come."

So they all thought it over. All of them said, "Keśav Nāyak is a great man. We should do what he says. We'll have to go."

So Nyāya Bhāratī said [to Keśav Nāyak], "Go ahead. We'll come."

So Keśav Nāyak returned. He made all the preparations at his house. The renouncers came to the Devāḷe tank, and stayed there.

Then all the cooking was done, and Keśav Nāyak's wife was sitting on a small cot folding crêpes, when the Gosāvī came there. She got up from the small cot, and the Gosāvī sat down on it. He began to fold crêpes.

First he unfolded them, then he refolded them. First he counted them backwards, then he counted them forwards.

The renouncers came when it was time for their meal. Keśav Nāyak spread coarse woolen blankets for them to sit on. They all sat down, with Nyāya Bhāratī at their head.

Then a circular area[3] was prepared. First the Gosāvī's holy feet were washed in the circle, then Nyāya Bhāratī's were washed, then all the others' were washed.

Then a mark was made, first on the Gosāvī's forehead, and then on everyone else's, and consecrated rice was applied [to the marks].

Then the plate at the head was prepared for the Gosāvī, and they all sat below the Gosāvī. Leaf plates were set before them, and they were all served. Then Keśav Nāyak said to start eating. And the Gosāvī ate a proper meal. They all ate. Then the Gosāvī rinsed his mouth. They all rinsed their mouths.[4]

There was a single water stand with nine water jars. The [used] water flowed into a single drain. The Gosāvī was seated over it.

Then pan was offered, first to the Gosāvī, and then to everyone else. They were given a mouth freshener of cloves and nutmeg. Then the Gosāvī wiped the pan leaves on the grass, then wiped them on his knee, and then made rolls with them and put them into his holy mouth.

And the renouncers said, "[This] man has great equanimity with respect to the world. [To him], that world[5] is the same as this world." With that, they took their leave.

Then the Gosāvī returned to the monastery. They all followed him to the monastery. Then Mhāïṃbhaṭ spread thick cloths in front of the Uñcamaḍh for them to sit on. They all sat down. The Gosāvī sat apart from them, on a cushioned seat. A two-piece shawl of blue-green silk was draped over him. His holy mouth was full of pan.

Then the Gosāvī looked at Mhāïṃbhaṭ, but Mhāïṃbhaṭ did not understand. So Bhaṭ said, "Mhāïṃbhaṭ, the Gosāvī wants you to say something to them."

So Mhāïṃbhaṭ asked about the *jīvanmukta.*[6] "What is the *jīvanmukta* like?" asked Mhāïṃbhaṭ.

They had a discussion of this point. [Nyāya Bhāratī] said, "The *jīvanmukta* is of such-and-such a kind."

"He's not like that," replied Mhāïṃbhaṭ, raising objections. Finally he silenced [Nyāya Bhāratī].

And the Gosāvī laughed. As the Gosāvī did so, the betel roll spat out of his holy mouth. The devotees took it as *prasād*. Then [Mhāīṃbhaṭ] pointed toward the Gosāvī and said, "The reality of the *jīvanmukta* is like that."

[Nyāya Bhāratī] said, "Sure it is."[7]

Then the Gosāvī said, "Oh, drop dead! You're rolling stones![8] Rolling stones, I tell you!"

"Sure, Lord," he said. "We're the only ones who are rolling stones."

"Oh, drop dead! You're cleaners of harrow blades! Cleaners of harrow blades, I tell you!"

"Lord," he said, "we're the only ones who are cleaners of harrow blades. The only renouncer is the Gosāvī."

Then Mhāīṃbhaṭ put forehead marks on all of them, and applied consecrated rice [to the marks]. Then he brought out a plateful of cloves and nutmeg, and offered it to them as a mouth freshener. Then Nyāya Bhāratī prostrated himself to the Gosāvī. They all left.

280. He sprinkles at the Śimagā[1] festival.

When the Gosavi had gotten old, the Śimagā festival came. All the children, and the people playing Śimagā games, began to shout at the gate.

So the Gosāvī got up, shaking, from his cot, and went to the gate. The gate was closed, its bar stuck into the ground. He was [trying to] open it on the wrong side.

Bhaṭ said to Mhāīṃbhaṭ, "The Gosāvī wants to play." So they opened the gates.

And the players clapped their hands. "Hey! A great man! A great man!" they said, and sprinkled the Gosāvī with syringes.

Then the Gosāvī said, "Oh, drop dead!" and hid in a corner.

Then they took the Gosāvī out in his palanquin, and the Gosāvī's childhood playmates came out in their old age to play. Then all night long, they played games like the childrens'. They played with mud, dirt, ashes, and dung; then they played with camphor, musk, sandalwood paste, and red lead; and then they played two-ended drums, kettledrums, ḥorns, and clapsticks.

Then [the Gosāvī] returned to the monastery, and had his massage and his bath. Then his regular worship service was performed.

281. He meets a Dravidian.[1]

A certain Brāhman of the Dravidian country saw in the *Bhaviṣya Purāṇa*[2] (according to some, he found it in the *kalpa* literature[3]) that an incarnation of Īśvara had descended at the foot of the Vindhyas,[4] in the region of Varhāḍ,[5] in the village of Kheḍ Rīdhaureṃ, in the home of a Kāṇvā Brāhman.[6]

So that Brāhman said, "I must see whether this scripture is true or false," and he set out, along with his family. In his search, he came to the region of Varhāḍ. With him were his wife, his two children, and an ox to carry his baggage.

When they arrived, the Gosāvī was playing at the Five Pipals near the Telāḷe tank. They met to the north of the northernmost pipal tree. [The Brāhman] checked him for all the marks mentioned in the scripture, and then said, "Who are you?"

Then the Gosāvī spoke a verse:

> I am not a man, nor a god or Yakṣa,
> Nor a Brāhman, a Kṣatriya, a Vaiśya or a Śūdra.
> I am not a celibate; I am not a householder or a forest hermit,
> Neither am I a mendicant, I who am innate knowledge.[7]

So the man prostrated himself. He touched the holy feet. He made his wife and children fall at the holy feet. Then the Gosāvī said, "Drop dead! Now this is right, I tell you."

With that, the Gosāvī returned to the monastery. They came with him. (According to some, they met on the verandah, to the right as you enter.)

No one could understand his language, so Mhāïṃbhaṭ questioned him in Sanskrit,[8] and he told Mhāïṃbhaṭ everything. Then they gave him lodgings in the Trīpuruṣa[9] temple.

He sprinkled the Gosāvī's holy feet with water. Then he offered *tuḷasī* to them. He drank the foot water. Then he praised [the Gosāvī] in his own language: "Today my study of the scriptures has borne fruit, in that I have met the Gosāvī." Then he went to his lodgings.

282. He accepts the Dravidian's food.

Then early the next morning he came for *darśan* of the Gosāvī. He prostrated himself to the Gosāvī, then invited him to eat. The Gosāvī accepted the invitation.

Then [the Brāhman] returned to his lodgings. He prepared porridge in the cooking water from the rice he had brought from his own country. He cooked a vegetable dish of the leaves of bean plants. He gave the Gosāvī a meal [of this, along with] five lumps [of jaggery], a seer of sugar, thirteen plantains, and a cupful of ghee. Then he offered the Gosāvī a garment which he had brought with him from his country. In this way, he worshipped him well.

He stayed for five days. Then, when he was leaving, he approached the Gosāvī. He touched his holy feet. He circumambulated [the Gosāvī] five times. Then [the Gosāvī] placed both his holy feet on his forehead, and the man left. His name was Kṛṣṇabhaṭ.

283. He accepts a three-piece garment from a Māṅg from Kure.

Once a year, a Māṅg from Kure used to weave three cloths [for the Gosāvī]. Mhāïṃbhaṭ would give him sixty quadruple silver coins[1] for the three cloths.

Then one day [the Māṅg] said, "I won't take the twenty silver coins[2] for one of the cloths. One of my cloths must be an offering to the Gosāvī. If it can't be, I won't sell it to you." (According to some, ". . . I won't weave it.")

Once a year, he would be given forty silver coins. Once a year, he would offer a three-piece garment made of two pieces of cloth for those forty silver coins, and one piece given by him.

284. He makes a cripple walk.

One day a cripple was seated at the gate. His mother had gone into the village. The Gosāvī went up to him and gazed at him, then said, "Drop dead! Stand up! Stand up! Stand up, I tell you!"

And he stood up. He prostrated himself to the Gosāvī. He touched the holy feet. Then he walked to where his mother was.

His mother said, "Hey, what is this?"

"The Rāüḷ just made me walk," he said. "The Rāüḷ is our Mother. The Rāüḷ is our Father. The Rāüḷ is powerful. There is nothing the Rāüḷ cannot do."

So she came to the monastery. She made an offering of a silver coin[1] to the Gosāvī. She prostrated herself. Then she left.

285. He gives speech to a dumb boy.

One day the Gosāvī was sitting at the main gate. A certain Brāhman's boy was dumb. He could say, "Oo, oo," but he couldn't speak words. He was light-skinned, fair, sallow; but since he could not speak, he became unattractive. His mother said to her [husband], "What is this? Take him to the Rāüḷ, and ask the Rāüḷ to do something about him."

So one day he brought him. They had *darśan* of the Gosāvī. They prostrated themselves. When [the boy's father] was about to make his request of the Gosāvī, the Gosāvī said, "Oh, drop dead! Go away!" and thumped the child and ran at him.

And the boy cried out, "Help! Help!"

The Gosāvī gave him speech.

Then his father said, "Hey! The Rāüḷ has given you speech. The Rāüḷ is our Mother. The Rāüḷ is our Father." Then he prostrated himself to the Gosāvī, then took the boy and left.

286. He calls Lakṣmīndrabā['s[1] food] fodder.[2]

Lakṣmīndrabā was eating spoiled food, stale food, pot scrapings, and husks. The Gosāvī went over to him. "Oh, drop dead!" the Gosāvī said. "It's fodder! Fodder, I tell you! Oh, drop dead! You're a leather[3] thief! A leather thief, I tell you!"

He was a great adulterer.

So Lakṣmīndrabā said, "Yes, Lord, I have stolen a lot of leather. Such a sinner am I, Lord." And he touched the holy feet.

287. He is guided down and up.

One day when the Gosāvī was walking back and forth, he stumbled. And the Gosāvī said, "Oh, drop dead! No one tells me where to go down, I tell you. No one tells me where to go up, I tell you."

From that day on, the devotees would guide him down and up. When he was going down from the verandah near the threshold of the Rājamaḍh,[1] the devotees would say, "Go down, Lord." When he was climbing onto the verandah, they would say, "Go up, Lord." They would tell him this way.

288. He plays with his reflection.[1]

The Gosāvī used to go up to a small well. He would stand at the edge and look at his holy face in the well. He would talk to himself. He would say things to himself. He would comb his beard with his fingernails. He would laugh. He would put his holy hand into the well. Sometimes he would sit at the edge of the well, dangling his holy feet.

He would play this way, and then he would leave.

289. He stops Īśvar Nāyak's disease.

Īśvar Nāyak's wedding was performed, and he and his bride were brought home in a procession. Then the bride and groom were brought to prostrate themselves to the Gosāvī.

[Īśvar Nāyak] had a disease. He looked emaciated. He ate good food, ghee and rice, but the disease had made him as thin as a stick.

The Gosāvī was sitting on his cot when the bride and groom arrived. They prostrated themselves to the Gosāvī, and touched his holy feet. And [the Gosāvī] thumped Īśvar Nāyak on the back and said, "Oh, drop dead! Go away! Go away, I tell you!"

And his disease left him. He became big and strong.

290. He eats bread[1] of golden wheat.

One day a woman named Sītomīto had made bread of golden wheat. Then she had wrapped it in a sari and covered it with a winnowing fan.

The Gosāvī went there. He took out the bread and ate it. "Oh, no," she began to cry. "The Rāüḷ has eaten my bread. What will I do now?" She began to cry this way.

The Gosāvī left. Then Mhāïṃbhaṭ gave her back the wheat.

291. He calls scented paste vomit.

They used to mix for the Gosāvī a scented paste of camphor, musk, sandalwood, vermilion powder, saffron, and fragrant seeds. And the Gosāvī would say, "Oh, drop dead! This is vomit! Vomit, I tell you!"

Then they would anoint [the Gosāvī's] whole body and draw a mark on his forehead. They would put civet in the part of his hair. He would feel it with his holy hand and say, "Oh, drop dead! That's right, I tell you," and he would laugh.

292. He calls civet phlegm.

One day the Gosāvī had his massage and his bath. His whole body was anointed with sandalwood paste. A half-moon mark was drawn on his forehead. Then civet was put in the part of his hair.

He felt it with his holy hand, and said, "Oh, drop dead! This is phlegm! Phlegm, I tell you!" and he wiped the civet from the part of his hair onto the wall.

293. He asks for camphor.

One day the Gosāvī had a desire for camphor. The local camphor had run out. So the Gosāvī said, "Oh, drop dead! Go to Devgiri Cantonment,[1] I tell you. There's a merchant there named Keśav Nāyak. In the cellar of his house there is a certain chest. [In it] is a certain box, [with] Rising-Sun [camphor in it]. Bring that, I tell you. . . . Don't bring it, I tell you. . . . Yes, do bring it, I tell you."

So Bhaṭ and Mhāïṃbhaṭ went to Devgiri Cantonment. Then, making inquiries, they found their way to Keśav Nāyak's house. They asked him, "Do you have any Rising-Sun camphor?"

"No," he said.

Then Bhaṭ and Mhāïṃbhaṭ said, "In your cellar there's a certain chest [with] a certain box [in it]."

He remembered. "How do you know?" he said. "And for whom are you getting such an expensive kind?"

Bhaṭ and Mhāïṃbhaṭ said, "Our Rāüḷ. He told us. We're getting it for him."

Then he said, "If you'll take a berry-weight[2] of camphor as my [gift to] the Rāüḷ, and if you'll accept alms from me, I'll let you have some camphor."

Then Mhāïṃbhaṭ looked at Bhaṭ. Bhaṭ said, "Take it. It may be taken out of one's own desire, or it may be taken because of someone else's liking, or it may be taken to prevent one's own sin, or it may be taken to prevent the sin of another.[3] Besides, what may not be done for the sake of Parameśvara?"

So Bhaṭ and Mhāïṃbhaṭ said, "Give us alms."

He said, "You must eat it right here."

Bhaṭ and Mhāïṃbhaṭ agreed, and answered, "All right."

He was a member of a left-handed sect.[4] He prepared fine foods, and then prepared the plates. He poured ghee into the metal cups. He poured liquor into one cup for each of them. When he had prepared their plates this way, he called Bhaṭ and Mhāïṃbhaṭ, and they sat down. He poured them water to sip.

Then Bhaṭ and Mhāïṃbhaṭ took [the liquor] with purifying grass knotted on their fingers,[5] and then set down their metal cups. And [Keśav Nāyak] was overjoyed.

Then they ate their meal, rinsed their mouths, and were given a mouth freshener.

Then he sold them two berry-weights of camphor, and gave them his berry-weight of it. Then they brought the camphor to Ṛddhipur and offered it to the Gosāvī. And the Gosāvī said, "Now this is the way I like it, I tell you." And he accepted it.

294. He punishes the barber who cuts his nails.

One day the Gosāvī was sitting on the verandah, to the left as you enter. Mhāïṃbhaṭ had the barber come. He cut [the Gosāvī's] nails very nicely. Mhāïṃbhaṭ gave him a copper coin.[1]

And the Gosāvī slapped him and said, "Oh, go away, I tell you."

He said, "Yes, Lord, I took too much [money], and so you've punished me, Lord Gosāvī. You've done right, Lord." And he touched the holy feet.

295. He plays with his reflection in a mirror.[1]

He used to sit on the verandah, to the left as you enter. He would go over to the mirror that was there. He would squat down and look at his holy face in the mirror. He would comb his beard with his holy hand. He would smooth his hair.

Then he would talk to himself. "Oh, he's talking, I tell you," he would say. "He's saying things, I tell you. Oh, he's laughing, I tell you. Oh, he's acting, I tell you." And he would touch the mirror with his holy hand.

He would play this way; then he would leave.

296. He says, "Drink buttermilk, Māïlā. Drink buttermilk, Lukhī."

Māïlā was a relative of Keśav Nāyak.[1] Lukhī was a maidservant. Māïlā would be eating a plateful of buttermilk gruel; and Lukhī, too, would be eating. The Gosāvī would come along and sit between them. And he would slurp up the buttermilk gruel and say, "Now this is the way I like it, I tell you." He ate this way with the two of them every day.

Then when they had both died, the Gosāvī would eat in the monastery. At the end of his meal, he would have buttermilk and rice. At that point, he would pour three handfuls of buttermilk on the post at his eating place, and then he would say, "Drink buttermilk, Māïlā. Drink buttermilk, Lukhī." He would say this three times.

He did this every day.

297. He drinks water from a coconut shell cup.

There were stones beneath the gutter of the Uñcamaḍh. Among those stones, at the top of the pile of stones, was a coconut shell cup. The Gosāvī used to come in from outside and squat near the coconut shell. He would take the coconut shell in his holy hands and say, "Oh, drop dead! Come up! Up, I tell you!" And [water] would slosh up [into the cup].

And he would put the lip [of the cup] to his holy mouth and take water. Then he would say, "Now this is the way I like it, I tell you," and he would let go of it. And the coconut shell would clatter back down. Then he would go into the monastery.

This is the way he would play with the pile of stones.[1]

298. He plays with Mahākāḷa Mahālakṣmī.[1]

The Gosāvī used to go to Mahākāḷa Mahālakṣmī's temple, touch Mahākāḷa Mahālakṣmī with his holy hand, and say, "Oh, you're here. Oh, go die![2] Speak, I tell you. Oh, speak! Speak, I tell you." And he would laugh.

He would say to Mahākāḷī,[3] "Oh, he's a black one. You're Mahākāḷī, I tell you."

He would play this way; then he would leave.

299. He makes Maheśvarbhaṭ let go of his sacred thread.[1]

One day the Gosāvī had had his massage. He was having his bath. The Gosāvī had taken his sacred thread from his holy neck and put it on a square stool.

At that point, Maheśvarbhaṭ[2] came along. He took the sacred thread and started washing it. And the Gosāvī acted angry and said, "Oh, go die! Let go of it! Let go! Let go, I tell you!"

So he put down the sacred thread. Tīpurārībhaṭ washed the sacred thread and placed it on the [Gosāvī's] holy neck.

Then his bath was completed.

300. He brings a corpse to life at the burning ground.[1]

One day Paras Nāyak's[2] son died. He was taken to the Nagareśvara temple, in the northeast corner of the village. A pyre was built, and he was placed on it. Then the rice-ball to be given at the burning ground was offered. A fire was lit at the foot of the pyre. Then a stream of water was poured out, and the water pot was broken at his feet.[3]

At that point, the Gosāvī arrived there, and said, "Oh, go die! Pull him off! Pull him off, I tell you!"

"But, Lord," they said, "why do you want him pulled off now? It's too late, Lord."

The Gosāvī said, "Oh, go die! Pull him off, I tell you," and he reached his holy hand up to the topmost pieces of cow dung. He turned them over, and slapped him on the face with his holy hand, and said, "Oh, go die! Get up! Get up, I tell you."

And he came to life. He jumped up, startled. He wrapped some clothes around himself.

They were amazed. "Hey! The Rāüḷ has saved Paras Nāyak's son. The Rāüḷ is our Mother. The Rāüḷ is our Father. The Rāüḷ is powerful. There is nothing the Rāüḷ cannot do."

301. He uproots a snake gourd and replants it.[1]

One day the Gosāvī went to a certain Brāhman's house. He had planted a snake gourd over the water stand. The Gosāvī pulled it up, and [the Brāhman's wife] cried out. "Rāüḷ," she said, "why did you uproot a fruit-bearing, blooming plant?"

And the Gosāvī acted angry.[2] "Oh, go die! You're shouting, I tell you," he said, and he ran at her. She ran into the house and shut the door. The Gosāvī stood at the door and banged on it with the bottoms of his fists. Then he left. He dropped the snake gourd [somewhere].

Then on the third day, he brought back the snake gourd. Then he dug near the water jar with a stick. He planted its roots. He poured on three handfuls [of water] from that same water jar.

Then the woman said, "It's dried out, Rāüḷ. How can it take root now?"

On the third day, it revived. Flowers and fruits burst forth. Then she said, "The Rāüḷ is our Mother. The Rāüḷ is our Father. There is nothing the Rāüḷ cannot do."

302. He makes peace between a mother and her son.

A certain old woman's son became angry with his mother and left. The old woman left too, following him.

As she was catching up with him, the Gosāvī was going toward Dābh well. They met at the side of the road, at the southeast corner of the Pīvaḷ tank. The old woman prostrated herself to the Gosāvī. She touched his holy feet. Then she pleaded, "Oh, Lord, my son is leaving me in anger. He won't stay. So what should I do, Lord?" and she began to cry.

So the Gosāvī said [to him], "Oh, drop dead! Why are you angry?" Then the Gosāvī took hold of him with his holy hand and brought him over to her. Then he made peace between them, and they both went to the village.

The Gosāvī went to the monastery.

303. He plays in the Bhūjāḍeṃs' house.

The Bhūjāḍeṃs were merchants. Their house was to the west of the Paraśurāma temple. They were three brothers. The three brothers had three houses built on a single foundation.

The Gosāvī went there. He fell asleep on [one brother's] bed. He had a proper meal, with a lampstand at his plate. That one's name was Paras Nāyak.[1] He built Paraśurāma's temple.

304. He eats a snack in the blacksmith's house.

The blacksmith's house was to the north of Bhadra.[1] It faced east. The Gosāvī went there and sat down on a square stool. Then [members of the household] put together on a plate a snack of *cār* seeds, *goḍaṃbī* seeds,[2] dried date powder, bits of coconut, jaggery, and sugar. And they offered it to the Gosāvī.

Then the Gosāvī said, "Now this is the way I like it, I tell you," and he ate it. He rinsed his mouth, and he was offered pan. Then he returned to the monastery.

305. He plays in Mhāïṃbhaṭ's shop.[1]

Mhāïṃbhaṭ would put a long loose robe on his body. He would put a cap on his head. He would put ten-finger ornaments on his hands. Taking his money pouch under his arm, he would go to his shop. He would sit in his shop and change money.

The Gosāvī would come there, and Mhāīṃbhaṭ would get up. The Gosāvī would sit in [Mhāīṃbhaṭ's] place and take out the silver coins. He would hold them in his holy hand and describe them: "This one is bent. This one is filed down. This one is light. This one is all right. This one [too] is all right. This one isn't."

He would play this way for a while; then he would leave.

306. He plays in goldsmiths' shops.

He used to go to the place where all the goldsmiths sat. The goldsmiths would stand up, and the Gosāvī would sit down in their places. Then he would take out the touchstone; he would take out pieces of gold. He would touch the gold to the touchstone. He would test the gold's purity, saying, "This has been purified fifty-two times;[1] this has been purified forty-eight times."

Then he would put it on the scales and weigh it. He would say to himself, "This is the right weight. This is not enough." He would play with berry-weights,[2] *vāl*-weights,[3] barleycorn-weights,[4] *toḷā*-weights,[5] two-*toḷā*-weights, and *māṣ*-weights.[6]

He would do the same things in all the shops; then he would leave.

307. He asks for carrots and radishes.[1]

When the Māḷī women of the village and from neighboring villages were sitting in the market, the Gosāvī would come along and say, "Oh, give me a carrot! Give me one, I tell you!" And he would put in his holy hand and take out carrots.

Those who let him take some would double their profits. Those who would not let him, would not sell any.

He would take some womens' radishes. He would take a bite of one right there, and say, "Oh, drop dead! It's hot, I tell you!" And he would throw them down and say, "Oh, drop dead! Take them! Take them, I tell you!"

And they would say, "Yes, Lord, it's great *prasād,*" and they would take them and keep them. Then, when they had sold their vegetables, they would go home and eat them with their gruel.

308. He plays with unmarried girls.

The unmarried girls of the village used to go to Odyāḷe tank to worship sand.[1] Sheltered in the northern corner of the western embankment, they would worship the sand there.

The Gosāvī would go there. He would play among them. They would play clapsticks by clapping them together. Some would clap them against the wet [sand?]. He would grab some of them by the waist and then let them go. And he would say, "Now this is the way I like it, I tell you."

He would play this way; then he would leave.

309. He startles the Poḷā festival[1] bullocks.

On the new moon day of the Poḷā festival, they would decorate the village bullocks. The Gosāvī would go to the embankment of Odyāḷe tank. Hiding in the northwest corner of the northern embankment, he would stand up, saying "Hoo! Hoo!" He would startle the bullocks, and they would run off into the wild.

Then [their owners] would turn them around and bring them back. Again he would do the same thing.

The Gosāvī would do this three times; then he would leave. And they would take their bullocks home.

310. He plays with a stiff brush.

The Gosāvī used to have his massage. Then a square stool would be set outside. Sometimes a low stool would be set out. The Gosāvī would sit on it, and a cleansing mixture would be applied to his holy hair. Then his holy hair would be brushed with a stiff brush.

Then he would take the brush in his holy hands and bend it in half. He would put it on his holy head. He would put it on his holy neck. He would put it back on his holy head and brush [his hair with it] with his holy hand. And he would say, "Oh, drop dead! This is right, I tell you!" and wipe his holy hair. Then he would throw the brush into the water.

He would play this way; then he would have his bath.

311. He sleeps in the Bandeśvara[1] temple.

The Gosāvī used to go to the Bandeśvara temple. He would go to sleep oriented east to west. He would sleep curled up in the foetal position. Then he would wake up.

Then he would sit in a seat and think out loud: "Oh, drop dead! I'm going to go away now, I say. Oh, what will these people from Sīvana[2] do? Where can I send them now? To whom can I entrust them?"

The Gosāvī worried this way; then he returned to the monastery.

312. He gives silver coins to a Brāhman.[1]

One day the Gosāvī took his afternoon nap in the Bandeśvara temple. When he had awakened, a Brāhman came up to him and said, "I'm poor. I'm destitute. I have nothing to eat. I don't even get gleanings. And my daughter has reached the age for marriage. So please give me something to eat."

And the Gosāvī got up immediately and said, "Go die, I tell you." With that, he went to a hillock to the west of the Bandeśvara temple, and dug in the ground with the big toe of his holy foot. And he said, "Oh, go die! Take it! Take it, I tell you!" and gave him three handfuls of silver coins.[2] (According to some, he gave him only two silver coins.)

Then the man said, "Patron,[3] you've given me exactly as much as I deserve."

And the Gosāvī laughed, and then left. The man left.

313. He goes to the braziers' quarter.

Kamaḷseṭi left the village to travel abroad. When he returned from abroad, he brought back a great many rubies, pearls, corals, inlaid gems, and so on. He stopped to the west of the two water jars.

The Gosāvī went there. He gave his contact[1] to all the things. Then, seeing his favorable disposition, the man invited him, saying, "Oh, Lord, please come to my house. Please let your glance rest on my children."

And the Gosāvī accepted his invitation. The man took him home with him. His house was on a hillock to the west of the rose-apple tree in the orchard.[2]

He took him there. Then he set out a bed and mattress, and [the Gosāvī] sat down on it. Then he washed the holy feet, drank the foot water, and sprinkled the whole house [with it]. Then he said, "Today, Lord, this place has become the purest of the pure."

Then rice was put on to cook. *Poḷī*-breads were prepared. Carrot greens were cooked. The Gosāvī ate a meal of this, with a spiced dish of gram, and ghee. Green muskmelon was put on his plate. Then the Gosāvī said, "Now this is the way I like it, I tell you." And so he finished his meal. Then he rinsed his mouth and was offered pan.

Then the man asked him, "Lord Gosāvī, please go through the braziers' quarter. Please let your merciful glance rest on everyone."

The Gosāvī agreed to his request, and went, amusing himself and playing his games, from house to house. Then he left.

314. He stays in Caṇḍikāpur.[1]

The Gosāvī stayed for seven days in Caṇḍikāpur. He would touch Gaṇeśa[2] and Caṇḍikā[3] with his holy hand and say, "Oh! Oh, drop dead! You're here, I tell you." And he would sleep right there in the sanctuary.

315. He demands milk from Ābāïseṃ.

One day the Gosāvī was sitting on his cot, with his holy feet hanging over the side. And he got a desire for milk. So he said, "Bring me milk! Bring it to me, I tell you." He insisted, so Ābāïseṃ brought him some milk.

Then he had his meal and said, "Now this is the way I like it, I tell you," and accepted [the milk]. Then he rinsed his mouth and chewed pan.

316. He milks a cow from a distance.[1]

The Gosāvī used to go up to a stone cow. He would touch her with his holy hand. He would caress her and make her milk flow, and then he would say, "Oh, drop dead! They'll come, I tell you. And it will come down, I tell you."[2]

And he would go off a ways and squat down. Then he would make the motions of milking, and then he would stop himself, saying, "Hey, there! Enough! Enough! Hey, there must be some for the calf, I tell you. Hey, untie the calf! Untie it, I tell you." And he would laugh.

He would play this way; then he would leave.

317. The maidservant's maidservant speech.[1]

One day Sādheṃ gave Māhādāïseṃ a task, and the Gosāvī overheard. So the Gosāvī said, "Oh, drop dead! A maidservant's maidservant! A shaven-headed widow. A shard of pottery." The Gosāvī spoke angrily this way.

And so everyone should do his own work. Everyone should do his appointed task. In this incident, the Gosāvī prescribed an item of the code of conduct.[2]

318. He eats a meal in the house of an Āndha[1] in Utaravāḍī.[2]

The Gosāvī went to Aḷajpur. The houses of the Āndhas were in Utaravāḍī. He went there, to the house of one of them. The Āndha was in his house, eating, and he got up as soon as he saw the Gosāvī. He stood and said to his wife, "Get up! The Rāüḷ has come."

She got up. They touched the holy feet. They spread a coarse woolen blanket for him to sit on. The Gosāvī sat on the seat.

Then [the woman] got rice from the stack of storage pots. She put it on to cook. She prepared *poḷī*-breads.[3] She made a spicy dish of split *vāl*-pulse.[4] She got out honey. Then she gave the Gosāvī the meal.

And the Gosāvī said, "Now this is the way I like it, I tell you," and ate the meal. He rinsed his mouth. He was offered pan. Then he left.

319. He tells the story of the bugs.

One day the Gosāvī went to the Kaḷaṅkeśvara temple. All the devotees were with him. Then the Gosāvī said, "Oh, drop dead! There were two bugs here, I tell you. At night they would come out. They would bite anyone who was staying here. They bit a good many this way, and they swallowed some of them. That's what they used to do."

Then Māhādāïseṃ asked, "But, Lord, how could there be bugs like that?"

The Gosāvī answered, "Oh, drop dead! They were an incarnation of a deity,[1] I tell you."

So Māhādāïseṃ kept silent.

320. He sleeps in the Rāmnāth temple.

The Gosāvī ate his meal in a leather tent, and then went to the Rāmnāth temple. He fell asleep in the temple hall, curled up in the foetal position. Then, when he woke up, he went to the monastery.

Sometimes he would go to the Dābh well. On his way back, he would go to the Rāmnāth temple. He would sleep in the temple hall for a while, or he would sit on the crossbar [of the doorway] with his holy feet hanging down. Then he would go to the monastery.

321. The shaven-headed widow etc. speech.

One day a certain woman was sitting to the south, outside the wall of the compound, when the Gosāvī came along. He saw her, and picked up a stone in his holy hand.

And she was frightened. She got up and started to run away. The Gosāvī ran after her and abused her, saying, "Oh, go die! Clear out! Clear out! Clear out, I tell you. A shaven-headed widow! A shard of pottery! A servant girl at the door! A wretch!"[1]

But she kept running. When she had run away, the Gosāvī left.

322. He goes home.[1]

Then, in due course, the Gosāvī became old. In due course, his holy neck, his holy head, and his holy hands trembled shakily. Then he could no longer digest the food he ate, and he got diarrhea.[2]

He was sick this way for thirteen days. Then all the devotees, from

Ābāïseṃ on down, pleaded, "Oh, Lord, please take medicine. Please stop this affliction. Please change your inclination, Gosāvī."

The Gosāvī answered, "Oh, go die! Why are you saying this? Why? Oh, I will go now, I tell you." So the Gosāvī himself accepted the diarrhea.

Then the Gosāvī would squat on a low stool. He would hold onto his cot with his holy hand, and he would defecate. Then Ābāïseṃ would offer him water in a metal dish. He would make use of the water in the shelter of a curtain.

Then one day Bhaṭ asked, "Lord, Śrī Cakradhar Rāyā[3] entrusted us to you. Now you're leaving, Gosāvī. So to whom have you entrusted us?"

The Gosāvī answered, "Oh, drop dead! I've entrusted all these others to you, and I've entrusted you to Śrī Dattātreya Prabhu."[4] (According to some, the Gosāvī said, "Oh, go die! Go to Mātāpur,[5] I tell you!")

And with that, on the fourth day of the dark half of the month of Bhādrapad, in the Vyaya year,[6] the Gosāvī left.[7]

323. His grief-stricken daughter comes.

The Gosāvī's daughter[1] was in Sāvaḷāpur. She heard in the house that the Gosāvī had gone home.[2] (According to some, she heard the news at the place where she had gone to get water, and she left her water pot there.)

She came to Ṛddhipur. Her eyes were blinded from her sorrow. She cried the whole way on account of her father; she was still crying when she arrived.

Meanwhile, his whole body had been anointed with sandalwood paste. Flowers were offered to him. Pan was crushed and put into his holy mouth. A new fine silk garment was draped over his holy body. Then he was laid on a bier, and Bhaṭ, Mhāïṃbhaṭ, Lakṣmīndrabhaṭ, and it's not known who the fourth was, carried away the bier. They stopped at the foot of a tamarind tree, near its eastern branches.

The Gosāvī's daughter arrived as they were digging the grave. She saw the bier and threw herself down with a loud thump. She fainted. Bhaṭ and Mhāïṃbhaṭ ran up to her and revived her. Then she began to sob and moan. She threw herself onto the holy body and began wailing, "My maternal home is gone."

Seeing her suffer this way, Bhaṭ and Mhāïṃbhaṭ were brokenhearted. The devotees were all very sad. Bhaṭ and Mhāïṃbhaṭ said, "She truly is the Gosāvī's daughter." And Bhaṭ said, "He fondled us and kept us happy. We know that he was Īśvara. [But] our grief is not as great as [hers]."

Finally the grave was dug. Bhaṭ cut a piece of padding an arm's length wide, and placed it in the bottom. The holy body was laid on it, and draped with the fine silk garment. (According to some, he was buried with his holy body naked.)

Then all the devotees, beginning with Bhaṭ and Mhāïṃbhaṭ, set off for the monastery. Bhaṭ and Mhāïṃbhaṭ tried to lead the Gosāvī's daughter away, but she would not budge. They offered her a sari and a blouse, but she refused them. "How can I take anything now? Is this my maternal home?" And she left.

Afterwards, Bhaṭ and Mhāïṃbhaṭ deliberated, and said, "The headmen are watching." So they took him out and buried him at the wall of the compound, south of the original grave. Now, Īśvara's body is like camphor,[3] so what could have been left behind? There must have been some reason for it.

Later the village headmen built a temple over [the original grave].

Notes to the Translation

An explanation or identification is given in these notes at the first occurrence of a name or term; for subsequent occurrences, consult the glossary or the appropriate index.

The edition on which this translation is based relies primarily on one manuscript and gives a few variants from two others. The translation chooses freely between the readings of the first manuscript and the others. Only when the differences between the readings are of particular interest are they pointed out in these notes.

Abbreviations used in these notes are as follows:

Abbott J. Abbott. *The Keys of Power: A Study of Indian Ritual and Belief.* 1932; repr. ed. Seacaucus, N.J.: University Books, 1974.

Enthoven R. E. Enthoven. *The Tribes and Castes of Bombay.* 3 vols. 1920–1922; repr. ed. Delhi: Cosmo Publications, 1975.

Hobson-Jobson Henry Yule and A. C. Burnell. *Hobson-Jobson: A Glossary of Colloquial Anglo-Indian Words and Phrases, and of Kindred Terms, Etymological, Historical, Geographical and Discursive.* 1903; repr. ed. New Delhi: Munshiram Manoharlal, 1979.

Kane Pandurang Vaman Kane. *History of Dharmaśāstra (Ancient and Medieval Religious and Civil Law in India).* 5 vols. 2nd ed. Poona: Bhandarkar Oriental Research Institute, 1968–1975.

Kolte (Notes) Mhāïṃbhaṭ. *Śrī Goviṃdaprabhu Caritra,* ed. V. B. Kolte. 5th ed. Malkapur: Aruṇa Prakāśana, 1972. "Spaṣṭīkaraṇātmaka Ṭīpā," p. 130–48.

LC Mhāïṃbhaṭ. *Līḷācaritra,* ed. V. B. Kolte. Bombay: Mahārāṣṭra Rājya Sāhitya Saṃskṛti Maṃḍaḷa, 1978.

***LC*, P.** "Pūrvārdha."

***LC*, U.** "Uttarārdha."

Molesworth J. T. Molesworth. *A Dictionary, Marāṭhī and English.* 2nd ed., 1857; repr. ed. Poona: Shubhada-Saraswat, 1975.

Monier-Williams Monier Monier-Williams. *A Sanskrit-English Dictionary.* 1899; repr. ed. Oxford: Clarendon Press, 1970.

ms., mss. manuscript, manuscripts.
MSK Y. R. Date, C. G. Karve et al. *Mahārāṣṭra Śabdakośa.* 7 vols. and supplement. Pune: Mahārāṣṭra Kośamaṃḍaḷa, 1932–1938; supplement, 1950.
p.c. personal communication.
Russell and Lal R. V. Russell and Rai Bahadur Hīra Lāl. *The Tribes and Castes of the Central Provinces of India.* 4 vols. London: Macmillan, 1916.
Sūtrapāṭha Anne Feldhaus. *The Religious System of the Mahānubhāva Sect: The Mahānubhāva Sūtrapāṭha.* New Delhi: Manohar, 1983. Parts II and III.

1. *Śrī Pareśa.* Parameśvara, the Mahānubhāvas' one God.

Chapter 1

1. Cf. *LC,* P.15.
2. *He.* Parameśvara.
3. *Womb incarnation.* One of three types of Parameśvara incarnations named in *Sūtrapāṭha* X.104–05. See introduction, section I, under "Guṇḍam Rāüḷ in Other Mahānubhāva Texts."
4. *Kāṇva Brāhman.* A follower of the Kāṇva branch (*śākhā*) of the White Yajurveda.
5. *(According to some . . . according to others).* The text was originally written as a compilation of various people's recollections of Guṇḍam Rāüḷ and was later reconstructed on the basis of several people's memories of the original version. Here and at several other places, the text gives evidence of the variety of sources of either the original version, the reconstruction, or both. See introduction, section IV, under "History of the Text."
6. *A few miles.* Literally, "at a distance of one and a half *gāvs.*" A *gāv* is the normal distance between two villages. According to Molesworth, it varies "from four kos or nine miles to five or four miles."
7. *The Gosāvī.* Guṇḍam Rāüḷ, the subject of this biography.
8. *Guṇḍo.* A *guṇḍā* is "a rolling or roundish stone" (Molesworth). S. G. Tulpule (p.c.) suggests that this is an example of an unattractive name given to protect a child from the envy of evil forces. M. Emeneau discusses such names, which he calls "apotropaic names," in "Towards an Onomastics of South Asia," *Journal of the American Oriental Society,* 98 (1978): 113–30.
9. *Mother's brother and sister. māmā* and *māüsī.*
10. *Seven years later.* The version of this account in *LC,* P.15, states that the thread ceremony was performed "within several [literally, "seven or five"] years" of the time his parents died. The age at which it is generally prescribed that Brāhman boys should have their thread ceremony is eight years (Kane, vol. II, p. 274f).
11. *Thread ceremony.* The initiation ritual for Hindu boys of the castes which are called "twice-born" because of their use of these rites. In the course of the ceremony, the boys are invested with the thread (worn draped over the left shoulder, hanging down on the right side below the waist), which is the mark of their high ritual status. For a discussion of the texts relating to this ceremony, see Kane, vol. II, p. 268f, and R. B. Pandey, *Hindu Saṃskāras,* 2nd ed. (Delhi: Motilal Banarsidass, 1969), p. 111f. For an early twentieth-century ethnographic description, see Mrs. Sinclair Stevenson, *The Rites of*

the Twice-Born (1920; repr. ed. New Delhi: Oriental Books Reprint Corporation, 1971), p. 27–45.

12. paḷasulā *ritual.* A ritual performed on the fourth day of the thread ceremony (Molesworth).
13. *"Om, give me alms, good woman!" voṃ bhavati bhīkṣāṃ dehī.* The (Sanskrit) words *bhavati bhīkṣāṃ dehī* are those with which it is prescribed that an initiated Brāhman boy should beg in his new career as a celibate student (*brahmacārin*). See Kane, vol. II, part I, p. 309. As to why the Gosāvī would not say "Om," Kolte (Notes, p. 130) has three suggestions: (1) that "Om" is used in praising the formless Parameśvara, but Mahānubhāvas worship Parameśvara not as formless but as having form; (2) that the Gosāvī was himself an incarnation of Parameśvara (and hence it made no sense for him to say "Om"); and (3) "Om" praises the deities Brahmā, Viṣṇu, and Śiva (whom the Mahānubhāvas regard as distinct from and inferior to Parameśvara).

Chapter 2

1. Cf. *LC,* P.15, where it is stated that Bopa Upādhyāya, Rāma Upādhyāya, and Tīka Upādhyāya were brothers, and that the Gosāvī studied under all three of them.
2. *Upādhyāya.* A kind of traditional teacher.
3. *Was extraordinarily talented.* Literally, "accepted extraordinary talents." As Parameśvara, the Gosāvī needed to learn nothing.
4. *Īśvara.* God, Lord. Equivalent to "Parameśvara."
5. *Incarnation of a deity.* Of a *devatā,* one of the many gods distinct from and inferior to Parameśvara, the one God in the Mahānubhāva doctrinal system.
6. *Drop dead.* The expression translated this way throughout the text, *melāl-līl-le jāe,* means literally, "Go away dead."
7. *More than others.* A possible interpretation of the syllables *ya-ta-ra-pa-speṃ* (*-syeṃ* in the second edition of Kolte's version of the text), which appear in all the mss. Kolte has seen (Kolte, p.c.). Cf. Bhau Mandavkar, " *'Yatarapasye' Mhaṇaje Kāya?*" in *Ciṃtanī* (Amaravati: Sevā Prakāśana, 1980), p. 60–64.

Chapter 3

1. *Incarnation of a deity.* See notes to 2, above.
2. *Laughed.* Literally, "accepted laughter." As Parameśvara, the Gosāvī is not affected by emotions.

Chapter 4

1. Cf. 32, below.

Chapter 5

1. *Rāüḷ.* A name for the Gosāvī used more by townspeople than by his devotees.
2. prasād. Food tasted by a deity, holy person, and so forth, and distributed as his leftovers to his devotees. A deity "makes *prasād*" by tasting food without eating it all.

Chapter 6

1. *Sādheṃ.* Elhāïseṃ, a female disciple of Cakradhar and Guṇḍam Rāüḷ, mentioned frequently in the *LC* as well as in the present text (see especially 174–85). See V. B. Kolte, *Śrīcakradhara Caritra,* 2nd ed. (Malkapur: Aruṇa Prakāśana, 1977), p. 81–84.
2. *Kuṇbī.* A caste of peasants. See Russell and Lal, vol. IV, p. 16–50, and Enthoven, vol. II, p. 284–315. A Brāhman would normally not eat food prepared by a member of this or other castes lower than Brāhmans in the purity-pollution hierarchy. This episode is but the first of several instances in the text where the Gosāvī or his devotees ignore the pollution rules of Brāhman orthodoxy.

Chapter 7

1. Cf. 9.

Chapter 8

1. Cf. 57, 96, 245, and 300.
2. *Vājeśvara.* A local form of the deity Śiva? The temple could also be that of the goddess(?) Vājā mentioned in 134.

Chapter 9

1. Cf. 7.

Chapter 11

1. *Māḷī women.* Women of the gardener caste. See Russell and Lal, vol. IV, p. 159–71, and Enthoven, vol. II, p. 422–26.

Chapter 12

1. *Vināyaka.* "Remover of obstacles," a name of Gaṇeśa, the elephant-headed deity.

Chapter 13

1. The tamarind seed game seems to have been analogous to the game of flipping coins, where the person calling "heads" or "tails" wins the coin if it falls the way he has predicted and loses if it falls the opposite way (Kolte, p.c.).

Chapter 14

1. This conversation, which occurred in a later period of the Gosāvī's life than that of most of the stories among which it is found in the text, appears to have been placed here because it is about the Gosāvī's youth.
2. *Māhādāïseṃ.* A female disciple of Cakradhar and Guṇḍam Rāüḷ, and a cousin (father's brother's daughter) of Nāgdev, the leader of Cakradhar's disciples (See Kolte, *Śrīcakradhara Caritra,* p. 69, 79–81). See 85 for the story of her meeting Guṇḍam Rāüḷ.
3. *Rājamaḍh.* Rājamaṭh, literally, "Royal Monastery," the temple which served Guṇḍam Rāüḷ and his devotees as a monastery after the events related in 102–20. See R. C. Ḍhere, "Rājamaṭhāce Rahasya," in *Lokasaṃskṛtīcī Kṣitije* (Pune: Viśvakarmā Sāhityālaya, 1971).

4. *He got a cramp. khāṃca paḍalī.* I am grateful to I. M. P. Raeside for suggesting this interpretation. It is not clear exactly what the Gosāvī used to do with his hand, or what happened when he tried.
5. *The Cripple.* Ābāïseṃ. See 127.
6. *Ābāïseṃ.* Another female disciple, Nāgdev's mother (*Smṛtisthaḷa* 1; Kolte, *Śrīcakradhara Caritra,* p. 78–79). See 212 for the story of her coming to serve the Gosāvī.

Chapter 15

1. *Had fallen asleep, went to sleep.* Literally, "accepted sleep." As Parameśvara, the Gosāvī does not need sleep.

Chapter 16

1. Orthodox Brāhmans consider menstruating women ritually polluting and do not allow them inside the house. (See Kane, vol. II, p. 802–05.) This explains Gāvitrī's mother's concern over Gāvitrī's sitting on the Gosāvī's platform, as well as Gāvitrī's remark about the verandah. Note that the Gosāvī seems angered by Gāvitrī's polluting action, but reacts by doing something which would normally cause more pollution—although, since the Gosāvī did it, it is considered instead to have sanctified the water.
2. *Sāvitrī* is identified in 82 as Tīka Upādhyāya's daughter; hence, the "teacher," here, would be Tīka Upādhyāya, not Bopa Upādhyāya, even though 2 states that the Gosāvī studied under Bopa Upādhyāya.

Chapter 18

1. *"Horse".* A stone that the Gosāvī pretends is a horse.

Chapter 19

1. *Ghāṭe Haribhaṭ* is mentioned in *LC,* P.154, P.156, and U.323. P.154 describes his first meeting with Cakradhar, in the Kodeśvara temple in Sīṅgṇāpur. U.323 summarizes the present episode and gives a fuller account of the events preceding it: the reason Ghāṭe Haribhaṭ dresses and acts as he does is that he has persuaded Cakradhar to give him forgetfulness of the world (*prapañcācī vismurti*). Hence the title of the present chapter.
2. *Sīṅgṇāpur.* In the *LC,* this appears to be Ghāṭe Haribhaṭ's village.

Chapter 20

1. Cf. 23.
2. *Keśav Nāyak.* An important householder in Ṛddhipur.
3. Not only is putting one's feet into a water jar unsanitary, but in India, it would also normally be a cause of ritual pollution.

Chapter 21

1. *Sāmānyeśvara.* A form of the deity Śiva.
2. *Contact. saṃbandha.* Among the objects Mahānubhāvas revere are those which have Parameśvara's *saṃbandha,* i.e., those which have been touched by an incarnation of Parameśvara. See Feldhaus, "The Orthodoxy of the Mahānubhāvas," in *The Experience of Hinduism,* ed. E. Zelliot and M. Berntsen (forthcoming).

Chapter 22

1. *Bhadra.* A locality in Ṛddhipur.
2. *Syrup, etc.* Rich foods, hence inappropriate for an ascetic.

Chapter 23

1. Cf. 20.
2. *Māṅgs.* Members of an "untouchable" caste considered so polluting that they must have their own separate drinking water. See Russell and Lal, vol. IV, p. 184–89, and Enthoven, vol. II, p. 434–47.
3. *Two animal horns.* I do not know of any special significance to these, or why they would be placed at a water stand.

Chapter 24

1. Cf. 58, 301.

Chapter 25

1. This is the first of several such "economic miracles" reported in the text. In none of the cases is it explained by what mechanism the miracle occurs. It is possible that the goods are considered more desirable after they become the Gosāvī's *prasād* (see glossary); but in 26, the curds not offered to the Gosāvī undergo a real physical change.

Chapter 26

1. *"It was with* us *the Rāüḷ was playing."* Cf. Kṛṣṇa's *rāsa krīḍā,* in which each of many milkmaids (*gopīs*) thinks she is the one dancing closest to Kṛṣṇa. *Bhāgavata Purāṇa* X.33.

Chapter 27

1. *Śrīprabhu.* The Gosāvī, Guṇḍam Rāüḷ.
2. *Keśava.* "Long-haired," the deity Kṛṣṇa or Viṣṇu.

Chapter 28

1. *Telī women.* Women of a caste who press and sell oil. See Russell and Lal, vol. IV, p. 542–57, and Enthoven, vol. III (Bombay, 1922), p. 371–74.
2. *Direct knowledge, knowledge of particulars.* Two early stages on the path of knowledge leading to release (*mokṣa*). See *Sūtrapāṭha* VIII.21f. Who and where the "beings" are is not clear, but it seems that they are invisible.
3. *Contact.* See notes to 21.

Chapter 29

1. The Telīs are low in the ritual-purity hierarchy, and so the woman is shocked that the Gosāvī, a Brāhman, would eat their food. But he indicates that such considerations are not important. Cf. 6.
2. bhākrī. The simplest of the flat breads, usually made of *jondhḷā* (Holcus sorghum, according to Molesworth) or *bājrī* (Holcus spicatus, according to Molesworth) dough cooked on a griddle.
3. lā̃k. Molesworth identifies this grain as Lithyrus sativus.

Chapter 30

1. *Śrāddha ceremony.* A ritual in which offerings are made to and in honor of dead ancestors.
2. *Declaration of purpose.* A formal part of rituals, usually called *saṃkalpa.* Here the verb form *kalpīleṃ* is used.
3. *Panic-seed rice.* "Rice" made of boiled *rāḷe,* identified by Molesworth as Panicum Italicum. According to the *MSK,* p. 2625, this is commonly used among poor people in this region as a substitute for rice.

Chapter 31

1. *Eleventh day.* The vigil on this day is normally in honor of Viṣṇu (or, in the Vārkarī sect now prevalent in Maharashtra, Viṭhobā). Note that the Gosāvī's miracle makes this vigil seem pointless, except to the one person who "wouldn't come."
2. *"Horses".* See notes to 18.

Chapter 32

1. Cf. 4.

Chapter 33

1. *Haṭakeśvara.* A form of the deity Śiva.

Chapter 34

1. *Thinking rock.* Cf. 201, 263, and 264.

Chapter 35

1. *Śrāvaṇī.* A ceremony performed on the full-moon day of the month of Śrāvaṇa (July–August) in which Brāhmans change their sacred threads (see notes to 1, under "Thread ceremony"). The old threads are thrown away, not to be used again (as, in the present episode, *all* the Gosāvī's old clothes are most definitely not to be used again). For a description of the ritual, see Stevenson, p. 307–08.

Chapter 36

1. *Sūtak well.* The well normally used for bathing after funerals. See 41. Molesworth states that "*sūtak*" normally refers to the impurity arising from a birth in the family, but that it can also refer to the impurity associated with a death. See Kane, vol. IV, p. 269, for meanings of the term in Sanskrit legal literature. Kane states that in Marāṭhī and some other modern Indian languages, the word is used only for the impurity associated with death. In taking a normal bath and performing an auspicious ritual at this well, the Gosāvī is once again flaunting the orthodox rules about ritual purity and pollution.
2. *Saṃdhyā rites.* A ritual performed by Brāhman men at sunrise, sunset, and other "junctures" (*saṃdhyās*) of the day. It consists primarily of sipping water and reciting certain formulas.

Chapter 37

1. *Dheḍ.* Kolte's edition has *dheṇḍa.* Russell and Lal, vol. IV, p. 129, give "Dhed" as an alternate name for "Mahār" (see notes to 46). Enthoven, vol. I (Bombay, 1920), p. 322–28, lists them as a separate caste ("Dheda"), and also (vol. II, p. 401) gives the name "Dhed" as a synonym for "Mahār." In either case, the Dheḍs are an "untouchable" group.
2. S. G. Tulpule (p.c.) points out that it is normal for Brāhmans' houses to be to the west of Untouchables' houses, rather than to their east, because the wind, which generally blows from west to east, will then be less likely to blow pollution toward the Brāhmans.

Chapter 38

1. *Vīṭhalu Joïsī.* From his name, this man appears to be a Brāhman with the hereditary occupation of astrologer.

Chapter 39

1. Cf. 72, 129, 177, and 251 for other stories of the Gosāvī fulfilling people's unspoken wishes.

Chapter 41

1. Cf. 81, 165.
2. *Sūtak well.* See notes to 36.
3. *Sīndak well.* Cf. 83.

Chapter 42

1. *Kaḷaṅkeśvara.* A form of the deity Śiva.
2. *Contact.* See notes to 21.

Chapter 43

1. *Trance. stīti.* Cf. 73 and a number of episodes in the *LC.*

Chapter 44

1. *Rāmṭek.* A major Hindu pilgrimage place on a large hill about one hundred miles east of Ṛddhipur. The chief deity of the place is Rāma. See 73 and 207 for other pilgrims who do not need to go on to Rāmṭek once they have gotten to Ṛddhipur.
2. *Nagareśvara.* Literally, "Lord of the town," a form of the deity Śiva.

Chapter 45

1. *Dhoti.* The lower garment worn by men, consisting of a cloth which is draped and folded and tucked between the legs.

Chapter 46

1. *Mahārs.* Members of the largest "untouchable" caste of Maharashtra. See Russell and Lal, vol. IV, p. 129–46, and Enthoven, vol. II, p. 401–18.
2. *Mahārs' quarter. mahāravāḍā.* Usually outside a village.
3. In *LC,* P.589, Nāgdev describes the Gosāvī doing this kind of thing but does not specify that he did it in Māṅgs' and Mahārs' houses.

Chapter 47

1. Note the village headmen's reluctance (or inability) to restrain the Gosāvī, as well as their cavalier attitude toward the Mahārs and Māṅgs. Rather than control the Gosāvī, the headmen cause great inconvenience to several households of Untouchables.

Chapter 48

1. Cf. 23, 164. The Untouchables of a village must have their own separate wells.

Chapter 49

1. Carcasses are particularly polluting to a Brāhman, as are people who handle them. Once again, the Gosāvī is violating the rules of orthodoxy.
2. *His error,* apparently, was not to realize the Gosāvī's omnipresence.

Chapter 50

1. cār *seeds.* Identified by Molesworth as seeds of Chirongia sapida.
2. goḍaṃbī *seeds.* Identified by Molesworth as seeds of the marking-nut plant or Semecarpus.

Chapters 52, 53

1. More "economic miracles." See notes to 25.
2. *Seer.* A weight varying greatly by region, but roughly equivalent to a little more than one kilogram. See *Hobson-Jobson.*

Chapter 54

1. Cf. 305.
2. *Silver coins.* āsus.

Chapter 55

1. Cf. 77.
2. *He ate his own food as* prasād. That is, he ate what was left of his food after the Gosāvī had had some.

Chapter 56

1. Cf. 114.
2. After correctly following all the orthodox rituals (*karma*) for bowel movements, the Gosāvī urinates in an incorrect position. See Kane, vol. II, p. 649f.
3. *Brahman.* The impersonal Absolute, in reference to which correct ritual procedures are meaningless.

Chapter 57

1. Cf. 8, 96, 245, and 300.
2. "*Horse.*" See notes to 18.

Chapter 58

1. Cf. 24, 301.
2. kohaḷī. Identified by Molesworth as the Cucurbita Pepo ("pumpion gourd") plant.

Chapter 59

1. *Acts afraid.* As Parameśvara, the Gosāvī is not really affected by emotions. Although the wording of the title reminds us of this theological fact, the wording in the story itself does not.
2. *Uñcamaḍh.* Literally, "Tall Monastery," one of the temple-monasteries of Ṛddhipur.

Chapter 60

1. *"Horses."* See notes to 18.

Chapter 62

1. *Bhairava.* A form of the deity Śiva.
2. *Patron. yajamāna.*

Chapter 63

1. *Acts angry.* As Parameśvara, the Gosāvī does not really get angry. Again, the title, but not the text, reminds us of this (cf. 59). Cf. also 137, 195.

Chapter 64

1. *Śimagā festival.* Holī, a festival characterized by boisterous pranks, including inferiors' sprinkling colored water or urine on their superiors. The festival occurs during the month of Phalgun (February–March). Cf. 280.
2. *Paraśurāma.* Rāma-with-an-axe, a hero-deity usually considered to be an incarnation of Viṣṇu.

Chapter 65

1. Cf. 112, 228, 238, 247, and 314. A story which resembles these, but which, unlike them, has a clear theological point, is found in *LC,* P.168. After touching the ears, nose, eyes, and so on of various temple images, the Gosāvī says to each of them, "You're a God? Drop dead, I tell you! You're not a God, I tell you." Then he touches Cakradhar the same way, and says, "This is God." See introduction, section I, under "Guṇḍam Rāüḷ in Other Mahānubhāva Texts."
2. *Temple for making offerings. bhogasthāna.*

Chapter 66

1. *Dādos.* Also called Rāmdev, a disciple of Cakradhar who appears frequently in the *LC. LC,* U.428 mentions the two metal cups and explains that Dādos always got two of everything, one for Cakradhar and one for himself. See also Kolte, *Śrīcakradhara Caritra,* p. 66–69.
2. *Telugu country.* The region where the Telugu language is spoken, modern Andhra Pradesh.
3. *Our Gosāvī.* Cakradhar.

Chapter 68

1. Cf. 268.

Chapter 69

1. *Dhānubāï* is mentioned in *LC,* P.48, where she worships Cakradhar in her

home in Aḷajpur. She is identified in this *LC* passage as the wife of (the? a?) "Pāñcauḷī." Kolte (*LC*, "Vyaktisūcī") takes "Pāñcauḷī" to be a person's name, but it seems more likely to be a designation of Nemāḷ Pāṇḍīyā. Kolte (Notes) identifies Nemāḷ Pāṇḍīyā as a minister (*pradhān*) of Aḷajpur, and refers to the *LC* story of Dhānubāī's worship of Cakradhar. This same (or another?) Dhānubāī is said in *LC*, P.74, to live in the same compound as Rām Daraṇā, whose son appears in 99.

2. darśan. Seeing (and being seen by) a deity, holy person, and so forth.
3. *Devgiri.* The capital of the Yādava dynasty, near present-day Aurangabad. The text has *ṭeṃka,* "the hill," naming the place for the small isolated mountain which is its outstanding geological feature.

Chapter 70

1. Cf. 7 and 9.

Chapter 71

1. *A series of meals. parīkhā nimantraṇa* or (Kolte, Notes) *parīkṣā nimantraṇa.* This is elucidated in *LC*, P.414, where one person after another invites a group of ascetics for a meal.

Chapter 72

1. Cf. 39, 129, 177, and 251 for other stories of the Gosāvī fulfilling people's unspoken wishes.
2. The ritual pollution of the family and the confinement of mother and child after birth last ten or twelve days. According to Abbott, p. 497, the pollution lasts ten days among Brāhmans and twelve days among Kṣatriyas. During this period, the mother and the new baby are kept in a closed room, with a plate of hot coals under the bed (Stevenson, *The Rites of the Twice-Born,* p. 3). I have been unable to find an explanation of, or another reference to, the practice of touching the storage pots with the plate of coals.

Chapter 73

1. *Trance. stīti.* See 43.
2. *Act like Īśvara.* Act like a god. Cf. *LC*, P.27, where an untouchable Carmakāra (= Cāmhār, leatherworker) put into *stīti* by Cakradhar acts the same way, and is worshipped as a god until people find out his caste.
3. *Rāmṭek, Rāma.* See notes to 44. See 44 and 207 for other pilgrims who do not need to go on to Rāmṭek once they have gotten to Ṛddhipur.

Chapter 74

1. *Solitary period, leadership.* Phases of the life of Guṇḍam Rāüḷ which are not precisely distinguished in the present text. The period of "leadership" would seem to be the period after Cakradhar's demise, when his disciples came to stay with Guṇḍam Rāüḷ.

Chapter 75

1. *Official. adhikārī.*

Chapter 76

1. Cf. 158, 260, 288, and 295.

Chapter 77

1. Cf. 55.

Chapter 78

1. *His clothes, his neck.* The Gosāvī is comparing female water buffaloes to orthodox, learned (male) Brāhmans (*pāṭhaks*, here translated "pandits"), with their forehead marks and their various types of baths.

Chapter 79

1. The beginning, which seems to be missing from this story in Kolte's edition, has been supplied in square brackets in the translation.
2. *Śūdra.* A member of one of the castes lower than the twice-born (see notes to 1, "Thread ceremony"), but not as low as Untouchables.

Chapter 80

1. *Umāïseṃ.* Kolte (Notes) suggests that this is a different Umāïseṃ from Nāgdev's sister Umāïseṃ, who is mentioned later in the present text (121, 122, 132, 133, and 150) as well as in the *LC.*

Chapter 81

1. Cf. 41, 165. A similar episode, or another version of this one, is found in *LC,* P.415.
2. *Tīka Upādhyāya.* The teacher's teacher of Bopa Upādhyāya, the Gosāvī's teacher. See 2. According to *LC,* P.15, Tīka Upādhyāya was the brother of Bopa Upādhyāya, and himself one of the Gosāvī's teachers.
3. *An evil woman.* This remark is not clearly explained in the present text, nor can I find an explanation of it in the *LC.* If the "teacher" in 16 is Tīka Upādhyāya (see notes to 16), then this is the woman who complains there that the Gosāvī has polluted her water jar.

Chapter 82

1. Tīka Upādhyāya believes that the food, as leftovers, is polluted, and so he does not eat any himself. Apparently, he tricks his guests into eating it. But his ancestors reveal, without explicitly invoking the notion of *prasād,* that the Gosāvī's leftovers are better than other food. And so Tīka Upādhyāya completes the ritual by partaking of the food himself.

Chapter 83

1. *Triangular sling.* For carrying the pot of hot coals to the cremation ground.

Chapter 84

1. This story is repeated and continued in *LC,* P.380. Dādos (= Rāmdev) arrives in Kānaḍī Bhālugā̃v after Cakradhar has already left. In the *LC* version, Dādos sets off for Kānaḍī Bhālugā̃v immediately, but stops along the way.
2. *Our Gosāvī.* Cakradhar.

Chapter 85

1. *Bhaṭ.* Nāgdev, Cakradhar's chief disciple. See Kolte, *Śrīcakradhara Caritra,* p. 69–78.
2. *Cāṅgdev Rāūḷ.* Cakradhar. It seems that Guṇḍam Rāūḷ is recognizing Nāgdev and Māhādāïseṃ as Cakradhar's disciples.
3. *Dārbheśvara.* A form of the deity Śiva.
4. *When she brought Bhaṭ from Bhānkheḍ.* This episode, which occurred after Cakradhar's death, is narrated in *Smṛtisthaḷa* 2–4. In *Smṛtisthaḷa* 4, on meeting Nāgdev, the Gosāvī says, "Cāṅgdev Rāūḷ's."

Chapter 86

1. Cf. 93.

Chapters 87–92

1. These episodes are also recorded in *LC,* P.585.

Chapter 88

1. dhīḍareṃ, āhītā. The preparation of what the Gosāvī (but not Māhādāïseṃ) meant by the term *dhīḍareṃ* is described in the story. This episode illustrates dialectical variation in Old Marāṭhī as well as the geographical spread of the early followers of Cakradhar and Guṇḍam Rāūḷ.
2. *Gaṅgā.* The Godāvarī River.
3. *Varhāḍ.* Berar or Vidarbha, the northeastern part of the Marāṭhī-speaking region.

Chapter 91

1. *Acted angry.* See notes to 63.
2. *Rupai.* Māhādāïseṃ. Dādos (= Rāmdev) was her guru as well as Ābāïseṃ's, Umāïseṃ's, and Nāgdev's before they all became followers of Cakradhar. See *LC,* P.238 and *Smṛtisthaḷa* 1.
3. *Lion-faced stone block. sīhāḍā (siṃhāḍā).*
4. *Our Gosāvī.* Cakradhar.
5. *Mother.* A term of respect and affection, not indicating (in this context) an actual filial relationship.
6. *Loads* [*of grain*]. *khaṇḍīs.* A *khaṇḍī* or candy is a large measure of weight and volume. It varies greatly by region, but is roughly equivalent to five hundred pounds. See *Hobson-Jobson,* "Candy."
7. *Rīdhaureṃ.* Ṛddhipur.
8. *Naming ceremony.* The *bārseṃ,* held on the twelfth day (Marāṭhī *bārā* = twelve) after birth.

Chapter 93

1. Cf. 86.
2. *Dāïṃbā.* A disciple of Cakradhar and Guṇḍam Rāūḷ, mentioned frequently in the *LC* as well as in the present text. See Kolte, *Śrīcakradhara Caritra,* p. 98–100.
3. *Paiṭhan.* Cakradhar's headquarters during the latter part of his life.
4. *By the Gosāvī to Śrīprabhu.* By Cakradhar to Guṇḍam Rāūḷ.

Chapter 94

1. *Our Gosāvī.* Cakradhar.
2. *Bhojā.* Dāïṃbā's nickname. See *LC,* P.485, for the story of Cakradhar giving him the name.
3. *Kāśī.* Benāras or Vārāṇasī, the holiest of Hindu cities.

Chapter 95

1. Cf. 312.
2. *Niṣkalaṅka.* "The stainless one," a name of the deity Śiva.
3. *Patron. yajamāna.*

Chapter 96

1. Cf. 8, 57, 245, and 300.
2. *Kamaleśvara.* A form of the deity Śiva.

Chapter 97

1. This episode is narrated in greater detail in *LC,* U.564.
2. *Mhāïṃbhaṭ.* The author of the present text. See introduction; see Kolte, *Śrīcakradhara Caritra,* p. 96–98.
3. *Bhāvaī fourteenth.* The eve of the no-moon day of the month of Jyeṣṭha (May–June).
4. *Bhaṭ.* This name, which the text usually uses to refer to Nāgdev, here refers to Mhāïṃbhaṭ. It means simply "Brāhman."
5. *Our Gosāvī.* Cakradhar.

Chapter 98

1. *"Horse."* See notes to 18.

Chapter 99

1. *Rām Daraṇā.* See *LC,* P.74–77, for the story of Cakradhar meeting Rām Daraṇā and accepting his hospitality for ten months at Aḷajpur.
2. *Touch-the-post.* See 21.
3. *Rāmnāth.* A form of the deity Śiva.

Chapter 102

1. *Followers of the Veda.* That is, orthodox Hindus.
2. *Navacaṇḍī festival.* Navarātra, a goddess festival held during the first nine days of the month Āśvin (September–October). See Kane, vol. V, p. 154–87.
3. *Acted angry.* See notes to 63.
4. *Sīvana.* The Godāvarī Valley. See 235. Note the local headmen's possessiveness toward the Rāüḷ and their resentment of the immigrant devotees.

Chapter 103

1. Notice that the invitation to Deūḷvāḍā is engineered by Nāgdev and Mhāïṃbhaṭ, and that all the devotees pressure the Gosāvī to accept it. This seems to be a direct response to the outrage committed by the Gosāvī in the preceding episode.

Chapter 104

1. "*Horse.*" See notes to 18.

Chapter 105

1. *Wave trays of lights. ovāḷaṇeṃ.* Here, a way of doing homage.
2. *Prostitutes.* These women are considered auspicious, as they are never widowed. See Abbott, p. 112.
3. *Pratimaṭh.* Apparently, like the Rājamaḍh (see notes to 14), a temple of Narasiṃha, the man-lion incarnation of Viṣṇu. See 107, 111, and 112.

Chapter 106

1. *Everyone ate in the same row.* I.e., they did not observe the normal caste-related restrictions on commensality.

Chapter 107

1. *Narasiṃha.* The man-lion incarnation of Viṣṇu.

Chapter 109

1. *When he was there.* I.e., in Ṛddhipur, where his behavior caused trouble for his disciples. See 102.
2. *Bhaṭ and Mhāïṃbhaṭ were very happy,* not just because Dāmurt had been appeased, but because the Gosāvī had miraculously appeared in two places at once.

Chapter 110

1. Cf. 118.
2. *Navacaṇḍī.* See notes to 102. An important part of the Navacaṇḍī festival is feeding a meal to unmarried girls (Kane, vol. V, p. 170–71). It is unclear whether the meal recorded here and in 118 occurred during the same nine-day period as the events recorded in 102. Another Navacaṇḍī festival is sometimes held during the first nine days of Caitra (March–April) (Kane, vol. V, p. 154); this could be the one referred to here. According to 105, the Gosāvī stayed in the Pratimaṭh in Deūḷvāḍā for six months, and his stay began after the (Āśvin, presumably) Navacaṇḍī festival of 102. It is also possible that the present episode and that in 118 did not occur in Deūḷvāḍā; in this case, there is no indication as to when they occurred.
3. *Brides'* foreheads are decorated with red powder, and the part of their hair with vermilion. The Gosāvī is teasing the girls, who are as yet unmarried.

Chapter 111

1. The priest apparently thought that the food sampled by the Gosāvī was thereby ritually polluted. Cf. notes to 82. The implication of the priest's dream is that Narasiṃha, like several of the Gosāvī's human devotees (for example, in 163 and 262), refuses any food except the Gosāvī's *prasād.*

Chapter 112

1. Cf. 65, 228, 238, 247, and 314.

Chapter 113

1. *Vāghikā.* From *vāgh,* tiger.

Chapter 114

1. Cf. 56. It is unclear whether the Gosāvī introduces some innovation into the purification procedures, or whether the Brāhmans (of Deūḷvāḍā?) had been unaware of the ritually correct procedures.

Chapter 115

1. *Keśav Nāyak, Vīṭhal Nāyak.* Influential men who appear to have been among the devotees accompanying the Gosāvī to Deuḷvāḍā. Keśav Nāyak was a resident of Ṛddhipur; Vīṭhal Nāyak (see 269), of Taḷegā̃v.
2. *The capital. kaṭak.* According to Kolte (Notes), this term is used for Devgiri, the Yādavas' capital. Cf. notes to 293.
3. *Quadruple silver coins. āsu cauthariyā.* Cf. 283.
4. *Copper plate.* Inscribed with a record of the transaction.

Chapter 116

1. *The doors,* presumably, are those of the Pratimaṭh. The text does not explain why the doors are closed, nor why Nāgdev did not want the Gosāvī to go to Ṛddhipur yet.
2. *Harimā.* A nickname for Nāgdev. Cf. 277.

Chapter 117

1. *Southernwood festival. davaṇeyācem̥ parva.* Worship, using the southernwood plant (*davaṇā,* identified by Molesworth as Artemisia abrotanum and derived by him from Sanskrit *damanaka,* which is identified by Monier-Williams as Artemesia indica), of various deities, performed on or near the full-moon day of the month of Caitra (March–April). See Kane, vol. V, p. 310–11.

Chapter 118

1. Cf. 110, text and notes.

Chapter 119

1. *Kamaḷā Rāṇī.* Dāmurt's wife? (Tulpule, p.c.)
2. [*One morning*]. The morning of a full-moon day, it seems; thus not the morning after the events of 118, since the Navacaṇḍī festival ends six days before the full moon. Possibly the morning after the Southernwood festival in 117. 118, which duplicates 110, would seem to be an interpolation here.
3. *Full-moon day.* A particularly auspicious and meritorious day for performing rituals.

Chapter 120

1. *Rājamaḍh.* See notes to 14.
2. *He stays in the Rājamaḍh for fear of a snake.* This sentence is not found in the base ms. of Kolte's edition, but it is in one of the other mss. used for the edition.
3. *The flowers.* Used in worshipping the Gosāvī.

Chapter 121

1. *Umāïseṃ.* Nāgdev's sister and Ābāïseṃ's daughter; a widow (*Smṛtisthaḷa* 1; cf. Kolte, *Śrīcakradhara Caritra,* p. 78–79). Note the jealousy among the women of this family over their service of the Gosāvī.
2. *The Cripple.* Ābāïseṃ. See 127.
3. *God gave me a God.* Cakradhar sent Ābāïseṃ to serve Guṇḍam Rāüḷ. See 212, text and notes.
4. *Rupai.* Māhādāïseṃ.
5. *Umai.* Umāïseṃ.
6. *Māhādī.* Māhādāïseṃ.

Chapter 122

1. *Our Gosāvī.* Here, Guṇḍam Rāüḷ.
2. *Cāṇḍā, Pāṭaṇ, Pusadā.* Market towns?
3. *Silver coins. āsus.*
4. *The Cripple.* Ābāïseṃ. See 127.
5. Bhaṭ is pointing out that the Gosāvī's generosity to Ābāïseṃ exceeds the call of duty.

Chapter 123

1. *No one knows where.* The text is based on people's recollections, and none of those people remember where the Gosāvī was sitting—including, it seems, Mhāïṃbhaṭ, the author of the text, who was there at the time. According to a variant noted in Kolte's edition, "The Gosāvī was sitting on his cot."

Chapter 124

1. "*Give away loot.*" *mogarasul vousāveṃ.* A way of practicing almsgiving (*MSK*).

Chapter 125

1. dovai. The context explains what the Gosāvī means by this term, which may be a dialectical variant of *dūrvā.* Cf. 88.
2. *Bhāvaī festival.* See notes to 97. The celebration of the festival (the Gosāvī's way, at least) is described in the present chapter.

Chapter 126

1. *The presence of two Gods.* The *sannidhāna* of Cakradhar and Guṇḍam Rāüḷ. In Mahānubhāva liberation doctrine, it is through *sannidhāna* that Parameśvara's incarnations give liberation. See *Sūtrapāṭha* VIII.16 and Appendix A, "Purvī."

Chapter 129

1. Cf. 39, 72, 177, and 251 for other stories of the Gosāvī fulfilling people's unspoken wishes.

Chapter 131

1. *Māhādāï, Rupai, Māhādī.* Māhādāïseṃ.
2. *One watch. pahār* (*prahara*). Three hours.
3. *Devakī.* The mother of Kṛṣṇa, whom Mahānubhāvas consider to be, like Guṇḍam Rāüḷ and Cakradhar, an incarnation of Parameśvara.
4. "*Or did Māhādī bite the snake?*" Cf. 191.

Chapter 132

1. For the jealousy between Ābāïseṃ and her daughter Umāïseṃ over their service to the Gosāvī, cf. 121.

Chapter 133

1. *"The Gosāvī has destroyed your karma."* As the transcendent Parameśvara, the Gosāvī can suspend the normal workings of the universe: not just the laws of nature, as in 71, 209, 210, 211, 266, and so forth, but also the laws of karma, according to which the results of actions must be experienced.

Chapter 134

1. purī-*bread.* A puffed wheat bread prepared by deep-frying thin flat circles of dough in oil.
2. *Vājā.* A local goddess? The deity of the Vājeśvara temple (in 8 and 267)?
3. *Crossed the threshold seven times, had a child throw stones.* As remedies for the Gosāvī's complaint, it seems. Abbott, p. 425, states, "To-day the threshold in common belief is the abode both of beneficent and of evil *śakti* [power]." And chapter 10 of Abbott's book is devoted to "The Power of Stones."

Chapter 135

1. *"The seed. . . ."* This is not a verse of the *Bhagavadgītā* itself, but rather, apparently, of Mhāïṃbhaṭ's commentary.
2. *Kurus and Pāṇḍavas.* The two sides of the family at war in the *Mahābhārata,* the epic which includes the *Bhagavadgītā.*
3. *Gītā.* The *Bhagavadgītā,* which Mahānubhāvas revere as revelation, since it is the words of Kṛṣṇa, whom Mahānubhāvas consider an incarnation of Parameśvara. (See Feldhaus, "The Mahānubhāvas and Scripture," *Journal of Dharma* (Bangalore), 3 (1978): 295–308.) Perhaps it is only Mhāïṃbhaṭ's commentary, and not the *Gītā* itself, which the Gosāvī is mocking.

Chapter 136

1. *Dhanañjayā.* "Conqueror of wealth," a name of Arjuna, the *Mahābhārata* hero to whom the *Bhagavadgītā* is addressed. But the Brāhman in this episode was probably reciting from a scripture earlier than the *Bhagavadgītā.* The name is given here in the Marāṭhī vocative (*-jayā*). In the *Ṛg Veda,* the name appears in the (Sanskrit) vocative at 9.46.5, but it is not repeated there, as it is here. (I am indebted to Acharya V. P. Limaye for the *Ṛg Veda* reference, and to Professor S. G. Tulpule for asking him for it.)
2. *Nāgujayā.* Nāgdev? This also is a Marāṭhī vocative. As in the previous episode, here too the Gosāvī is punning, but if he is playing on the words of the *Ṛg Veda,* he is ridiculing a scripture which is not authoritative for Mahānubhāvas. See Feldhaus, "The Mahānubhāvas and Scripture."

Chapter 137

1. Cf. 63, 317, and 321.

Chapter 138

1. Cf. *LC,* P.317, where Cakradhar promises Dāïṃbā that he will perform Sobhāgeṃ's funeral rites. Guṇḍam Rāüḷ can carry out Cakradhar's prom-

ise since both Guṇḍam Rāüḷ and Cakradhar are incarnations of Parameśvara.

2. *Sobhāgeṃ.* Cakradhar gives her this name, which means "wifehood," "the auspicious condition of an unwidowed married woman," in *LC,* P.316. He calls her a "potful of *sobhāgeṃ*" when she describes to him how much her husband loves her.
3. Mahānubhāvas normally bury, rather than burn, their dead. In this they follow the usual practice of Hindu ascetics (see Kane, vol. II, p. 965; and vol. IV, p. 229–31); cremation is usual for Hindu householders.
4. *Bhojā.* = Dāïṃbā. See notes to 94.
5. *"The Gosāvī said. . . . The Gosāvī has made it come true."* Cakradhar made the promise, and Guṇḍam Rāüḷ fulfilled it.
6. *The ball of rice, the stream of water, and so forth.* These are all parts of the orthodox cremation rite. Cf. 300 and, for the bath, 41. See Kane, vol. IV, p. 189–231.

Chapter 139

1. *Patron. yajamāna.*

Chapter 140

1. *Mahātmā.* "Great-souled one." Here, possibly, a Mahānubhāva, as this name was used by Cakradhar and others to refer to his followers. See V. B. Kolte, " 'Mahānubhāvapaṃtha' kī 'Paramārga'?" in *Mahānubhāva Saṃśodhana: 1* (Malkāpūr: Aruṇa Prakāśana, 1962), p. 25–29.
2. Cf. 145.
3. *Nāgā Rāüḷ's wife.* A ms. variant noted in Kolte's edition has "sister" for "wife." *LC,* U.543, states that Nāgā Rāüḷ's sister, Kamalbhairav, wore men's clothes. *LC,* U.330, uses feminine grammatical forms to refer to Naga Rāüḷ, while a ms. variant noted in Kolte's edition of the *LC* states that Nāgā Rāüḷ was a woman but wore men's clothes. See also *LC,* U.462.

Chapter 141

1. *Stringed instrument. sarivīṇā.*
2. *Mode. rāga.*

Chapter 142

1. *Contact.* See notes to 21.

Chapter 143

1. Another "economic miracle." See notes to 25.
2. *Contact.* See notes to 21.

Chapter 144

1. kubā. Identified by Molesworth as Careya arborea.

Chapter 145

1. Cf. 140.
2. *Mahātmā.* See notes to 140.

Chapter 146

1. Poḷī-*bread.* Flat wheat bread baked on a griddle.
2. *Demāïseṃ.* This may be Mhāïṃbhaṭ's wife, Demāïseṃ, mentioned in 197, or another Demāïseṃ (= Dematī), a disciple of Cakradhar mentioned several times in the *LC.*
3. The passage does not make clear what "the difference" was between the two sets of *poḷīs*, unless the second pair was not stacked one on top of the other.

Chapter 148

1. darbha-*grass.* A grass, identified by Molesworth and Monier-Williams as Poa cynosuroides, used in orthodox rituals. It is worn looped around the finger next to the smallest, on the right hand or on both hands (Kane, vol. II, p. 657).

Chapter 150

1. *Thinking rock.* See 34.
2. *Twisted the end of her garment.* Tulpule (p.c.) points out that this is a gesture used by children in making demands of their mothers.
3. *On another day, she prepared his plate.* "She," here, seems to be Umāïseṃ, not the other woman.

Chapter 151

1. tūr-*pulse.* Identified by Molesworth as Cytisus cajan.

Chapter 152

1. *Waving a tray of lights. ovāḷaṇeṃ.* See notes to 105.

Chapter 154

1. *Bharāḍī.* The text has *bhrīḍī.* A type of wandering religious mendicant and entertainer. See Enthoven, vol. I, p. 113–17, and R. C. Ḍhere, *Marāṭhī Lokasaṃskṛtīce Upāsaka* (Pune: Jñānarāja Prakāśana, 1964?), p. 69–88.
2. *"Horse."* See notes to 18.
3. prasād. Here, not food, but a gracious gift.

Chapter 155

1. This episode illustrates that the Gosāvī knew very well the rules of the orthodoxy which he so often violated.
2. Widows wear white clothes; brides, red.
3. *Set* [*the village*] *on fire.* Be promiscuous (Tulpule, p.c.).

Chapter 156

1. dhīḍareṃ. See 88.

Chapter 157

1. *Vesa Paṇḍit.* Vesa Nāyak. See 163.
2. āvaḷā. The tree from which this fruit comes is identified by Molesworth as Phyllanthus emblica or Emblic myrobalan. The Sanskrit form, *āmalaka,* is used in the title.

Chapter 158

1. Cf. 76, 260, 288, and 295.

Chapter 160

1. *Vanījārs.* Brinjārīs, itinerant carriers and traders of grain. See *Hobson-Jobson,* "Brinjarry"; Russell and Lal, vol. II, p. 162–92, "Banjāra"; and Enthoven, vol. II, p. 331–43, "Lamani."
2. *Paraśurāma.* See notes to 64.

Chapter 161

1. rāyaṇī-*trees.* Molesworth identifies these as Mimusops hexandra or kanki.

Chapters 162, 163

1. tulasī. Holy basil, a plant which is used in the worship of Viṣṇu and Kṛṣṇa, and which is itself worshipped as a goddess.

Chapter 163

1. *Vesa Nāyak.* A variant noted in Kolte's edition has "Īśvar Nāyak" in both the title and the text.
2. Cf. 262.

Chapter 164

1. Cf. 48.

Chapter 165

1. Cf. 41, 81.
2. *Lambodara.* "Long-stomached," a name of the elephant-headed, pot-bellied deity, Gaṇeśa.

Chapter 167

1. *Mendicant.* This episode gives evidence of the existence of a distinction among the earliest disciples of Cakradhar and Guṇḍam Rāüḷ between mendicant ascetics (here, *bhīkṣuka*s) and other, nonmendicant, devotees. The episode also shows that on becoming a *bhīkṣuka,* a disciple gave up his rights and possessions.

Chapter 169

1. *The Cripple.* Ābāïseṃ. See 127.

Chapter 170

1. *Bandeśvara.* A form of the deity Śiva.

Chapter 171

1. *Dhāno, Āpe.* Neither of these is mentioned elsewhere in this text or in the *LC.*

Chapter 172

1. mohāḷu*s,* pothī*s.* The title identifies both(?) of these as tubers of some sort. Kolte's glossary identifies *mohāḷu* as "a fruit" (*phaḷa*) and *pothī* as *camakorā*

or *āḷū;* the *Mahārāṣṭra Śabdakośa* gives *aḷūṃ* as a synonym for *camakorā;* Molesworth identifies *aḷū* as Arum campanulatum and Calladium esc.
2. *Copper coin. dāma.*

Chapter 173
1. Another "economic miracle." See notes to 25. Cf. 216.

Chapter 174
1. *Gaṅgā.* The Godāvarī River.
2. *Govinda.* Guṇḍam Rāüḷ, sometimes called Govindaprabhu.
3. *Elho.* Sādheṃ (= Elhāïseṃ).
4. *All the devotees had a meal.* A ms. variant recorded in Kolte's edition substitutes (adds?) "had *prasād.*"

Chapters 175, 176
1. prasād. Here, not food, but a gracious gift. Relics of this sort are reverently preserved by Mahānubhāvas to this day.

Chapter 177
1. Cf. 39, 72, 129, and 251 for other stories of the Gosāvī fulfilling people's unspoken wishes.
2. *Would be holding.* This translates "*dharitī,*" a variant noted in Kolte's edition. The base ms. of Kolte's edition reads "*ṭīṃbakārīti,*" which, his glossary suggests, means "would be sounding," "would be playing," as a musical instrument.

Chapter 178
1. *Pancake. āhītā.* See 88.

Chapter 179
1. *Govinda.* This could be Guṇḍam Rāüḷ, as in 174; or Kṛṣṇa, whose devotees practice imagining themselves in various relationships to him; or both, since Mahānubhāvas understand both to be incarnations of Parameśvara.

Chapters 180, 181
1. *"Can there be anything wrong with Īśvara? Does he like this kind of thing?"* The questions appear to be rhetorical, indicating the opinion that the Gosāvī must be displeased with Sādheṃ.

Chapter 182
1. *Brahman.* The impersonal Absolute; here, equivalent to Parameśvara, incarnated in the Gosāvī.
2. *Elho.* Sādheṃ (= Elhāïseṃ).

Chapter 183
1. *Black bull.* That is, fat and dark-skinned (Tulpule, p.c.).

Chapter 184
1. *Māṅg's chicken.* Again, this seems to be a form of abuse.

Chapter 185
1. Cf. 175–77.

Chapter 186
1. *Āüseṃ.* A devotee of Cakradhar. In the *LC,* she addresses Cakradhar with the same phrase with which she here addresses Guṇḍam Rāüḷ: "*jī jī svāmī jagannāthā!*" ("O Swami, Lord of the World!"). Toward the end of his life, Cakradhar sends her to Guṇḍam Rāüḷ (*LC,* U.639; *Sūtrapāṭha* XII.208).
2. *Gaṅgā.* The Godāvarī River, which seems to Āüseṃ to burn after the loss of Cakradhar.
3. *Hail! udo!* Cakradhar says this to Āüseṃ in *LC,* U.524.
4. *Cakra Swami.* Cakradhar.

Chapter 187
1. Cf. *LC,* U.524, where Āüseṃ does this same kind of worship of Cakradhar.
2. *Guṇḍam Swami.* Guṇḍam Rāüḷ.

Chapter 188
1. Food is to be eaten with the right hand, not the left; but while eating, one should not use one's right hand to touch anything but the food on one's own plate. Thus, by taking more with her left hand, Āüseṃ avoided polluting the portion she had set aside for the Gosāvī.

Chapter 191
1. Mahānubhāva ethics places great emphasis on *ahiṃsā,* not injuring living beings. See *Sūtrapāṭha,* XIII.105–06, and so forth, and Feldhaus, *The Religious System of the Mahānubhāva Sect,* p. 67.
2. "*You've bitten it.*" Cf. 131.

Chapter 192
1. *Midwife.* That is, not an ascetic.

Chapter 193
1. Cf. 213.
2. *Money-changers.* Mhāïṃbhaṭ himself was one. See 249, 250, and 305.
3. *Sīdhanāth.* A form of the deity Śiva.
4. liṅga. The phallic image of the deity Śiva.

Chapter 195
1. Cf. 63.
2. *Loads* [*of grain*]. *khaṇḍī*s. See notes to 91.
3. "*You're lucky, blessed, fortunate.*" Mhāïṃbhaṭ's point is apparently the same here as in the previous episode: Kothaḷobā is lucky to get attention from the Gosāvī, even if the attention takes the form of abuse.

Chapter 197
1. *Demāïseṃ.* See notes to 146.

Chapter 198
1. *His sin.* Mhāïṃbhaṭ's sin, of suspicion.

Chapter 199

1. *Bhusāres.* Enthoven (vol. I, p. 197) reports that these are members of "a sub-division of Lamānis or Vanjāris." See notes to 160.

Chapter 200

1. *Plantains* are among the foods that may be eaten during a fast. See Kane, vol. V., p. 99f.
2. *Maiḷbhaṭ's sister . . . Rāṇāïseṃ.* This translates a ms. variant noted in Kolte's edition. Kolte's base ms. reads, "Maiḷbhaṭ's wife . . . Elhāïseṃ." The variant has been translated here for consistency with the mention of Rāṇāïseṃ later in the story. Aside from this chapter and the next, Maiḷbhaṭ is not mentioned again in this text or in the *LC,* but there is a Rāṇāïseṃ who appears several times in the *LC* as a devotee of Cakradhar.

Chapter 201

1. *Thinking rock.* See 34, 263, and 264.
2. tulasī. See notes to 162.
3. cavaḷā-*beans.* Molesworth identifies these as "a large variety" of Dolichos catjang or sesquipedalis, or of Portulaca quadrifida.

Chapter 203

1. *Gaṅgā.* The Godāvarī River.
2. *The capital.* See notes to 115.
3. *Rāmṭek.* See notes to 44.
4. *Māhādev Pāṭhak.* Apparently the Māhādevobā of 202, 204, and 205. He is a learned man who is mentioned several times, with the honorific Pāṭhak, in the *LC.*

Chapter 204

1. *Tīpurārībhaṭ.* A disciple mentioned several other times in the text, always in connection with stories about which disciple should perform which service for the Gosāvī. See 273, 274, and 299.

Chapter 205

1. *Lakhudevobā.* A devotee of Cakradhar mentioned several times in the *LC.* A ms. variant noted in Kolte's edition at *LC,* P.472, explains that Lakhudevobā was the son of Gāṅgāïseṃ, Ābāïseṃ's sister, and that he was thus a cousin of Nāgdev.

Chapter 206

1. *The capital.* See notes to 115.
2. *Silver coins. āsus.*

Chapter 207

1. *A son-in-law* is greatly honored in his wife's parents' house, in hope that he will treat their daughter well.
2. *Rāmṭek.* See notes to 44. See 44 and 73 for other pilgrims who do not need to go on to Rāmṭek once they have gotten to Ṛddhipur.

Chapter 208

1. *Mahārs' quarter*. See notes to 46.

Chapter 211

1. *Rāmnāth*. See notes to 99.

Chapter 212

1. *Our Gosāvī*. Cakradhar.
2. *Gaṇapati monastery*. In Pratiṣṭhān (Paiṭhaṇ) (*LC*, U.321).
3. *Śrīprabhu, Śrīprabhu Gosāvī*. Guṇḍam Rāüḷ. The episode in which Cakradhar sends Ābāïseṃ to Ṛddhipur is narrated in *LC*, U.326. As she is leaving, Ābāïseṃ asks Cakradhar, "I've heard that it's difficult serving there. So how should I behave there?" And Cakradhar answers, "My woman, first show Śrīprabhu a dish that you're going to offer him. His inclination (*pravṛtti*) is not to put anything into his mouth without inspecting it. As Śrīprabhu gets used to you, Śrīprabhu accepts your service. You'll be able to serve Śrīprabhu."
4. *Tīka Upādhyāya's compound*. The Gosāvī's disciples acquire a monastery in 115, and the Gosāvī moves into it in 120. If the Gosāvī was still staying in Tīka Upādhyāya's compound when the present episode occurred, it must have taken place before the move to the monastery.
5. *Śrī Cakradhar Rāyā*. "King Cakradhar."

Chapter 213

1. Cf. 193.
2. *Narasiṃha*. The man-lion incarnation of Viṣṇu. The temple is probably the one in which the Gosāvī stayed during his six months in Deüḷvāḍā (104–19).
3. purāṇa. One of a number of long Sanskrit texts dealing with mythological and philosophical topics.
4. *Lakṣmīndrabās*. Lakṣmīndrabhaṭ.
5. *Took a man with her*. This translates the reading of the base ms. of Kolte's edition. The other two mss. specify, respectively, that the man was a Ṭhākūr (see notes to 217) and a Brāhman.
6. *Put the red paste on your forehead*. Adorn you for your wedding. Cf. notes to 110.

Chapter 214

1. *Caitra and Vaiśākh*. March–April and April–May. The hottest months of the year, before the coming of the monsoon.

Chapter 215

1. *Gaṇeśa*. The elephant-headed deity, apparently a Gaṇeśa image installed near the marketplace.

Chapter 216

1. Another "economic miracle." See notes to 25. Cf. 173.
2. *Acted angry*. See notes to 63.

Chapter 217

1. *Ṭhākūr.* A member of a certain tribe. See Enthoven, vol. III, p. 376–81. Russell and Lal, vol. IV, p. 411, explain that "Thākur, or lord, is the common Rājpūt title, and that by which they are generally addressed." For Rājputs, see notes to 278.

Chapter 219

1. *Caitra and Vaiśākh.* See notes to 214.

Chapter 220

1. *Bhādrapad.* August–September.
2. *Śrāvaṇ.* July–August. This is late for mangoes to form on the trees.
3. *Vāḷukobā.* This disciple appears in no other episodes in this text or in the *LC.*
4. *Silver coin. āsu.*
5. *Bhaṭ knew well the right time for stealing.* Because he had been "*mahā-dhāṃḍāḷācā*" (*LC,* U.595), a rogue, before joining Cakradhar.

Chapter 221

1. Cf. 88, text and notes.
2. āḷakavasā, taravaṭā. The context makes it clear that these are synonyms. Molesworth does not have an entry for *āḷakavasā,* and he identifies *taravaṭā* simply as "an esculent and medicinal herb." Monier-Williams identifies (Sanskrit) *taravaṭa* as Cassia auriculata.

Chapters 222, 223

1. *Govindbhaṭ Toḍole, Govindbhaṭ.* These may well be the same person. No other Govindbhaṭ is mentioned elsewhere in this text, or in the *LC.*

Chapter 224

1. *Wedding bracelet, betel nut, and so forth.* Parts of the marriage ritual. See Kane, vol. II, p. 527f. and Stevenson, *The Rites of the Twice-Born,* p. 58f for textual and ethnographic accounts, respectively, of the rites. See also Pandey, *Hindu Saṃskāras,* p. 199f.
2. *Kṛṣṇa and Rukmiṇī.* A Hindu god who is, to the Mahānubhāvas, an incarnation of Parameśvara, their one God; and his wife.
3. *Engagement ceremony. svayaṃvara,* a ceremony in which a young woman chooses for herself the man she will marry. See Kane, vol. II, p. 523–24. Rukmiṇī's *svayaṃvara* is a favorite topic of Mahānubhāva poets.
4. "*Surely he touched her in her soul.*" "Pūrvārdha" 31.4 in the collection of Māhādāïseṃ's songs (*ḍhavaḷe*) in V. N. Deshpande, *Ādya Marāṭhī Kavayitrī* (Yeotmal, 1935). (I am indebted to Professor Tulpule for this reference.) See *Smṛtisthaḷa* 174 for another version of the story of Māhādāïseṃ composing a song about Rukmiṇī's engagement ceremony.
5. "*I* [*ate*] *in Rukmiṇī's palace.*" That is, in his earlier incarnation as Kṛṣṇa.
6. *Dvāpara, Kali.* The second and fourth, respectively, of the four *yuga*s (ages) of Hindu cosmology. For statements that Kṛṣṇa's incarnation was in the Dvāpara Age, cf. *Sūtrapāṭha* X.101 and (appendix A, Feldhaus edition) "Pañcakṛṣṇa" 1 and "Pañcanāma" 1.

7. bhākrī-*bread.* A much simpler and less festive food than those already on the Gosāvī's plate.
8. *Final rites of the wedding. sāḍe,* held, according to Molesworth, "about the fourth day" after a wedding, and involving presentations of clothing and other rites.
9. *They suddenly went out in a band.* The text adds "*nāsāvayākāraṇeṃ,*" which may mean "to digest the food" (Tulpule's suggestion, p.c.), or "to wreak destruction."

Chapter 225

1. The preceding episode ends with a somewhat awkward transition to this one, which begins a series of chapters (225–47) narrating events during the Gosāvī's journey.

Chapter 227

1. Cf. 69.

Chapter 228

1. Cf. 65, 112, 238, 247, and 314.
2. *Nāgnāth.* A form of the deity Śiva.
3. liṅga. See notes to 193.

Chapter 229

1. *Gopāḷa.* The Hindu god Kṛṣṇa as a cowherd.
2. The child's confusion is quite proper from the point of view of Mahānubhāva theology, according to which both Kṛṣṇa and Guṇḍam Rāūḷ are incarnations of Parameśvara, the one God.

Chapter 231

1. Cf. 1.

Chapter 235

1. *Gaṅgā.* The Godāvarī River.
2. *Varhāḍ.* See notes to 88.
3. *Sīvana.* Here this name is clearly a synonym for the Godāvarī Valley. For Varhāḍ natives' feelings about the immigrants from Sīvana, cf. 102.

Chapter 236

1. The text gives no explanation for the Gosāvī's behavior in this episode.
2. *Umbarāvatī.* Identified by Kolte (*Śrī Goviṃdaprabhu Caritra,* p. 164) as modern Amarāvatī/Amrāotī.

Chapter 237

1. *He stays in Rāhāṭgāv.* Here the title tells all that is recorded about the stop.
2. *Koḍeśvara.* A form of the deity Śiva.
3. *(Or . . .).* Here the sort of variant normally introduced by the phrase "*ekī vāsanā,*" "according to some" (see notes to 1), is introduced by the single word *tathā.*

Chapters 237, 238

4,1.*Vaḍajaṃbā.* A goddess.

Chapter 238

1. Cf. 65, 112, 228, 247, and 314.

Chapter 240

1. The first three titles tell of other stops on the journey before that at Bhīsnaur. Cf. 237.
2. *Eleventh-day vigil, fast.* See notes to 31. Note that Bhaṭ encourages the people to break their vigil, and the housewife to break her fast. The vigil and the fast had been in honor of a mere deity (*devatā*), not of the Mahānubhāvas' one God, Parameśvara. Cf. 31.
3. "*How could it not be so . . . ?*" For what appears to be sarcasm on Bhaṭ's part, cf. 270.

Chapter 241

1. *He did not take food from the fourth.* The text does not explain this remark.

Chapter 242

1. tūr-*pulse.* See notes to 151.
2. vāl-*pulse.* Molesworth identifies this as "a small variety" of Dolichos spicatus.

Chapter 243

1. *Ṭhākūr.* See notes to 217. This is the reading of the base ms. of Kolte's edition. Another ms. used for the edition has "Brāhman" in the text, though not in the title.
2. *Kaḷaṅkeśvara.* A form of the deity Śiva.

Chapter 245

1. Cf. 8, 57, 96, and 300.

Chapter 246

1. *Uncooked food.* Although Brāhmans are polluted by food cooked by members of lower castes, they can accept uncooked food from anyone. It is impossible to be certain that Kamaḷ Nāyak and his wife were non-Brāhmans, or that all the Gosāvī's devotees were Brāhmans, but it appears that the devotees were observing the sort of pollution rules which the Gosāvī himself regularly ignored.
2. *Dīghī.* Kolte's fifth edition has *dīdhī,* though the "Sthalasūci" in the same volume, p. 165, has *dīghī.* In 193, Dīghī is named as one of the villages visited by Nāgdev on his begging rounds, but he actually meets Kothaḷobā in Vāṅkī.

Chapter 247

1. Cf. 65, 112, 228, 238, and 314.
2. *Māṅgjāī.* A goddess.

Chapter 248

1. *Three names.* It is unclear what the third name is. Tulpule (p.c.) suggests that it may be simply "Īśvar Nāyak," or that it may be the name which appears to be given to Mhāïṃbhaṭ in the next episode (249). Kolte (p.c.) agrees with the first suggestion.
2. prasād *names.* Names given, like *prasād,* as a gracious gift.

Chapter 249

1. Cf. 305.
2. *He would beg alms. He would beg right away, in a hurry.* The text may be corrupt here, as similar sentences appear in a more fitting context in the next episode (250).

Chapter 250

1. *Fodder.* Cf. 286. In *LC,* U.564, Mhāïṃbhaṭ tells Cakradhar how he made himself get accustomed to eating food obtained by begging. The first time he tried to eat such food, he vomited.

Chapter 251

1. Cf. 39, 72, 129, and 177 for other stories of the Gosāvī fulfilling people's unspoken wishes.

Chapter 252

1. *Māhāṇḍuḷ, Māhāṇḍuḷeṃ.* Orthographic and phonetic variation is common in Old Marāṭhī; and thus the two names may be exactly the same. As the context does not really make this clear, I have left the two different spellings as they are found in Kolte's edition.
2. *Gaṅgā.* The Godāvarī River.
3. The variant included in the narration of this episode illustrates Mhāïṃbhaṭ's research methods. Kolte (p.c.) suggests that the variant dates not from Mhāïṃbhaṭ's original text, but from the rewriting of the text after the theft of the manuscripts (see introduction, section IV).

Chapter 253

1. One of the few episodes with an obvious moral, this one encourages *ahīṃsā* ("nonviolence"), an important element of Mahānubhāva ethics. See note to 191.

Chapter 254

1. *Sānubāï.* Tulpule (p.c.) suggests that this might be a goddess; Kolte (p.c.) thinks she is a woman, possibly a mad woman. The Gosāvī acts as if she is a dog.

Chapter 255

1. The goddess of Mātāpur (Māhūr) is named Reṇukā; that of Kolhāpur, Mahālakṣmī. In *Sūtrapāṭha* XII.25, Cakradhar forbids his followers to go to either of these places, but in 322, Guṇḍam Rāüḷ tells them to go to Mātāpur after his death.

Chapter 260

1. Cf. 76, 158, 288, and 295.

Chapter 262

1. *15*. This number in this position should indicate that the list preceding it contains fifteen items. But it actually contains eighteen or twenty items, depending on whether the two copper pots and the two cows count as one each or two each.
2. *Act angry*. See notes to 63. The text gives no explanation for the Gosāvī acting angry with himself at this point.
3. For a parallel to Jagaḷ Daraṇā's vow, see 163.

Chapters 263, 264

1. *Thinking rock*. See 34; cf. 201.

Chapter 265

1. *Nāthobā*. A disciple of Cakradhar who is mentioned frequently in the *LC*, but nowhere else in the present text.
2. *Four watches*. *pāhār*s (*prahara*s). Twelve hours.

Chapter 266

1. *One watch*. *pāhār* (*prahara*). Three hours.

Chapter 267

1. *Bhutānandeṃ*. A female disciple of Cakradhar mentioned several times in the *LC*, but nowhere else in the present text. Her original name was Māïbāïseṃ. *LC*, "Ajñāta Līḷā," 57, narrates the story of Cakradhar giving her the name Bhutānandeṃ.
2. *Lion-faced stone block*. *sehāḍā;* ms. variant, *sīhāḍā*.

Chapter 268

1. Cf. 68.

Chapter 270

1. *Jog Nāyak*. There are three Jog Nāyaks in the *LC*. This could be one of them, or a fourth.
2. *In a tube*. Keeping fine silks in a closed tube is a way of preserving them (Tulpule, p.c.).
3. "*How could you not* [*be satisfied*] *now?*" For what appears to be sarcasm on Bhaṭ's part, cf. 240.

Chapter 271

1. *Person*. *jīva,* a "soul," which, through transmigration, can be embodied as a human, an animal, or (see 253) a plant.
2. *Cācaleśvara*. A form of the deity Śiva.

Chapter 272

1. *Silver coins*. *āsu*s.
2. *Acted angry*. See notes to 63.

Chapter 273

1. Cf. 317.

Chapter 274

1. Cf. 299.
2. *Sacred thread.* See notes to 1, under "Thread ceremony."

Chapter 275

1. *Sāraṅg Paṇḍit.* A disciple of Cakradhar. *LC,* P.194, relates the story of Cakradhar pointing out Guṇḍam Rāüḷ to him.
2. *Vārāṇasī.* Benaras or Kāśī, the holiest of Hindu cities.
3. *Lion-faced stone block. syāhāḍā.*
4. The verse is in Sanskrit.
5. *Incense and a plate of lamps were waved before him.* See notes to 105.

Chapter 276

1. Tulpule (p.c.) suggests that Ṭhulubāï might be a nickname appropriate for a fat woman. The base ms. of Kolte's edition reads "Ṭhalubāï"; a variant reads "Dulubāï."

Chapter 277

1. *Harimā.* A nickname for Nāgdev. See 116.
2. *Vairāgyadev.* Nāgdev's son. The story of Cakradhar giving him his name is related in *LC,* U.342, which also reports that he became a disciple at age twelve, and that three and a half years later, he went to have *darśan* of "the Gosāvī."
3. *Thread ceremony.* See notes to 1.
4. *Religion. dharma.*
5. *Parameśvara.* Neither here nor at *LC,* U.342, is it clearly specified which Parameśvara-incarnation Vairāgyadev went to have *darśan* of, but the *LC* passage makes Cakradhar seem more likely.

Chapter 278

1. *Rājput.* A member of a military caste/tribe. See Russell and Lal, vol. IV, p. 410–70, and Enthoven, vol. III (1922), p. 269–97.
2. uḍīd-*pulse.* Identified by Molesworth as Phaseolus radiatus.
3. cavaḷā-*beans.* See notes to 201.
4. As Voḍaṇ Jhaḍap is not a Brāhman, neither he nor his wife can cook for the Gosāvī, Bhaṭ, or Mhāïṃbhaṭ, all of whom are Brāhmans; but neither should he eat in the same line with them. So the Brāhmanical purity rules are followed in one instance and broken in the other. Cf. 246.

Chapter 279

1. *Cleaners of harrow blades.* I.e., rustics.
2. *Nyāya Bhāratī.* The name Bhāratī (the text spells it Bhārathī) indicates that this man belongs to one of the ten orders of renouncers claiming descent from Śaṅkarācārya. See Kane, vol. II, p. 948.
3. *Circular area. maṇḍala.*
4. *Ate, rinsed mouth.* The vocabulary used for the Gosāvī's eating, mouth rins-

ing, and so forth, is different from that used for the others'. This contrast, used throughout the text, is particularly striking here. See introduction, section I, under "Divinity."

5. *That world.* The "other" world, transcending this one. From the context, it is impossible to tell exactly what is meant.
6. jīvanmukta. A person who has obtained release (*mokṣa*) but is still alive.
7. *"Sure it is."* In the Marāṭhī, as in the English, this and Nyāya Bhāratī's other remarks could be sarcastic or straightforward.
8. *Rolling stones. ṭoḷe.*

Chapter 280

1. *Śimagā.* See 64, text and notes.

Chapter 281

1. *Dravidian.* South Indian.
2. *Bhaviṣya Purāṇa.* A *purāṇa* (see notes to 213) predicting future events.
3. kalpa *literature* gives rules for performing Vedic rituals. A ms. variant noted in Kolte's edition substitutes "poetry," *kāvya.*
4. *Vindhyas.* Mountains running roughly east-west across the northern edge of the Deccan plateau.
5. *Varhāḍ.* See notes to 88.
6. *Kheḍ Rīdhaureṃ, Kāṇvā Brāhman.* See 1, text and notes.
7. *"I am not a man. . . ."* Brāhman, and so forth, are the four classes (*varṇa*s) of classical India. Celibate, and so forth, are the four classical stages of life (*āśrama*s), with *bhīkṣu* (mendicant) here replacing the more usual *saṃnyāsī* (renouncer). A Yakṣa is a kind of demigod. The Gosāvī is stating that he transcends the *varṇāśrama* orthodoxy of Hinduism as well as other nonabsolute categories of beings. This verse occurs as the last *sūtra* of the "Vicāra Mālikā" chapter of the *Sūtrapāṭha* (XI.a61); the verse is in Sanskrit, not Marāṭhī.
8. *Sanskrit.* Like other medieval devotional sects, the Mahānubhāvas took great care to use the vernacular in their religious teachings, and thus to make their teachings available to others besides learned Brāhman men (see Feldhaus, "The Mahānubhāvas and Scripture," p. 300). Of necessity, however, Sanskrit was still their common language with Brāhman men from other linguistic regions of India.
9. *Trīpuruṣa.* The three deities Brahmā, Viṣṇu, and Śiva.

Chapter 283

1. *Quadruple silver coins. cauthariyā . . . āsu*s. Cf. 115.
2. *Silver coins. āsu*s.

Chapter 284

1. *Silver coin. āsu.*

Chapter 286

1. *Lakṣmīndrabā.* Lakṣmīndrabhaṭ. Note that in the account of Lakṣmīndrabhaṭ's conversion in 213, it is by threatening adultery that Lakṣmīndrabhaṭ's wife attempts to prevent him from leaving her to become a renouncer.

2. *Fodder.* Cf. 250.
3. *Leather.* Skin; or, in the English idiom, "flesh."

Chapter 287

1. *Rājamaḍh.* See notes to 14.

Chapter 288

1. Cf. 76, 158, 260, and 295.

Chapter 290

1. *bread. roṭīs* (pl.).

Chapter 293

1. *Devgiri Cantonment. kaṭak devgiri.* See notes to 115.
2. *Berry-weight.* See notes to 306.
3. *"It may be taken out of one's own desire. . . ."* As the subsequent narrative makes clear, the "alms" Keśav Nāyak proposes to give Bhaṭ and Mhāiṃbhaṭ include liquor. For the prohibition on drinking liquor, see Kane, vol. II, p. 791–99. Kane does not mention the exceptions named by Bhaṭ.
4. *Left-handed sect. vāḍamārga,* glossed by Kolte (p. 125) as *vāmamārga.* A sect using forbidden practices and substances, including liquor, in its rituals.
5. *purifying grass knotted on their fingers. pavītrā āṃguḷīyā karuni.* See note to 148.

Chapter 294

1. *Copper coin. dāma.*

Chapter 295

1. Cf. 76, 158, 260, and 288.

Chapter 296

1. *Keśav Nāyak.* Not the Devgiri merchant in 293, but the resident of Ṛddhipur mentioned elsewhere in the text (in 20, 35, 67, and so on).

Chapter 297

1. This seems to be a miracle story, but it is not clear what the miracle is. Perhaps, as the translation suggests, the cup fills with water at the Gosāvī's command.

Chapter 298

1. *Mahākāḷa Mahālakṣmī.* Kolte suggests (p.c.) that this is a single goddess, Mahālakṣmī, the wife of Mahākāḷa.
2. *"Go die!"* The Gosāvī's favorite curse changes slightly in the final episodes of his biography. Beginning here, he often drops the "*jāe*" of "*melā/ī/e jāe*" (see notes to 2). According to Molesworth, whose dictionary reflects nineteenth-century Brāhman usage, this curse is typically used only by women; it is not clear whether this was the case in the Gosāvī's time as well.
3. *Mahākāḷī* is the same goddess as Mahākāḷa Mahālakṣmī. *kāḷā*(m.)/*kāḷī*(f.) means "black." The Gosāvī is punning, saying that the goddess is black since her husband's name means "black."

Chapter 299

1. Cf. 274.
2. *Maheśvarbhaṭ.* This may be Maheśvar Paṇḍit, a son of Nāgdev (Kolte, *LC*, p. 803) mentioned a few times in the *LC*.

Chapter 300

1. Cf. 8, 57, 96, and 245.
2. *Paras Nāyak.* This may be a devotee of Cakradhar mentioned several times in the *LC*. For instance, *LC*, P.294, reports that Cakradhar stayed four months in Paras Nāyak's cell, behind the Mahālakṣmī temple in Bīḍ. See also 303, text and notes.
3. *Rice-ball, stream of water, and so forth.* See notes to 138.

Chapter 301

1. Cf. 24, 58.
2. *Acted angry.* See notes to 63.

Chapter 303

1. *Paras Nāyak.* It is not clear whether or not this is the Paras Nāyak whose son is revived in 300. See notes to 300.

Chapter 304

1. *Bhadra.* See notes to 22.
2. cār *seeds,* goḍaṃbī *seeds.* See notes to 50.

Chapter 305

1. Cf. 249; cf. 54.

Chapter 306

1. *Purified fifty-two times. bāvanakasa.* The best gold (*Mahārāṣṭra Śabdakośa*).
2. *Berry-weight. guñja.* Molesworth identifies this as "the smallest of the jeweler's weights, . . . considered as equal to three barleycorns." The *Mahārāṣṭra Śabdakośa* identifies it as one-sixteenth of a *toḷā*-weight (see below).
3. vāl-*weight.* Molesworth defines this as equal to three *guñja*s, but states that "popularly it is computed at two or two and a half *guñja*."
4. *Barleycorn-weight. jaü.* According to Molesworth, this is "considered as equal to six mustard seeds."
5. toḷā-*weight.* According to Molesworth (1831; 2nd ed., 1857; repr. ed., 1975), this "is stated in books at 16 *māṣ* of 5 *ratī* or 6½ grains each; amounting therefore to 105 grains Troy," but "in practice it is calculated at 12 *māṣ* jeweler's weight; amounting therefore to 210 grains." The *Mahārāṣṭra Śabdakośa* (1935) adds that it is equal to 193½ (Troy) grains in Puṇe and Ahmadābād, 188½ in Ahmadnagar, 184½ in Jalna, 180 in Bombay, and so on.
6. māṣ-*weight.* According to Molesworth, this is "variously reckoned at five, eight, or ten *ratī* (seeds of Abrus precatorius)." A *ratī,* according to Molesworth, "averages nearly 2¼ grains Troy." According to *Hobson-Jobson,* under "Tola," "The Hindu scale is 8 *rattīs* . . . = 1 *māsha,* 12 *māshas* = 1 *tolā*. . . . The proper weight of the *rattī,* which was the old Indian unit of

weight, has been determined by Mr. E. Thomas as 1.75 grains." See also *Hobson-Jobson,* under "Ruttee."

Chapter 307

1. Another "economic miracle." See notes to 25.

Chapter 308

1. *Worship sand.* In order to obtain a good husband, suggests Tulpule (p.c.).

Chapter 309

1. *Poḷā festival.* A festival in which bullocks are decorated, paraded, and honored. According to Molesworth, the festival is held on the day of the new moon of Śrāvaṇ (July–August) or Bhādrapad (August–September). According to the *Mahārāṣṭra Śabdakośa,* it may also take place on the full-moon day of Āṣāḍh (June–July).

Chapter 311

1. *Bandeśvara.* See notes to 170.
2. *Sīvana.* See 102 and 235, text and notes.

Chapter 312

1. Cf. 95.
2. *Silver coins. āsus.*
3. *Patron. yajamāna.*

Chapter 313

1. *Contact.* See notes to 21.
2. *The rose-apple tree in the orchard.* The one in 142?

Chapter 314

1. Cf. 65, 112, 228, 238, and 247.
2. *Gaṇeśa.* The elephant-headed Hindu deity.
3. *Caṇḍikā.* "The fierce one," a goddess.

Chapter 316

1. Cf. the "horse" stones in 18, 19, and so on.
2. *"They'll come. . . . it will come down."* "They" might be calves, and "it" the milk.

Chapter 317

1. Cf. 273; for the curses, cf. 137 and 321.
2. *An item of the code of conduct. ācārasthaḷa.*

Chapter 318

1. *Āndha.* Russell and Lal (vol. II, p. 38) describe "Andh" as "a low cultivating caste of Berār." Enthoven (vol. I, p. 41) lists "Andhon" as "a synonym for Andvan" and lists "Andhvan" as "a subdivision of Mahārs" (see notes to 46).
2. *Utaravāḍī.* The "Northern hamlet," part of Aḷajpur.

3. poḷī-*breads.* See notes to 146.
4. vāl-*pulse.* Molesworth identifies this as "a small variety of . . . Dolichos spicatus."

Chapter 319

1. *Incarnation of a deity. vigraho,* distinct from an incarnation of the one God, Parameśvara. See notes to 2.

Chapter 321

1. For the curses, cf. 137 and 317.

Chapter 322

1. *Goes home.* Dies.
2. *Got diarrhea.* Literally, accepted it. As the subsequent paragraphs make clear, the Gosāvī could only get sick by his own will.
3. *Śrī Cakradhar Rāyā.* See notes to 212. *LC,* U.639, and *Sūtrapāṭha* XII.208 record Cakradhar's entrusting his disciples to Guṇḍam Rāüḷ.
4. *Śrī Dattātreya Prabhu.* Along with Cakradhar and Guṇḍam Rāüḷ, another of the five incarnations of Parameśvara recognized by Mahānubhāvas. Dattātreya is a god worshipped by non-Mahānubhāva Hindus.
5. *Mātāpur.* Māhūr. See notes to 255. Besides being the site of an important temple to the goddess Reṇukā, Māhūr is the site of a major Dattātreya temple.
6. *Dark half of the month of Bhādrapad, in the Vyaya year.* The fortnight of the waning moon in the month August–September. The Vyaya year (*saṃvatsara*) is the twentieth in the cycle of sixty years in the calendar linked to the movements of the planet Jupiter. See Kane, vol. V., p. 660–62. The text has "*vaya*" for "*vyaya.*" *Smṛtisthaḷa* 5 gives the date as the fourth day of the dark half of the month of Māgh (January–February) in the Vyaya year. Kolte discusses the date of Guṇḍam Rāüḷ's death in the introduction to his edition, p. 12–14, noting variant dates given in mss. of various Mahānubhāva texts. His conclusion is that Guṇḍam Rāüḷ died in *gata* Śaka 1208 (= 1286–1287 A.D.). Cf. introduction, section IV, under "History of the Text."
7. *The Gosāvī left.* That is, he died.

Chapter 323

1. *The Gosāvī's daughter.* See 156.
2. *Had gone home.* Had died.
3. *Īśvara's body is like camphor.* The text expresses wonder that the body of Guṇḍam Rāüḷ did not evaporate the way Kṛṣṇa's was said to have evaporated (*Sūtrapāṭha* X.93; *LC,* "Ajñāta Līḷā: Śrīkṛṣṇacaritra," 11). The disciples may have moved the body in order to prevent others' skepticism about this point of doctrine; but if so, reporting the fact would seem to counteract the disciples' intention.

People Named in *The Deeds of God in Ṛddhipur*

In the notes to the translation, people are identified, when possible, at the first occurrence of their names. Numbers refer to text chapters.

Places Named in *The Deeds of God in Ṛddhipur*

Places in Ṛddhipur

Āp well. 75, 76.

Bailaur road. 25.
Bandeśvara temple. 170, 311, 312.
Bhadra. 22, 304.
Bhairava temple. 62.

Cācaleśvara temple. 271.

Dābh well. 80, 85, 271, 302, 320.
Dābh well road. 73, 184.
Darbhāḷe tank. 78.
Darbheśvara (temple). 85.
Devāḷe tank. 31, 55, 70, 279.

Five Pipals. 85, 281.

Haṭakeśvara temple. 33.
High Lane. 31, 34, 57, 168.

Indur road. 45.

Jāṇāḷe tank. 130.

Kaḷaṅkeśvara temple. 42, 43, 319.
Kamaleśvara temple. 96.
Karaḍ well. 130.
Karaṇḍ orchard. 161.
Keśav Nāyak's water stand. 20.
Keśava temple. 27.
Kheḍ road. 26, 161.
Koḷ well. 100.

Lakṣmaṇ well. 45.
Low Lane. 34, 57.

Mahākāḷa Mahālakṣmī's temple. 298.
Mahārs' quarter. 46, 47, 208.
Māṅgs' water stand. 23.
Marketplace. 27, 28, 32, 49, 215.
Moḷīya well. 169.

Nagareśvara temple. 44, 300.
Niṣkalaṅka's temple. 95.

Odyāḷe tank. 167, 308, 309.

Paraśurāma temple. 64, 65, 101, 143, 160, 303.
Pīval tank. 302.

Rājamaḍh. 14, 94, 120, 287.
Rām well. 45.

Glossary

Bhādrapad: The sixth month of the Hindu calendar, usually falling in August and September.

bhākrī: A kind of bread, the simplest of the flat breads, usually made of *jondhḷā* (Holcus sorghum) or *bājrī* (Holcus spicatus) dough cooked on a griddle.

Bharāḍī: A type of wandering religious mendicant and entertainer.

Bhāvaī: A festival celebrated at the no-moon of the month of Jyeṣṭha (May–June).

Bhusāre: A kind of Vanījār.

Brahman: The impersonal Absolute.

Brāhman: A member of one of the highest, purest castes; a member of the highest, priestly class of the four-class "*varṇa*" system of classical Indian society.

Caitra: The first month of the Hindu calendar, usually falling in March and April.

***darbha*-grass:** A grass used in orthodox Brāhmanical rituals; Poa cynosuroides.

darśan: Seeing (and being seen by) a deity or holy person.

Dheḍ: A member of an untouchable caste.

dhoti: The lower garment worn by men, consisting of a cloth which is draped and folded and tucked between the legs.

Dīvāḷī: The "festival of lights," a festival of several days' duration occurring at the end of the month of Āśvin (September–October) and the beginning of the month of Kārttik (October–November).

Dvāpara Age: The second of the four *yugas* (ages) of Hindu cosmology.

Gosāvī: "The Gosāvī" is Guṇḍam Rāüḷ, the subject of this biography. "Our Gosāvī" is Cakradhar, the founder of the Mahānubhāvas.

Īśvara: God, Lord. In this text, equivalent to "Parameśvara."

***jīvanmukta*:** A person who has obtained release (*mokṣa*) but is still alive.

Kali Age: The fourth of the four *yugas* (ages) of Hindu cosmology; the current age.

Kāṇva Brāhman: A member of one of the several schools of Vedic priests; specifically, a follower of the Kāṇva branch (*śākhā*) of the White Yajurveda school.

karma: Action and the results of action; according to the law of karma, the results of actions must be experienced.

Kṣatriya: A member of the second-highest, warrior and princely class of the four-class "*varṇa*" system of classical Indian society.

Kuṇbī: A member of a caste of peasants.

***lā̃k*:** A grain, Lithyrus sativus.

***liṅga*:** The phallic image of the deity Śiva.

Mahār: A member of the largest untouchable caste of the Gosāvī's region, Maharashtra.

Māḷī: A member of the gardener caste.

Māṅg: A member of a certain untouchable caste.

***mokṣa*:** Final release from the round of birth, death, and rebirth.

Navacaṇḍī: A goddess festival held during the first nine days of the month of Āśvin (September–October).

pan: A masticatory composed of betel nut, lime, and spices folded in a betel leaf.

Parameśvara: "The highest Lord," the Mahānubhāvas' one God.

Poḷā: A festival in which bullocks are decorated and honored.

***poḷī*:** Flat wheat bread baked on a griddle.

***prasād*:** Food tasted by a deity or holy person and distributed as his leftovers to his devotees. For a deity to "make *prasād*" is for him to taste food which may then be distributed as *prasād*.

***purāṇa*:** One of a number of long Sanskrit mythological texts dealing with a variety of topics.

***purī*:** A puffed bread prepared by deep-frying thin flat circles of wheat dough in oil.

Rājput: A member of a military caste/tribe.

Rāüḷ: A name for Guṇḍam Rāüḷ used more by townspeople than by his devotees.

sacred thread: A long loop of thread worn by male Brāhmans and other upper-caste Hindu men. It is worn draped over the left shoulder and hangs down on the right side below the waist.

Saṃdhyā: A ritual performed by Brāhman men at sunrise, sunset, and other "junctures" (*saṃdhyā*s) of the day.

Sanskrit: The classical language of India, the language of learning and of Brāhmanical rituals in all regions of India.

seer: A weight, roughly equivalent to a kilogram.

Śimagā: A festival characterized by boisterous pranks. It occurs during the month of Phalgun (February–March).

Śrāddha: A ritual in which offerings are made to and in honor of dead ancestors.

Śrāvaṇ: The fifth month of the Hindu calendar, usually falling in July and August.

Śrāvaṇī: A ceremony, performed on the full-moon day of the month of Śrāvaṇ, in which Brāhmans change their sacred threads.

Śrīprabhu: A name for Guṇḍam Rāüḷ used less frequently in this text than "Gosāvī" and "Rāüḷ." "Śrī" is a form of respectful address and reference; "*prabhu*" means "Lord."

Śūdra: A member of the lowest, servant class of the four-class "*varṇa*" system of classical Indian society.

Telī: A member of a caste who press and sell oil.

Ṭhākūr: A member of a certain tribe; also a title of Rājputs.

***tulasī*:** The holy basil plant, or its leaves.

Upādhyāya: A kind of traditional teacher.

Vaiśākh: The second month of the Hindu calendar, usually falling in April and May.

Vaiśya: A member of the third-highest, mercantile and agricultural class of the four-class "*varṇa*" system of classical Indian society.

Vanījār: An itinerant carrier and trader of grain.

Yakṣa: A kind of demigod.

A Guide to Pronunciation

Most names and terms have been transliterated according to their Marāṭhī pronunciation, while a few (mostly names of gods) have been given in the Sanskrit forms more often found in English works on Indian religion. In both cases, the following general rules apply:

1. Pronounce:

   a like *u* in *cup*.
   ā like *a* in *father*.
   i like *i* in *hit*.
   ī like *ee* in *keep*.
   u like *oo* in *good*.
   ū like *oo* in *pool*.
   ṛ like *ri* in *river*.
   e like *ay* in *day*.
   ai like *i* in *fine*.
   o like *o* in *go*.
   au like *ow* in *cow*.
   c like *ch* in *church*.*
   g like *g* in *get*.
   gh like *gh* in *ghetto*.
   ṅ like *n* in *think*.
   ñ like *n* in *hinge*.
   ś and *ṣ* like *sh* in *ship*.
   th and *ṭh* like *th* in *Thomas* (never like *th* in *the*).
   other consonants more or less as in English.**

*Except in *Cāṅgdev,* in which the *c* is pronounced "*ts*" in Marāṭhī.
**There are differences between *t* and *ṭ*, *d* and *ḍ*, and so on, but to the untrained ear these are practically indistinguishable.

2. ˜ and -*ṃ* indicate nasalization: nasalize a vowel marked by ˜ or followed by -*ṃ*.

3. ¨ indicates a hiatus: in *aï, āï, aü,* and *āü,* pronounce the *ï* or *ü* separately from the *a* or *ā*.

[redacted]